GENTLE HIKES of Upper Michigan

Upper Michigan's most scenic Lake Superior hikes under 3 miles

Ladona Tornabene, Ph.D., CHES
Lisa Vogelsang, Ph.D., CMT
Melanie Morgan

Adventure Publications, Inc.
Cambridge, MN

ACKNOWLEDGMENTS

This book was made possible in part by a Faculty Summer Research Fellowship granted to Ladona Tornabene, Ph.D., CHES, from the University of Minnesota Duluth during the summer of 2004.

The authors would also like to thank those at the University of Minnesota Duluth (UMD), especially the Department of Health, Physical Education and Recreation for encouraging us with our third book in this series of health promotion guides. We would also like to express our appreciation and thankfulness to the employees of the following establishments for their assistance with the completion of this book: all State Parks in Michigan's Upper Peninsula, Mountain View Lodge, Nordic Bay Lodge, Blaney Lodge, Cedar Motor Inn, Eagle Harbor House, Pictured Rocks National Lakeshore, The Jampot, and individuals such as Dr. Bob Nara who not only provided information about Nara Nature Park to us, but donated the land to the City of Houghton in order to make those trails possible.

Many thanks to Adventure Publications for seeing the need for "Gentle Hikes" and working so closely with us throughout this project. You are awesome!

We would also like to express deep-felt appreciation to our families and friends for all their support and encouragement. We love you!

Thanks to Jack Canfield, Anthony Robbins, Brian Tracy, Dr. John Maxwell, Zig Ziglar, Joel Osteen, and Dr. Paul Deputy for being the motivators that you are to me (Ladona). Though I only know one of you personally, I have been inspired to set an outrageous goal to sell one million copies of our Gentle Hikes books!

And last, but certainly not least—The Creator of it all—to whom we give our utmost gratitude. Truly, "The heavens declare the glory of God and the firmament shows and proclaims His handiwork." Ps. 19:1

Please use caution and good sense when participating in outdoor recreational activities. The authors and Adventure Publications, Inc. assume no responsibility for accidents or injuries occurring on the trails, Almost Hikes, waysides, overlooks and picnic areas described in this book.

Learn as much information as you can about the activities and destinations to help prevent accidents and make your recreational experience more enjoyable.

Book design and illustrations by Jonathan Norberg; maps generated by Andrea Bong
Cover photo by Lisa Vogelsang

10 9 8 7 6 5 4 3 2 1
Copyright 2006 by Ladona Tornabene, Lisa Vogelsang and Melanie Morgan
Adventure Publications, Inc.
820 Cleveland St. S
Cambridge, MN 55008
1-800-678-7006
www.adventurepublications.net
Printed in the U.S.A.
ISBN-13: 978-1-59193-137-9
ISBN-10: 1-59193-137-1

DEDICATION

This book is dedicated to the glory of God.
As beautiful as His creation is, it pales in comparison to Him.
It is our hope that you experience both.
Megwich Hchi-Manitou.
Pasa Gweeg!

HELP US KEEP THIS GUIDE UP TO DATE!

Every effort has been made by the authors to make this guide as accurate as possible at press time. However, due to the dynamic nature of trails, etc. we would appreciate your feedback if you find a discrepancy with anything in this book. We would also love to hear your feedback regarding its usefulness to you. Please email Ladona Tornabene ltornabe@d.umn.edu and write "book feedback" in the subject line. Thank you very much.

TABLE OF CONTENTS

Bond Falls (see pg. 59). Photo by Ladona Tornabene

INTRODUCTION

Gentle Hikes was created out of a desire to share the outdoors with people of all ability levels.

Since this is the third of its kind in a series, we would like to explain how the original concept took form. It actually began on Minnesota's North Shore (which is where our first *Gentle Hikes* book was written) when we asked local merchants: "Do you carry a hiking book that focuses solely on short, relatively easy trails?" Very often, their reply was "Well, not exactly…"

All three authors call Duluth, Minnesota, home and it was the first summer of the new millennium. We had friends and family planning a visit and all of them wanted to go hiking! They wanted to experience scenic beauty via the trails; however, some had very limited time here and some had small children. They needed short hikes. Others had certain physical challenges or were totally new to hiking. They needed easier hikes with specific information about the trails such as inclines, steps and surface type.

We began thinking.

One of the authors has a physical limitation and another was temporarily plagued by sports-related injuries. This, combined with the above, made it clear that we needed to locate easier, shorter trails than those listed in most hiking books. Ideas began to flow and *Gentle Hikes* took form.

Although the term "gentle" is subjective, we have found the topography of Upper Michigan's Lake Superior region to be far more gentle than the diverse topography of Minnesota's North Shore. Keep in mind that hiking in the outdoors naturally involves inclines, declines, rocks, roots and uneven terrain. We have created a rating system (pg. 20) describing the extent of these elements so that you may choose a trail compatible with your personal abilities. We have also noted which trails meet Universal Design Standards (in other words, trails that meet accessibility standards for persons of all abilities as opposed to the "average" person). Furthermore, we specify which trails are multi-use, non-motorized paths (i.e. permitting bicyclists and in-line skaters, but prohibiting any motorized vehicles with the exception of motorized wheelchairs).

Whereas most of the trails in this book are well-marked and easy to follow, please be aware that we took the liberty to use parts of existing trails to form our own. We did this in order to meet the *Gentle Hikes* criteria. When this is the case, it's a good idea to familiarize yourself with the trail description to make sure you stay on course.

Whatever your hiking passion—be it continuous Lake Superior views, dramatic waterfalls, breathtaking vistas, rushing rivers, lush wooded paths or paved scenic trails—this book delivers all of these and much more.

Healthy trails to you always!

Ladona Tornabene, Lisa Vogelsang, Melanie Morgan

Ladona Tornabene, Ph.D., CHES, Lisa Vogelsang, Ph.D., Melanie Morgan

LAYING THE GROUNDWORK

Nara River Boardwalk (see pg. 76). Photo by Lisa Vogelsang

SUGGESTIONS FOR MAKING YOUR HIKE HAPPIER: CLOTHING & GEAR

Since all of our hikes are less than three miles and are on well-marked trails, we list fewer essentials than other resource guides. Remember to choose trails that are appropriate for your ability and fitness level. Start out slowly and gradually increase your walking speed to a comfortable level, pacing yourself throughout the hike.

Stretch

Stretching before a hike prepares the muscles for activity and stretching after can prevent muscle soreness. Not only does it feel good to stretch, but a flexible muscle is less likely to pull should you move suddenly or accidentally trip.

Rain Gear

Always pack a rain jacket, as weather conditions can change very quickly. Breathable, waterproof fabrics work best.

Clothing Fabric Type

Cotton feels great on a hot day, but when it gets wet, it stays wet. Synthetics are breathable, help wick perspiration from the skin and dry much faster than cotton.

Head Coverings and Sunscreen

It is important to protect the scalp from the sun's burning rays. Many styles of wide-brimmed hats and billed caps can be used. Sunscreens are a necessity in preventing sunburns, wrinkles and reducing the risk of skin cancer. Use a waterproof sunscreen with a minimum SPF 15. Apply before hiking and re-apply about every hour depending on perspiration levels. Remember sunblock for the lips, nose and ears as well as good quality sunglasses to protect your eyes.

Footwear

The shoes and socks you wear can make the difference between an enjoyable outdoor experience or a hike filled with possible blisters and discomfort. Athletic shoes are great for paved or flat trails without many roots or rocks and are appropriate for trails with a Lighter Side of Gentle rating. Sturdier shoes or hiking boots are a good idea for trails with a Moderate or Rugged Side of Gentle rating. Don't compromise when it comes to shoe or boot fit. Purchase your footwear from a merchant who is knowledgeable about hiking and try on the boots with the type of socks you plan to wear on the trail. Break in footwear prior to hitting the trails.

Cotton socks are not recommended because they absorb moisture and hold it next to your skin, which may cause blisters or cold feet. Synthetics or other natural fiber socks that are thick or made specifically for hiking are ideal. Some people prefer using a liner sock as well to ensure comfort and reduce the risk of blisters.

The Big Stick

There are several styles of hiking sticks and poles available. Many types have been shown to improve balance and reduce the risk of knee or ankle injury. They are especially useful on declines, inclines and uneven terrain. Most poles are adjustable and some have shock absorption capabilities, but their tips can damage tree roots. Hiking sticks are not adjustable and may be heavier to carry, but cause less damage to roots. Whichever you choose, being knowledgeable about proper usage is a must for your safety and the well-being of the environment.

Bug Beaters

Mosquitoes, black flies, gnats, biting flies, ticks, chiggers and sand fleas are all realities to consider when going outdoors. Prevent yourself from being the main course for the bugs' supper by testing which repellent works best for you. We recommend a product that is healthy for you and the environment. Use repellent on clothing as well as exposed skin. During times of high foliage, tuck your pants into your socks to prevent tick bites. Also check yourself for ticks after any trek into the woods, and know how to remove embedded ticks. Know the signs and symptoms of Lyme disease.

Water and Snacks

Drink whether thirsty or not because if you wait until you are thirsty, you are already dehydrated. A good rule of thumb is to bring 8 ounces (1 cup) of water for each 15 minutes of hiking expected. The Superior Hiking Trail Association (Two Harbors, MN) and other sources recommend allowing 1 hour for every 1.5 to 3 miles of trail covered. Since all of our trails are less than three miles, this means taking a minimum of 32 oz. of water with you (more on a hot day).

Sports drinks are OK, but soft drinks are not recommended, nor are any beverages containing caffeine or alcohol because you will lose more fluid than contained in the drinks. Do not drink water from streams, rivers or lakes unless you have a water purification device to clean the water of bacteria and other impurities.

Bring food on hikes lasting longer than an hour. Suggested snack items include dried fruits, crackers, granola, cereal, energy bars and trail mixes. To help keep trails beautiful, pack out anything you take in.

Safety Items

A readily accessible, genuine survival whistle is a necessity even on short hikes. The volume and pitch can scare away unwanted animals or alert others of your position in an emergency. Other items that we recommend bringing along are personal identification, a small first aid kit, trail maps/descriptions and a small flashlight.

Fun Items

While experiencing the spectacular scenic beauty of these trails, a camera and plenty of memory cards or film is an essential! If there's one bug we actually want to bite you, it's the shutterbug! Compact binoculars are also fun to have for identifying birds and butterflies. A small pocket notebook and pen are also nice for recording memories or thoughts.

Daypacks

Backpacks or waist packs are suggested and needed when carrying water or more than one pound of gear. Models with pockets especially for water bottles are convenient. The kind of pack needed depends on the type of hiking you'll be doing, how much gear you plan to carry and its comfort and functionality.

Conclusion

When out on the trail away from modern conveniences, an ounce of prevention is worth more than a pound of cure. Implementing the above suggestions may take a little planning and organizing initially, but you'll be glad you brought that pack along.

TRAILS

Region 1: Black River Harbor Area

1. Rainbow Falls
2. Sandstone Falls
3. Gorge Falls
4. Potawatomi Falls
5. Great Conglomerate Falls

Region 2: Porcupine Mountain Area

6. Government Peak Trail
7. Lake of the Clouds
8. Wilderness Visitor Center Nature Trail
9. Union Mine Interpretive Trail
10. Nonesuch Mine
11. Summit Peak Tower
12. Greenstone Falls
13. Suspension Bridge—Quick Route
14. Manabezho Falls, Presque Isle River & Suspension Bridge Loop
15. Manido Falls

Region 3: Keweenaw Peninsula Area

16. Bond Falls
17. Agate Falls
18. Canyon Falls
19. Falls River Falls
20. DeVriendt Nature Trail
21. Houghton Waterfront Trail
22. Peepsock Trail
23. Nara Nature Trail
24. Nara River Boardwalk
25. Bear Lake Trail
26. Breakwater & Fitness Trail
27. Fort Wilkins State Park Lake Superior Trail
28. Lake Fanny Hooe View Trail
29. Hunter's Point Trail

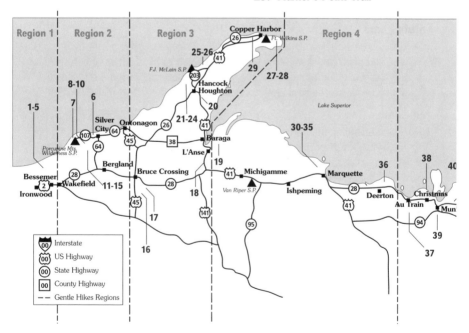

Region 4: Marquette Area

30. Presque Isle Bog Walk
31. Presque Isle Nature Trail
32. The Pedestrian Pathway (Wheelchair Accessible Route)
33. Sugarloaf Mountain
34. Little Presque Isle Song Bird Trail
35. Little Presque Isle Point
36. Laughing Whitefish Falls

Region 5: Munising/Pictured Rocks National Lakeshore Area

37. Au Train Songbird Trail
38. Bay Furnace Historic Site
39. Wagner Falls
40. Munising Falls
41. Sand Point Marsh Trail
42. Miners Falls
43. Miners Castle
44. Chapel Falls

45. White Pine Self-Guiding Nature Trail
46. Sable Falls
47. Grand Sable Dunes
48. Log Slide Overlook
49. Au Sable Light Station
50. Pine Ridge Nature Trail

Region 6: Tahquamenon Falls Area

51. Oswald's Bear Ranch Walk-About
52. Muskallonge Lake State Park Section of North Country Trail
53. Tahquamenon Falls (Upper)
54. Clark Lake
55. Tahquamenon Falls (Lower)
56. Tahquamenon Rivermouth Walk

Region 7: Sault Ste. Marie Area

57. Soo Locks Walk-About
58. Point Iroquois Lighthouse & Boardwalk

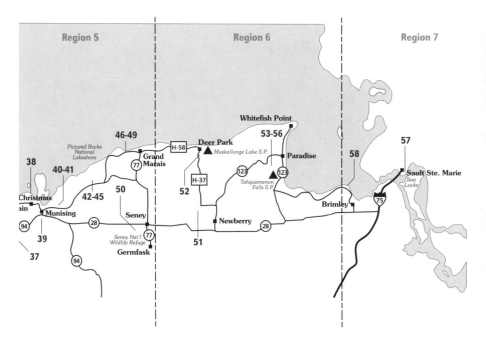

AUTHORS' CORNER

Best Lake Superior views:

Best waterfalls:

*wheelchair accessible

*wheelchair accessible

Best lake views (other than Superior):

Best harbor views:

Best interpretive trails:

Flattest trails:

*wheelchair accessible

*wheelchair accessible

Best dune views:

Sections of the North Country Trail

The following hikes feature sections of the North Country Trail. To identify these sections when hiking, look for the NCT eight-point star or hiker centered sign.

*wheelchair accessible

TRAIL USAGE INFORMATION

The following is general information about State Park Trails, the North Country National Scenic Trail (NCNST) Sections and regional areas. For specific questions regarding any particular trail, please contact respective trail headquarters (phone number provided after Trailhead Directions & Parking listed on all hikes in this section or see Appendix B, pg. 250).

State Park Trails:

We have included trails in five of Michigan's Upper Peninsula State Parks: Porcupine Mountains Wilderness, F.J. McLain, Fort Wilkins, Muskallonge Lake and Tahquamenon Falls. While we have featured some of the established trails, we have also strung together pathways to create loops or out-and-back treks to provide the most scenic routes we could find within the Gentle Hikes criteria (see pg. 20).

Certain state parks have multi-use trails (check with individual parks for policies). Motorized vehicles are prohibited on all state park hiking trails. Motorized wheelchairs are permitted on all state park hiking trails.

Michigan's State Forest system is the largest in the eastern United States covering 3.8 million acres and supporting the largest rustic recreation system in the Nation! These facts as well as camping and other recreational opportunities can be found at www.exploringthenorth.com/statepark/park.html

For camping reservations, call 1-800-44-PARKS (1-800-447-2757).

North Country National Scenic Trail (NCNST) Sections:

Putting footprints onto dreams, the NCTA (North Country Trail Association) is working closely with the National Park Service to complete the longest National Scenic Trail in the United States. When finished, its length will total over 4,500 miles! Named one of the 16 National Millennium Trails by the White House Millennium Council, the NCNST spans seven states (North Dakota, Minnesota, Wisconsin, Upper and Lower Michigan, Ohio, Pennsylvania and New York). Michigan has the largest percentage of the trail, with its Upper Peninsula having nearly 525 miles complete. Of those miles, almost 400 are certified. See page 16 for gentle sections of the North Country Trail that are featured in this book.

Motorized use on the trails is prohibited under the existing Forest Off-Roads Vehicle Policy. Horse use and mountain biking are discouraged. Mountain bikes may not be ridden where the trail crosses wilderness areas.

The NCTA is a nonprofit organization that relies primarily on volunteers to build and maintain the trail. Their national headquarters is located at 229 East Main Street, Lowell, MI 49331. For more information please contact the North Country Trail Association at 1-866-hikeNCT (1-866-445-3628) or www.northcountrytrail.org. When reported and available, trail conditions are posted on their website as well.

Pet Policies:

This is not a conclusive list of pet policies for all trails in this book. For more information, call the phone number listed at the beginning of a specific trail.

General Information: Please pick up after your pet at all times.

State Park trails: The DNR recommends contacting applicable state parks for their pet policies. If pets are permitted, they are required to be on a 6-foot leash. Pets are not allowed on beaches.

Dogs are not allowed on Presque Isle other than in an enclosed vehicle.

Pets are permitted on the following trails at Pictured Rocks National Lakeshore: Munising Falls, Miners Castle (to overlook area), Log Slide Trail (but not on the Log Slide). Pets are NOT permitted on Sand Point Marsh, Miners Falls, Chapel Falls, Au Sable Lighthouse and Sable Falls trails.

Trail Closures:

Generally, trails remain open for hiking until snow season begins. Trail reroutings, wildlife habitats, and/or hunting season could potentially close certain trails. Please check with contact listed on every trail regarding closures.

When Snowflakes Fly:

No trails are plowed for hiking during snow season.

Wagner Falls (see pg. 109). Photo by Lisa Vogelsang

HOW TO USE THIS GUIDE
Trail Rating:

To accommodate hikers of all levels, each trail follows a rating system. The rating system is governed by a set of criteria (see below) and offers three levels. Trails range from the Lighter Side of Gentle which includes all paved trails (and more) to the Rugged Side of Gentle which offers more challenge to those who desire it. The Moderate Side of Gentle, as you might expect, falls somewhere in between. All trails are under 3 miles in total length.

Regardless of the rating, each trail will always state the trail surface and width, number of inclines over 10 degrees, steepest and longest incline, safety concerns and all step and bench locations.

Our trail descriptions are very detailed and correspond to the trail in increments of tenths of a mile. We have made every attempt to locate and note trail aspects that may challenge some (e.g., inclines, rocks, roots, steps, etc.) as well as features that may be helpful (e.g., benches, handrails, paved trails, etc.). With this information, each person can make an informed decision based on his/her abilities as to how far to go on a certain trail or choose another altogether.

Icons:

The following icons represent our trail rating system.

 The Lighter Side of Gentle must meet all of the following criteria (excluding options):

Inclines: 10-12° (or less)
Rock/Root: Minimal (intermittent moderate sections)
Total number of steps encountered throughout the trail: <25
Trail surface: Even (intermittent uneven sections)

 The Moderate Side of Gentle meets ONE or more of the following criteria:

Inclines: 14-16° (or no more than 2 inclines between 18-22°, not exceeding 35' in length)
Rock/Root: Moderate
Total number of steps encountered throughout the trail: <175
Trail surface: Even or uneven

 The Rugged Side of Gentle meets ONE or more of the following criteria:

Inclines: 18-22°
Rock/Root: Moderate to Significant
Total number of steps encountered throughout the trail: <325
Trail surface: Even or uneven, laid log paths possible.

Icons in the Descriptions:

These icons, embedded in the trail description and mileage section for each trail, allow you to quickly see what's ahead on the trail.

 Inclines: Indicates the location of the steepest incline on the trail.

Steps: We note in the description if they ascend/descend, their composition and if they have handrails or not. Non-continuous indicates a brief resting area between sets of steps.

Benches: Indicates the location of benches on the trail.

Photo opportunities: On our trails we have chosen places where we thought the views were photo worthy. Some are obvious, others are purely subjective; we think you will be pleased with our suggestions. We have found it to be a great way of preserving and sharing memories for years to come.

Maps:

Provided for each trail, maps show mileage markers that correspond to selected trail descriptions. Not all mileage markers are shown on the maps, only those that will help you locate your position on the trail.

Other Items You'll Find:

 Foot Note:

Information that may be of interest or inspiration to our readers, including nearby sites to see. These are listed on the specific trail, Almost Hike, wayside or picnic area to which they pertain.

 SAYS WHO?

Professional information from reputable sources related to health education issues. These are scattered throughout the book.

🏔️ TRAIL NAME:*

*An asterisk means that the trail has been given a Gentle Hikes name because no name previously existed or it is part of another trail.

Location • The state of Michigan does not use mile markers on any of its highways or roads. We've divided Michigan into seven regions. The location of trails are listed in one of three ways: as one of these seven regions, or the city or state park in which it is located. Additionally, we list which major highway the trail is on or located near, and then we list the number of miles from a key city within that region.

• **Trail Highlights: Though subjective, we believe that these highlights give an account of the sights you can expect to see.**

TRAILHEAD DIRECTIONS & PARKING:

Directions are generally listed from U.S. 2 or MI 28 and the point of turnoff from those roads and the key cities nearby. Mileage is given for the purpose of proper navigation.

TRAILHEAD FACILITIES & FEES:

Unless otherwise noted, facilities are mentioned only if they are at trailhead parking area or on the trail. Fees pertain to parking and entrance. All Michigan state parks in this guide as well as some other locations (see individual trail description) require a use permit to enter. Day use or annual permits are available at state park offices, headquarters or self-pay boxes.

TOTAL TRAIL LENGTH, SURFACE & WIDTH:

Trail length is round trip distance to the nearest tenth of a mile. Trail surface varies from paved, gravel and hardpacked dirt to rock and root. When rock and root are present, they are reported in three categories: minimum, moderate and significant. Please note: paved trails are not plowed or de-iced during the snow season.

INCLINES & ALERTS:

Although inclines can be reported as % grade, we chose to use degrees (for conversion table, see Appendix C, pg. 253). The number of inclines exceeding 10° (18% grade), their degree ranges, the steepest incline (its length and location) and the longest incline (exceeding 30') is listed for every trail. Alerts include potential safety hazards or other matters of concern.

CONTACT:

For more information about the trail, state park or area, get in touch with this organization.

MILEAGE & DESCRIPTION:

This is your step-by-step description of what you'll encounter on the trail. Not every tenth of a mile is included, usually only those that help you locate your position on the trail or that offer amenities, potential challenges or spectacular views.

Footers help to orientate you throughout the book.

REGION ONE:
BLACK RIVER HARBOR AREA

Designated as a National Scenic Byway in 1992, this exceptionally beautiful Black River area is known for its series of five lovely waterfalls en route to Lake Superior. One of the most beautiful waterfalls, Potawatomi, is paved and wheelchair accessible. Guarding the river's borders are old-growth pine, hemlock and hardwood forests. The harbor offers one of the area's few boating access points to Lake Superior and its dockside store profits are used to fund interpretive projects in the Ottawa National Forest. We recommend starting your adventure at the Ottawa National Forest District Service in Ironwood where knowledgeable staff, more area information and a small gift shop await (see Appendix B, pg. 251 for address). Then head to the Black River Harbor (perhaps for a picnic, see pg. 202) and quick harbor tour via our Almost Hike (pg. 158). Then explore the falls and bring that camera along!

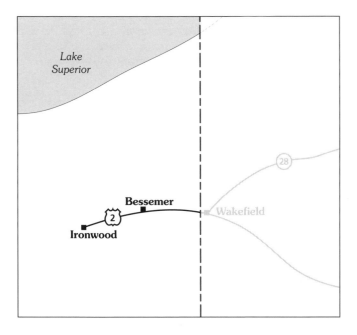

 **RAINBOW FALLS**

Black River Harbor Area • Off U.S. 2, 15.1 miles from Bessemer

- **See interesting kettles and rock formations of Rainbow Falls.**
- **Look for rainbow if conditions are right.**
- **Nice wooded hike.**

TRAILHEAD DIRECTIONS & PARKING:
From U.S. 2 in Bessemer, turn north on County Road 513 (Black River Road).
Drive 15.1 miles to paved parking area for Rainbow Falls.

TRAILHEAD FACILITIES & FEES:
Flush toilets nearby at Black River Harbor Picnic Area (pg. 202). Information kiosk.
No fees for trail use.

TOTAL TRAIL LENGTH, SURFACE & WIDTH:
0.3 mile; dirt and gravel; 4–6' wide. Minimum rock and root.

INCLINES & ALERTS:
There are no inclines over 10°, but there are a total of 194 steps; however, they
are non-continuous with a few resting platforms. Be aware that steps and trail drop
sharply to falls. Pace yourself and avoid overexertion. Dangerous waters and cliffs.
Stay behind barriers.

CONTACT:
Ottawa National Forest Visitor Center: (906) 358-4724

MILEAGE & DESCRIPTION

0.0   Trailhead begins at information kiosk on 4'-wide, hardpacked dirt and gravel
path. Note sign warning of dangerous waters. Stay behind barriers. From the
beginning of this trail, the wooded section is gorgeous. In 350', cross bridge
(wood, no handrail).

0.1   Find bench with a view of the forest in this section. Listen for falls. The North
Country Trail intersects just prior to steps. Continue toward steps and descend
194 (wood, double handrail, non-continuous) all the way down to viewing platform. We do not recommend leaving the steps as there are very steep drop-offs
with no guardrails in the area.

0.2   Overlook platform to Rainbow Falls. Interesting kettle formations and you may
see a rainbow if conditions are right. Retrace path to trailhead.

0.3   Trailhead.

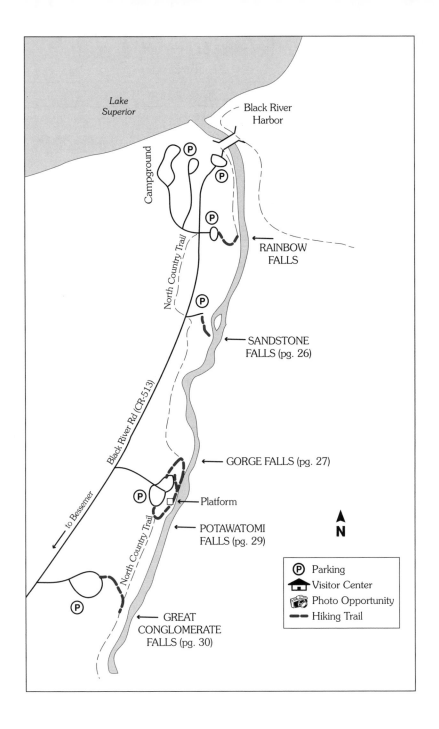

Lake
Superior

Black River
Harbor

Campground

North Country Trail

RAINBOW
FALLS

SANDSTONE
FALLS (pg. 26)

Black River Rd (CR-513)

GORGE FALLS (pg. 27)

to Bessemer

Platform

POTAWATOMI
FALLS (pg. 29)

North Country Trail

N

GREAT
CONGLOMERATE
FALLS (pg. 30)

Ⓟ Parking
Visitor Center
Photo Opportunity
Hiking Trail

SANDSTONE FALLS

Black River Harbor Area • Off U.S. 2, 14.4 miles from Bessemer

• **Sandstone Falls!**

TRAILHEAD DIRECTIONS & PARKING:

From U.S. 2 in Bessemer, turn north on County Road 513 (Black River Road). Drive 14.4 miles to paved parking area for Sandstone Falls.

TRAILHEAD FACILITIES & FEES:

Flush toilets nearby at Black River Harbor Picnic Area (pg. 202). No fees for trail use.

TOTAL TRAIL LENGTH, SURFACE & WIDTH:

0.1 mile; dirt and gravel; 4' wide.

INCLINES & ALERTS:

There is one incline (18° for 20') after descending 112 steps (non-continuous). This trail has a total of 140 steps. They are non-continuous with resting platforms and benches. All steps are composed of dirt and wood and although there is a single handrail, it is wide making it difficult to fully grasp. Steps have a variety of depth levels making them somewhat challenging to descend.

Steps and trail drop sharply to falls. Pace yourself and avoid overexertion. Because there are no high cliffs present at these falls, access to them is possible. Use caution when exploring as rock surfaces are very uneven and can be slippery when wet. There is no guardrail.

CONTACT:

Ottawa National Forest Visitor Center: (906) 358-4724

MILEAGE & DESCRIPTION

0.0 Trailhead begins at post indicating "¼ mile" on hardpacked dirt and gravel path

through a beautiful forest. In 200' find bench prior to descending 112 steps (non-continuous). There are two benches on steps. After steps, find incline (18° for 20'). Steps ease for 100' until descending 14 more. At this point, trail becomes loosely defined, but veer left and in approximately 200' find another set of 14 steps that leads down to falls area. Caution: Although the falls are not very high, they are lovely and powerful. Rocks near falls are very uneven and slippery when wet. Retrace path to trailhead.

0.1 Trailhead.

See map on page 25.

GORGE FALLS

Black River Harbor Area • Off U.S. 2, 13.7 miles from Bessemer

• **See beautiful Gorge Falls and Potawatomi Falls!**

TRAILHEAD DIRECTIONS & PARKING:
From U.S. 2 in Bessemer, turn north on County Road 513 (Black River Road).
Drive 13.7 miles to paved parking areas for Potawatomi Falls and Gorge Falls.
Follow signs to Gorge Falls. Wheelchair accessible parking available.

TRAILHEAD FACILITIES & FEES:
Vault toilet (wheelchair accessible), picnic area, grill. Flush toilets at Black River
Harbor Picnic Area (pg. 202). No fees for trail use.

TOTAL TRAIL LENGTH, SURFACE & WIDTH:
0.2 mile; dirt; 6' wide. Minimum rock, significant root in sections.

INCLINES & ALERTS:
There are no inclines over 10°, but there are a total of 187 steps. They are non-
continuous throughout the trail with many providing benches and/or resting platforms. All steps and boardwalk are composed of wood and have double handrails.
Some steps are very steep and some step-heights can be challenging. Dangerous
waters. Stay behind barrier.

CONTACT:
Ottawa National Forest Visitor Center: (906) 358-4724

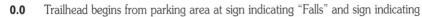

MILEAGE & DESCRIPTION

0.0   Trailhead begins from parking area at sign indicating "Falls" and sign indicating
"Caution! Dangerous waters." Stay behind barrier on 6' dirt path. In 200', turn
right at intersection and descend 10 steps. Immediately take another left and continue down 37 steps (non-continuous). Some steps are very steep and some step-
height can be challenging. Find bench, then descend 27 steps to platform #1,
which showcases beautiful Gorge Falls. You will soon see how it acquired its
name. Once back on main trail, expect significant root for about 100', then
descend 5 steps. Alert: These steps were uneven and loose at time of writing—
summer 2005). Continue down a stretch of decline to bench. Ascend 8 steps to
platform #2, which overlooks the gorge. From here, ascend 40 steps (non-continuous) to reach main trail. Veer left and look for another set of steps to the left.
Descend 41 steps (non-continuous), then ascend 17 to platform #3. From bench
descend 2 steps for the perfect photo op of Potawatomi Falls. After returning to
the main trail, turn left. Steps end and trail is now paved.

0.1   Read about "Geology of the Black River and Frontier Days" at the kiosk as you
find three benches. Follow pavement along railed ridge until it meets boardwalk,
which leads to the final observation platform featuring a simply stunning view of
Potawatomi Falls! Find two more benches. Upon return, do not retrace path to
trailhead as there is an easier way. Follow the blacktop and at the first paved
intersection, turn left.

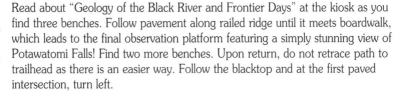

0.2 Continue to follow paved trail to parking area as you will have made somewhat of a loop. En route to parking area is a vault toilet (wheelchair accessible) and picnic area.

See map on page 25.

 SAYS WHO?

Make bones about it!

Regular physical activity helps to prevent/reduce osteoporosis and can decrease the risk of hip fracture in women by up to 50%.

World Health Organization [21]

Gorge Falls. Photo by Lisa Vogelsang

POTAWATOMI FALLS

Black River Harbor Area • Off U.S. 2, 13.7 miles from Bessemer

- **See beautiful and very picturesque Potawatomi Falls!**
- **This trail is wheelchair accessible.**

TRAILHEAD DIRECTIONS & PARKING:
From U.S. 2 in Bessemer, turn north on County Road 513 (Black River Road). Drive 13.7 miles to paved parking areas for Potawatomi and Gorge Falls. Important: For wheelchair accessible portion of Potawatomi Falls, follow sign to Gorge Falls. At the entry of Gorge Falls parking area is a paved trail that leads to the Potawatomi Falls viewing platform. If you park in the lot for Potawatomi Falls, there are steps en route to falls. However, you will end up at the very same viewing platform as the paved trail from the Gorge Falls parking area. Wheelchair accessible parking available.

TRAILHEAD FACILITIES & FEES:
Vault toilet (wheelchair accessible), picnic area, grill. Flush toilets at Black River Harbor Picnic Area (pg. 202). No fees for trail use.

TOTAL TRAIL LENGTH, SURFACE & WIDTH:
0.3 mile; paved; 5' wide.

INCLINES & ALERTS:
There are no inclines over 10°

CONTACT:
Ottawa National Forest Visitor Center: (906) 358-4724

MILEAGE & DESCRIPTION

0.0   Trailhead begins at sign indicating Potawatomi Falls Barrier Free Access on 5' paved path. In 90' find vault toilet and paved path to picnic table. At intersection, turn right.

0.1   Boardwalk (wood, double handrail), which leads to the observation platform. The first bench has a foliage-dependent view of part of the falls, but keep going as the view gets spectacular in just 40' at the next bench. The falls are very picturesque and quite nice. Retrace paved path to the first intersection and continue straight until pavement ends at information kiosk. Read about "Geology of the Black River and Frontier Days." There are three benches here. Trail turns to dirt beyond this point and has many steps. To maintain wheelchair accessibility, retrace path to trailhead.

0.3   Trailhead.

See map on page 25.

GREAT CONGLOMERATE FALLS

Black River Harbor Area • Off U.S. 2, 13 miles from Bessemer

- **Lovely Great Conglomerate Falls and breathtaking views of Black River.**
- **Hike in a beautifully wooded section.**

TRAILHEAD DIRECTIONS & PARKING:
From U.S. 2 in Bessemer, turn north on County Road 513 (Black River Road). Drive 13 miles to paved parking area for Great Conglomerate Falls.

TRAILHEAD FACILITIES & FEES:
Flush toilets at Black River Harbor Picnic Area (pg. 202). No fees for trail use.

TOTAL TRAIL LENGTH, SURFACE & WIDTH:
1.0 mile; dirt; 5–8' wide. Minimum rock, small section of significant root at end.

INCLINES & ALERTS:
There are no inclines over 10°, but there is a consistent upgrade on the return for about 1100'. There are a total of 102 steps; however, they are non-continuous throughout the trail with many providing benches and/or resting platforms. All steps are composed of wood and dirt and have no handrails unless otherwise noted. Viewing platform at falls is not decking but bare uneven rock. There are railings to help with balance. Dangerous waters. Stay behind barrier.

CONTACT:
Ottawa National Forest Visitor Center: (906) 358-4724

MILEAGE & DESCRIPTION

0.0
Trailhead begins at steps near information kiosk. Descend 12 steps (non-continuous) and find sign indicating "Conglomerate Falls." Trail continues through a very beautifully wooded forest.

0.2
Descend 5 steps.

0.3
Bench with view of forest prior to descending 14 steps (non-continuous). Alert: Dangerous waters. Stay on trail.

0.4
Descend 17 steps. In 300' descend 10 more steps (single handrail at times, non-continuous). Soon come to bench with partial river views. Listen for falls as they are not yet visible.

0.5
Descend 37 steps (single handrail). Shortly a section of significant root leads to the descent of another 7 steps (single handrail) and to falls viewing area. Alert: Last step height is steep and viewing area is not a platform, but simply a fenced area atop very uneven rock. Although the rails help with balance, use caution. The views are not only terrific of falls, but also look downstream for a glorious view of the Black River and its rocky borders. Retrace path to trailhead.

1.0
Trailhead.

See map on page 25.

REGION TWO:
PORCUPINE MOUNTAIN AREA

Welcome to 60,000 acres of wilderness and the last large tract of old-growth hardwood and hemlock forest in the Midwest! Porcupine Mountains Wilderness State Park has over 90 miles of foot trails for persons of all ability levels, but the most famous view—Lake of the Clouds—is wheelchair accessible and featured on pg. 34. The Porcupine Mountains were named by the Ojibwe and showcase incredible beauty, much of which can be seen from trails in this section of our book. Featured are virgin stands of massive old-growth forest, spectacular self-guided interpretive hikes, historical artifacts from mining era, access to the highest point in the Porcupine Mountains via Summit Peak Tower, stunning tree-lined drives to trailheads, exceptional scenic rivers, terraced-rock waterfalls, a suspension bridge and island exploration!

We recommend starting at the Wilderness Visitor Center for an amazing wildlife exhibit, well-stocked gift shop and lots of free information from an incredibly knowledgeable staff.

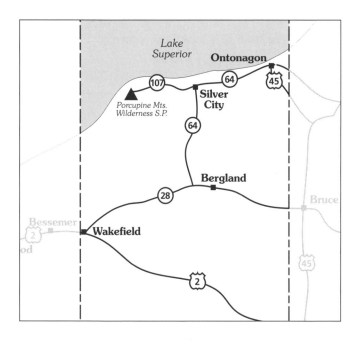

Porcupine Mountains Wilderness State Park • On MI 107, 6.3 miles from Silver City

- **Very beautiful wooded hike through old-growth forest.**
- **Quaint views of the Upper Carp River.**

TRAILHEAD DIRECTIONS & PARKING:

From MI 28 in Bergland, turn north on MI 64 and drive 17.7 miles to the junction of MI 64 and MI 107 in Silver City. Turn left (west) on MI 107 and drive for 6.3 miles to the small dirt and gravel parking lot near the sign for Government Peak Trail.

TRAILHEAD FACILITIES & FEES:

Information kiosk. Annual or day use state park permit is required and available at Wilderness Visitor Center, Park Headquarters and Presque Isle Ranger Station.

TOTAL TRAIL LENGTH, SURFACE & WIDTH:

1.8 miles; hardpacked dirt; 1–5' wide. Moderate rock (significant during first 800'), moderate root.

INCLINES & ALERTS:

There are no inclines greater than 10°. Some sections of boardwalk are narrow (1' wide) and overgrowth and mud may be problematic depending on conditions. Hiking pole advised as first 800' is uneven with loose rock. Trek carefully.

CONTACT:

Porcupine Mountain Wilderness State Park: (906) 885-5275

MILEAGE & DESCRIPTION

0.0   Trailhead begins from dirt parking area at sign indicating "Government Peak Trail" on 8'-wide rocky path up a gentle grade. Alert: Loose and uneven rock for the next 800'—trek carefully.

0.1   At intersection turn left as rocky surface continues.

0.3   Expect mud and narrow boardwalk (1' wide) in this section. Cross bridge (wood, no handrail) over small creek.

0.4   More narrow boardwalk with 5 step-like increments. In 200' note a marvelous stand of hemlock that lingers for 400'. Absolutely striking and good birding area!

0.5   At intersection, do not follow ski trail sign, but veer left and cross wider section of boardwalk. Dramatic stand of old growth ends. After significant root section, do not follow sign indicating "Overlook Trail," but peek around to read the other sign indicating "Trap Falls." You will not go all the way to Trap Falls (exceeds our trail length criteria) but proceed in that direction.

0.6   Alert: Narrow boardwalk, uneven in places. Expect mud, overgrowth, and a laid log path with uneven footing.

0.7   Uprooted tree at the time of writing (summer 2004); follow the small path behind it to give walking "under" a tree new meaning!

0.8   Alert: Large hole—pass carefully on right. Expect significant overgrowth as trail narrows to 1'. Many beautiful seasonal wildflowers here. Narrow boardwalk and another hole—pass on the left.

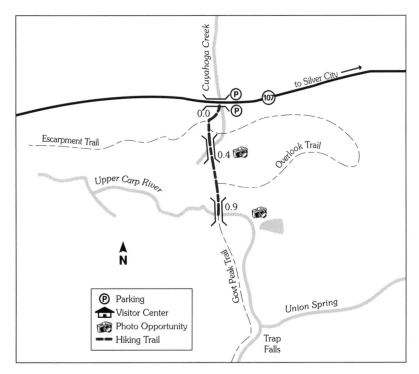

0.9   Five steps up to bridge (6' wide, wood, no handrail). Enjoy the Upper Carp River's quaint beauty. Retrace path to trailhead.

1.6   Alert: When approaching the same rocky section that began this trail, use caution as uneven and loose rock makes descent more challenging than ascent.

1.8   Trailhead.

Foot Note:

Many trails in this book showcase beautiful seasonal wildflowers. We recommend carrying a field guide (see Appendix A, pg. 246) for easy identification.

LAKE OF THE CLOUDS

Porcupine Mountains Wilderness State Park • Off MI 107, 10.5 miles from Silver City

* **See beautiful Lake of the Clouds!**
* **Wheelchair accessible observation platform via boardwalk.**
* **Scenic drive through the Porcupine Mountains to trailhead.**

TRAILHEAD DIRECTIONS & PARKING:

From MI 28 in Bergland, turn north on MI 64 and drive 17.7 miles to the junction of MI 64 and MI 107 in Silver City. Turn left (west) on MI 107, drive for 10.5 miles to the Lake of the Clouds paved parking area. Ample parking with wheelchair accessible parking available.

TRAILHEAD FACILITIES & FEES:

Vault toilets (wheelchair accessible), picnic tables, information kiosk, bench. Annual or day use state park permit is required and available at Presque Isle Ranger Station, Wilderness Visitor Center and Park Headquarters.

TOTAL TRAIL LENGTH, SURFACE & WIDTH:

0.2 mile; boardwalk; 7' wide.

INCLINES & ALERTS:

There are no inclines greater than 10°.

CONTACT:

Porcupine Mountain Wilderness State Park: (906) 885-5275

MILEAGE & DESCRIPTION

0.0   Trailhead begins from paved parking area at sign indicating Lake of the Clouds. There are two paths that lead to two different overlooks. We chose to include the boardwalk route as it is wheelchair accessible and the gentler of the two. The boardwalk is 7' wide (wood, double handrail) and meets ADA standards.

In approximately 150' you will encounter the first of six benches, which are spaced approximately 100' apart. Five have nice views of the forest and information markers are being added.

0.1   The view from the sixth bench is a jewel as you are now on the observation deck with commanding views of Lake of the Clouds and the rugged cliff face that towers above it to the north. Information signs showcase beautiful color photos of wildlife and the peregrine falcon. They also give info on the geology of the escarpment. Plan to spend some time up here as it's worth the view as well as the read. Afterward, retrace path to trailhead.

0.2   Trailhead.

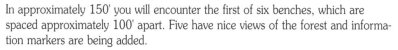

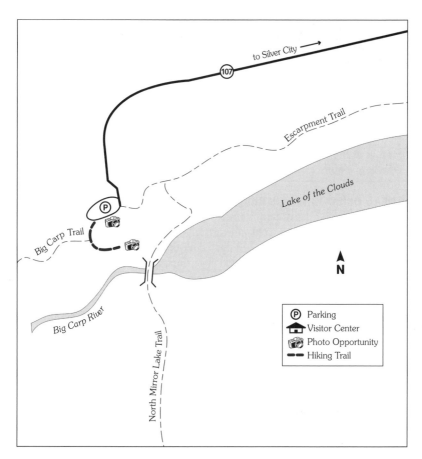

 SAYS WHO?

Feeling blue? Get into the green.

Just one brisk 30-minute walk can help lift your mood!

Medicine & Science in Sports & Exercise [30]

WILDERNESS VISITOR CENTER NATURE TRAIL

Porcupine Mountains Wilderness State Park • Off South Boundary Road, 3.6 miles from Silver City

- **Beautiful, wooded, self-guided interpretive hike; 25 colorful signs throughout reveal a wealth of information—all worth the read.**

- **Stop in at the Wilderness Visitor Center en route to trailhead to see an amazing wildlife exhibit.**

TRAILHEAD DIRECTIONS & PARKING:

From MI 28 in Bergland, turn north on MI 64 and drive 17.7 miles to the junction of MI 64 and MI 107 in Silver City. Turn left (west) on MI 107 and drive for 2.7 miles to the intersection of MI 107 and South Boundary Road (notice the sign that indicates Visitor Center). Turn left and drive along South Boundary Road for 0.4 miles, turn right at Entrance Road and a sign that indicates the Visitor Center. Drive 0.5 miles to paved parking for Wilderness Visitor Center area. Wheelchair accessible parking available. RV parking in separate nearby lot (follow signs).

TRAILHEAD FACILITIES & FEES:

Flush toilet (wheelchair accessible), water, incredible visitor center (see Wilderness Visitor Center, pg. 184), gift shop, small picnic area. Annual or day use state park permit is required and available at Wilderness Visitor Center, Park Headquarters and Presque Isle Ranger Station.

TOTAL TRAIL LENGTH, SURFACE & WIDTH:

1.3 miles; hardpacked dirt; 1–5' wide. Minimum rock and root.

INCLINES & ALERTS:

There are no inclines greater than 10°. Some sections of boardwalk are narrow (1' wide) and overgrowth and mud may be problematic depending on environmental conditions. Trail requires one road crossing.

CONTACT:

Porcupine Mountain Wilderness State Park: (906) 885-5275

MILEAGE & DESCRIPTION

0.0 Trailhead begins 100' south of Wilderness Visitor Center at sign indicating "Nature Trail" on 2' hardpacked dirt trail. The forest's beauty becomes apparent as you reach the first interpretive marker 120' into the trail. Sign #1 reveals interesting information about the Old-Growth Forest in which you are standing. In another 100', find Sign #2 and read the bio of an abundant energetic creature—the red squirrel.

Alert: Shortly you will come to the Visitor Center entrance road. Turn left and walk along side of road on grassy area for 60' until you see a bridge (wood, double handrail) on the other side of the road, which marks your re-entry onto the trail. Use caution when crossing road.

0.1 Sign #3 features info about a delicious forest delicacy—the Thimbleberry. In another 100', cross bridge over a lovely fern glade, followed by 4 steps up (all wood, double handrail). Shortly, Sign #4 tells about the Eastern Hemlock. Discover why they call him the Old Man of the Forest. Sign #5 gives info on the White Birch and its importance to the Ojibwe people. Soon, cross another bridge (wood, double handrail) over a lovely fern glade.

0.2 Find bench with nice views of the forest. Listen for the "cuk-cuk-cuk" sound of the large Pileated Woodpecker as you will most likely hear him before you see him. In 200', Sign #6 reveals his dietary delicacies and living quarters. Farther on, Sign #7 gives tips on identifying a Balsam Fir (as well as who prefers its delicacy) and Sign #8 tells of one of nature's riddles—Lichens. Did you know that healthy lichens indicate clean, healthy air?

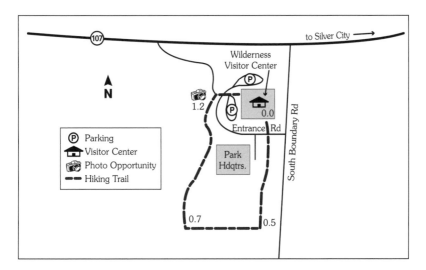

0.3 Intermittent sections of boardwalk continue for 350'. Alert: Boardwalk is narrow (1' wide). Use caution.

0.4 Alert: Muddy section. A good place to spot animal tracks. Overgrowth possible. Sign #9 reveals the Ancient Rock and how to differentiate between conglomerate and sandstone rock types. Sign #10 features the beloved Sugar Maple. We aren't the only species that love its sweetness. Read about what else depends on the most successful tree species in the Upper Peninsula.

0.5 At intersection, turn right, following trail marker. Sign #11 showcases the DNR's role in Black Bear management. In 200', cross bridge (20' wide, wood, no handrail) over Jamison Creek.

0.6 Sign #12 features the creature that the state park is named after—The Porcupine. It has 30,000 barbed quills (imagine being the person who had to count them all!). Cute, but definitely not cuddly.

0.7 Sign #13 provides info on the most widely distributed game bird in North

America—the Ruffed Grouse. It can often be seen on this trail. Listen for an explosive flurry of wing beats! Alert: Overgrowth and very muddy sections to come. At next intersection, turn right and follow sign for nature trail. Sign #14 reveals a very interesting fact. You have actually been walking on the Old Tram Road for the past few minutes. Can you spot traces of it? This sign boasts a great vintage photo accompanied by the history of Nonesuch Mining Company.

0.8 Descend 19 steps (wood and dirt, no handrail), expect more mud, cross boardwalk, then ascend 12 steps (wood and dirt, no handrail). This puts you atop a small ridgeline of lovely fern glade. Sign #15 features the Yellow Birch and tells how to recognize it.

0.9 Sign #16 contains interesting insect facts. Did you know that insects account for over half of all known living species of organisms and that most are actually beneficial? Ample photos are provided here. Have you seen any of these on your hike? Sign #17 reveals facts about the Bluebead Lily whose fruit is inedible to humans, but other creatures like it. Read to find out who.

As the small gorge shifts to the right side, notice the exceptional beauty through this part of the forest. Sign #18 explains what some of those colorful tree ornaments are that you may have noticed. These Decay Fungi play an important role in the forest ecosystem. Read how and enjoy the vivid color photos of the various fungi types. Sign #19 provides info on the most abundant wildflower in the park's old-growth hemlock forests: Canada Mayflower.

1.0 Cross boardwalk. Alert: May be loose in sections. Sign #20 may whet your taste buds for some of Dr. Chase's 1866 Root Beer as this marker proudly displays his authentic recipe! And it features none other than Wild Sarsaparilla.

1.1 Sign #21 tells of another common, but graceful presence—the White-tailed Deer. It is no stranger to most parts of the country. Fawns lose their spots at about 4 months old. At Sign #22, find out "who-cooks-for-you" as you listen for and read about the Barred Owl. At 17 inches tall, it boasts a 45-inch wingspan.

1.2 Sign #23 contains an image of the actual size of a wolf footprint. Michigan has more gray wolves than any other state except Alaska and Minnesota. Sign #24 provides color photos and great descriptions of Club Moss. There are 7 species within the park—which have you seen? The last sign, #25, provides info on the Big Tooth Aspen. Also known as poplar or popple, they are known for their ability to reclaim burned-over forestlands in northern Michigan.

At intersection, turn right to return to Wilderness Visitor Center. If you have not visited yet, we strongly encourage spending some time there. Descend 6 steps (wood and dirt, no handrail) onto boardwalk that crosses a wide variety of ferns. The multiple hues of green contrasted nicely with the gray bark, which makes for a nice photo. One more muddy section and 4 steps up (wood and dirt, no handrail) puts you back across entrance road to Visitor Center. Alert: Use caution when crossing road to return to parking area.

1.3 Parking area & trailhead.

 **Foot Note:**

Muddy places along various trails in this book can bring out an irresistible urge to linger while looking for animal tracks. Pick up a field guide (see Appendix A, pg. 246 for suggestions) for family fun!

Wilderness Visitor Center Nature Trail. Photo by Lisa Vogelsang

UNION MINE INTERPRETIVE TRAIL

Porcupine Mountains Wilderness State Park • Off South Boundary Road, 4.4 miles from Silver City

- **Fabulous interpretive trail (pick up guide from trailhead).**
- **Scenery abounds along the Union River as well as a glorious hemlock forest.**

TRAILHEAD DIRECTIONS & PARKING:

From MI 28 in Bergland, turn north on MI 64 and drive 17.7 miles to the junction of MI 64 and MI 107 in Silver City. Turn left (west) on MI 107 and drive for 2.7 miles to the intersection of MI 107 and South Boundary Road (notice sign for Visitor Center). Turn left and drive along South Boundary Road for 1.7 miles. Turn right into gravel parking area for Union Mine Trail.

TRAILHEAD FACILITIES & FEES:

Information kiosk. Annual or day use state park permit is required and available at Wilderness Visitor Center, Park Headquarters and Presque Isle Ranger Station.

TOTAL TRAIL LENGTH, SURFACE & WIDTH:

1.1 miles; hardpacked dirt; 1–3' wide. Moderate rock and root (significant in sections).

INCLINES & ALERTS:

There are no inclines greater than 10°. Expect overgrowth in sections. Must cross South Boundary Road twice. Steep cliffs with no guardrails along parts of river.

CONTACT:

Porcupine Mountain Wilderness State Park: (906) 885-5275

MILEAGE & DESCRIPTION

0.0   Trailhead begins near huge shovel at sign indicating "Union Mine Trail." Pick up an interpretive brochure here. At time of writing (summer 2005) the trail had two sets of interpretive signage. One set consisted of only numbers that corresponded to the brochure. The other set was actual interpretive signs with text and some photos. To maximize your historical experience, we recommend reading the brochure and interpretive signs on your journey.

Begin by reading about Union Mine at the information kiosk at trailhead. Grasp a sliver of life from a miner's diary: "May 27, 1846. Done various things, besides murdering 700 black flies." Depending on when you visit, history may repeat itself....

Expect overgrowth in this section. Find a reminder that "all America lies at the end of the wilderness road...."

0.1   For Marker #1, consult brochure and look for small shaft. Upon return, continue down hill (right) and find copper interpretive sign. The abundance of copper in Michigan enabled widespread distribution of electricity in the U.S.

In 400', consult brochure and find Marker #2. Look across the river for "trap" rock that held copper deposits sought by miners. Read about it and see photo on interpretive sign nearby. Soon encounter a section of significant root.

0.2 Now you are literally hiking along the river with photo-worthy views! For Marker #3, consult brochure and look for remnant of trench used to uncover copper ore. Interpretive sign gives history of Ontonagon's founding father—considered by some as "half horse and half alligator."

Expect sections of significant rock and root over the next 200'. Meanwhile, find bench with river views. Scenery in this area is absolutely gorgeous! For Marker #4, consult brochure and look for a remnant squared trough that once housed a water wheel. Interpretive sign gives photo of wheel and diary excerpts. Markers #5 and #6 as well as interpretive sign feature info on mine shaft and tunnels.

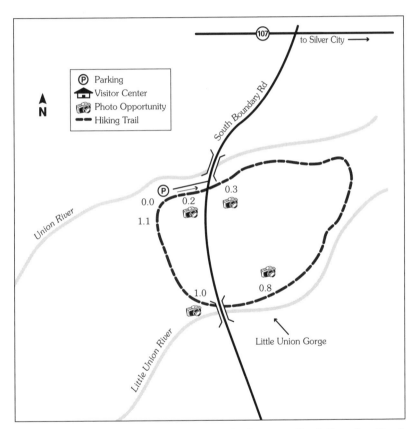

0.3 Ascend 5 steps (wood and gravel, no handrail) to cross South Boundary Road, then descend 2 steps (wood and gravel, no handrail).

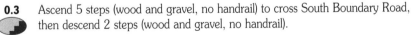 Some overgrowth and moderate root lead to Markers #7 and 8, which are 100' apart. Imagine... 100' under the very ground upon which you stand lies a 700' tunnel that was dug by hand-labor. Consult brochure for more information. Interpretive sign reveals photo of 1865 stamp mill.

Ascend 7 steps (wood, no handrail) to a marvelous photo op of the delicate, but beautiful falls. Alert: Steep cliff, no guardrail.

0.4 Descend 30 steps (wood, no handrail, non-continuous). Expect sections of moderate to significant rock and root over the next 400'. Alert: Near edge of cliff. Use caution.

0.5 Find bench with river views and Marker #9. Read brochure about the sandstone and copper deposits. In 300', interpretive sign showcases photo of the first road to this part of the mountains and brochure explains Marker #10. We speculate that it was this road that birthed the seatbelt concept!

In 100', trail turns off Nonesuch Road as you ascend 33 steps (wood and gravel, no handrail, non-continuous). Marker #11—read brochure for excerpts from Spalding's diary.

0.6 Narrow "treelike steps" lead over wet areas. Soon encounter interpretive sign showcasing more excerpts from Spalding's 1846 adventures. Stories range from an 80-year-old chief's fight with a bear and July 4th celebrations to the baby born next to the office. A rare glimpse into life some 140 years ago!

0.7 Note the massive hemlock in this area! In 200', find significant rock and root.

0.8 A bench with view of beautiful, delicate falls. This is a highly scenic area. Find Marker #12 and interpretive sign. Brochure and sign inform about mining companies, the latter featuring a photo of raising the copper!

0.9 Alert: Steep cliffs, no guardrails. Significant to moderate root.

1.0 Find bench and photogenic Little Union Falls. Marker #13—brochure reveals why mines were located near rivers.

In 100' ascend 5 steps (wood, no handrail), cross South Boundary Road, and then descend 4 steps (wood, no handrail). Soon find interpretive sign for #3 and #4 shafts that depicts a drawing of what is believed to be the tunnel structure for mines. In 200', consult brochure as Marker #14 reflects on the handful of serious mines in the Porcupine Mountains.

Soon cross narrow bridge (no handrail) before the final interpretive sign, which bids farewell to Mr. Spalding.

1.1 Parking lot and trailhead.

NONESUCH MINE

Porcupine Mountains Wilderness State Park • Off South Boundary Road, 6.9 miles from Silver City

- **This little jewel's trailhead is a bit challenging to find, but worth the effort as you will see the actual remnants of Nonesuch Mine and township.**
- **Read about intriguing history on trailhead kiosk and view sketch of Nonesuch during its heyday!**

TRAILHEAD DIRECTIONS & PARKING:

From MI 28 in Bergland, turn north on MI 64 and drive 17.7 miles to the junction of MI 64 and MI 107 in Silver City. Turn left (west) on MI 107 and drive for 2.7 miles to the intersection of MI 107 and South Boundary Road (note sign indicating Visitor Center). Turn left and drive along South Boundary Road for about 4.2 miles. This one is easy to miss. When you see a sign indicating a curve in the road and Speed Limit 30 mph, slow down and begin to look to the left for a small dirt road. Pull in and follow to gate, then park in dirt area.

TRAILHEAD FACILITIES & FEES:

Information sign on the history of Nonesuch Mine and township. Annual or day use state park permit is required and available at Wilderness Visitor Center, Park Headquarters and Presque Isle Ranger Station.

TOTAL TRAIL LENGTH, SURFACE & WIDTH:

1.0 mile; grass and hardpacked dirt; 12' wide (narrows to 2' on spur). Minimal rock and root.

INCLINES & ALERTS:

There are two inclines ranging from 13–16°. Steepest is 16° for 50' at 0.5 on the return. Danger: Do not climb on any rock walls or foundations or attempt to enter mine. Stay alert when near rock walls or foundations, as they are tall, old and unstable. Expect overgrowth and low hanging branches.

CONTACT:

Porcupine Mountain Wilderness State Park: (906) 885-5275

MILEAGE & DESCRIPTION

0.0   Trailhead begins from dirt parking area at sign indicating "Nonesuch Mine" near gate on 12'-wide, grassy (and overgrown) path. Follow this path for the next 0.4 mile. Expect to see many seasonal wildflowers.

0.4   A sign indicating "Do not climb on rock foundation" will be to the left. Immediately begin looking for a 1–2'-wide dirt spur trail to the left. Shortly you will descend 4 steps (dirt and wood, no handrail) and in about 100' look right for first sign of a wall. You will see more signs warning of not climbing on rock foundation. Please obey these signs for your safety as well as for the preservation of this historical relic. You will encounter more walls and in another 100' or so, the old mine. Alert: Danger, keep out.

0.5 A 150' trek through some overgrowth and low-hanging branches brings you to the Little Iron River. In high water conditions, you may be able to spot Nonesuch Falls, but at time of writing (July 2004) the falls were, er—nonesuch! Turn around here and retrace path to trailhead. In 200' you will encounter both inclines (16° and 13° respectively) that are very close together, each extending 50' on your return journey.

1.0 Trailhead.

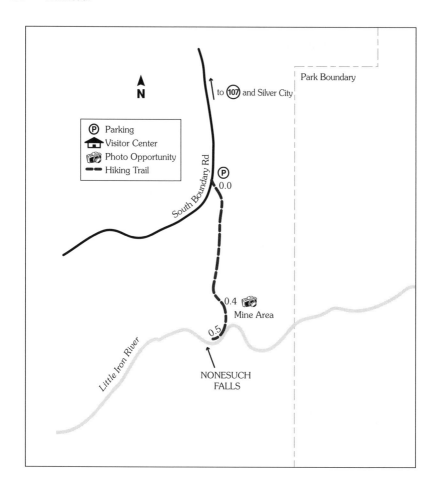

SUMMIT PEAK TOWER

Porcupine Mountains Wilderness State Park • Off South Boundary Road, 16.4 miles from Silver City

- **Lovely wooded picnic area and huge information kiosk showcasing field guide to bedrock, geological map, the ancient mountains and 1950s blowdown.**
- **Summit Peak Tower is the highest point (1,958') in the Porcupine Mountains overlooking Lake Superior and old-growth forest.**

TRAILHEAD DIRECTIONS & PARKING:
From MI 28 in Bergland, turn north on MI 64 and drive 17.7 miles to the junction of MI 64 and MI 107 in Silver City. Turn left (west) on MI 107 and drive for 2.7 miles to the intersection of MI 107 and South Boundary Road (notice sign for Visitor Center). Turn left and drive along South Boundary Road for 11.7 miles and turn right at Summit Peak Road. Notice the sign that indicates Summit Peak Scenic Area—park permit required. In 0.1 mile is a parking area designated for trailer unhitching (trailers over 6 feet are required to unhitch). RVs park here also but keep in mind that it is 1.9 miles to the trailhead. Continue straight on Summit Peak Road for 1.9 miles along a beautiful wooded drive and turn into ample paved parking for the Summit Peak Scenic Area. Wheelchair accessible parking available.

TRAILHEAD FACILITIES & FEES:
Unique composting and recycling toilet system (wheelchair accessible), is chemical- and water-free (see Foot Note), huge information kiosk, bench, small wooded picnic area. Annual or day use state park permit is required and available at Wilderness Visitor Center, Park Headquarters and Presque Isle Ranger Station.

TOTAL TRAIL LENGTH, SURFACE & WIDTH:
1.0 mile; hardpacked dirt, boardwalk; average 5' wide. Minimal rock and root.

INCLINES & ALERTS:
There are 7 inclines ranging from 12–18°. Steepest is 18° for 80' at 0.1 mile. All inclines are within the first 0.3 mile, making this a fairly steady moderate climb, but 5 strategically placed benches help. The trail has 229 steps. They are non-continuous throughout the trail and interspersed with benches and/or resting platforms. All steps on this trail are composed of wood, have double handrails and were in excellent shape at time of writing (summer 2004). Danger: Do not ascend tower during electrical storms.

CONTACT:
Porcupine Mountain Wilderness State Park: (906) 885-5275

MILEAGE & DESCRIPTION

0.0 Trailhead begins directly across from restroom at kiosk near sign indicating "Summit Peak Trail" up a gentle slope of hardpacked dirt and gravel. In 100', you will see a switchback. Do not take it at the request of park service. Stay on main trail to the right. The first incline (14° for 40') brings you to the first bench (all have views of forest). Next incline is 14° for 65'.

0.1 Two more benches in this section, which also has the steepest incline (18° for 80'). Find another incline of 14° for 80'.

0.2 Two more inclines (13° for 30' and 12° for 80') prior to bench with forest views. Just one more incline (14° for 55') and another bench mark the end of the slopes.

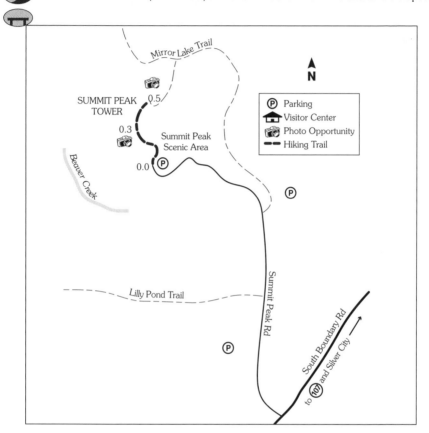

0.3 Now that the inclines are finally over, the stairs welcome you! But their ascent is worth the view. Ascend 48 steps and soon you will see an intersection located on the stairs. Turn left and descend 13 steps toward the first overlook for a fantastic mountain vista! A bench awaits for your viewing pleasure. Return to intersection and note sign indicating "Observation Tower." The tower's base is 690' from this location, making it a little over 0.1 mile to go. Ascend 41 steps, find a bench, boardwalk, and then ascend 31 more.

0.4 Another bench, 3 steps up, 7 down, another 32 up and 160' of boardwalk bring you to the tower's base.

0.5   Base of Summit Peak Tower. Ample benches make for a nice rest before the ascent of the final 54 steps to the top. Step width narrows as you begin the ascent to the highest point in the Porcupine Mountains. Alert: Do not ascend tower during electrical storms.

 The view from the top offers a sweeping panoramic vista of the Porcupine Mountains, extensive old-growth forest and Lake Superior (on a clear day). If it's exceptionally clear, you may be able to spot the Apostle Islands to the Northwest. The stack to the east is the White Pine Stack. The directional map here is very informative and worth the read. A small bench affords extended viewing pleasure. Normally we'd say it's a nice place to chill, but since we're atop the Porcupines, we'll say it's a nice place to "quill!"

When finished, retrace path to trailhead.

1.0 Trailhead.

 Foot Note:

The self-contained toilet system herein is flushless, saving thousands of gallons of water each year and functions without chemical additives. Invented in Sweden in 1937 by ecologist and artist R. Lindstrom, it does not produce sewage, but uses a natural air-fed biological decomposition to convert human fertilizers into an odor-free compost "tea"— similar in composition to topsoil.

SAYS WHO?

In 32 out of 44 studies, up to a 40% reduction in breast cancer risk was observed in women who were most physically active.

The Journal of Nutrition [13]

GREENSTONE FALLS

Porcupine Mountains Wilderness State Park • Off South Boundary Road, 19.6 miles from Silver City

- **Spectacular drive to trailhead!**
- **Exceptionally scenic hike along the Little Carp River leads to the intriguing Greenstone Falls.**
- **Bring the camera—the entire trail is one big photo op!**

TRAILHEAD DIRECTIONS & PARKING:

From MI 28 in Bergland, turn north on MI 64 and drive 17.7 miles to the junction of MI 64 and MI 107 in Silver City. Turn left (west) on MI 107 and drive for 2.7 miles to the intersection of MI 107 and South Boundary Road (notice sign for Visitor Center). Turn left and drive along South Boundary Road for 16.4 miles and turn right at the dirt road called, Little Carp River Road. Notice a sign that says Dead End No Trailers – park permit required. Do not take trailers or RVs as there is not enough room to turn around. Continue straight on Little Carp River Road for 0.5 miles along a beautiful wooded drive until you reach the parking area (also dirt) just before wooden bridge.

TRAILHEAD FACILITIES & FEES:

Info kiosk and bench. Annual or day use state park permit is required and available at Wilderness Visitor Center, Park Headquarters and Presque Isle Ranger Station.

TOTAL TRAIL LENGTH, SURFACE & WIDTH:

1.0 mile; hardpacked dirt; 2–3' wide. Minimal rock, significant root.

INCLINES & ALERTS:

There are no inclines over 10°; however, the trail has several sections of narrow (1' wide) boardwalk with some sections elevated 1–2' off the ground (no handrails). Expect some mud. Steep cliffs toward falls area.

CONTACT:

Porcupine Mountain Wilderness State Park: (906) 885-5275

MILEAGE & DESCRIPTION

0.0

Take time to note beautiful Blowdown Creek en route to trailhead—picturesque in its own right. To the left just prior to the bridge is a short path to Overlooked Falls (see pg. 161 for details on this Almost Hike). Pass bench and stop for lovely views of the Little Carp River from the bridge (wood, no handrail). Trailhead is just beyond bridge at sign indicating "Little Carp River Trail (Greenstone Falls)" on 3' dirt path.

As trail hugs river, views are simply gorgeous! In 200', find tree roots that can be negotiated like steps. Begin looking to the left for Overlooked Falls. Although the view is clearly better from the other side of the river, part of the falls can be seen here. Alert: Significant section of root shortly—use caution. Just prior to crossing a bridge (wood, no handrail), look left again to see the bottom of Overlooked

Falls. Immediately after this bridge, trail turns sharply to the right. Blue blazes on trees mark trail. You are still along the creek, but are now on a small ridgeline.

0.1   More root and muddy sections, but lovely wooded area.

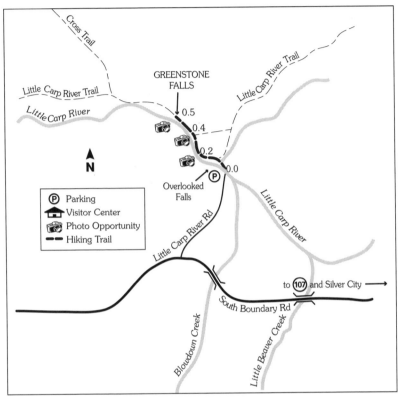

0.2   Encounter significant root and more mud in this section as trail nears river. In 150', cross boardwalk. Look left for small, picturesque falls. In another 200', find narrow section of elevated boardwalk (no handrail, uneven in places) with one step up. Trail turns away from river.

0.3   This section is filled with boardwalk and significant root. Boardwalk has single step increments (10 total) with one big step down in 250'. This section also contains a few steps (dirt and wood, no handrail).

0.4   At intersection, turn left and follow sign indicating "Greenstone Falls Cabin." In 200', encounter a leaning bridge (wood, single rope handrail) over picturesque creek. Alert: Step down at end of bridge has a 16-inch vertical drop; use caution. In the next 250', more significant sections of root lead to more tree root-like steps that take you up to a taller ridgeline. Alert: Steep cliffs. Gorgeous views of the Little Carp River. Stop on occasion and look over your left shoulder—incredible scenery abounds!

Expect more elevated boardwalk (2' above ground, no handrail) with three steps down throughout. Alert: In another 100', be prepared to step over a 12-inch-high tree root in the middle of the trail. One more section of boardwalk (2 steps down) brings you within 100' of viewing Greenstone Falls.

0.5 Greenstone Falls! This is a wonderfully scenic area. Look closely and you'll see how the falls acquired its name. Then bring on the camera! Afterward, turn around and retrace path to trailhead.

1.0 Trailhead.

Greenstone Falls. Photo by Lisa Vogelsang

SUSPENSION BRIDGE – QUICK ROUTE*

Porcupine Mountains Wilderness State Park • Off County Road 519, 28.1 miles from Silver City • *Gentle Hikes name

- **Unique opportunity to experience a suspension bridge with striking views of the Presque Isle River below.**
- **Self-exploratory island within beautiful forest area on Lake Superior.**

TRAILHEAD DIRECTIONS & PARKING:
From MI 28 in Bergland, turn north on MI 64 and drive 17.7 miles to the junction of MI 64 and MI 107 in Silver City. Turn left (west) on MI 107 and drive for 2.7 miles to the intersection of MI 107 and South Boundary Road (notice sign for Visitor Center). Turn left and drive along South Boundary Road for 24.4 miles and turn right (north) at County Road 519. Proceeding north you will pass the ranger station and the first parking area and come to a Y intersection in 0.9 mile. Go right and follow signs to paved picnic area parking lot.

TRAILHEAD FACILITIES & FEES:
Vault toilets (wheelchair accessible), beautiful wooded picnic area (see Presque Isle River Picnic Area pg. 204) information kiosk. Annual or day use state park permit is required and available at Presque Isle Ranger Station, Wilderness Visitor Center and Park Headquarters.

TOTAL TRAIL LENGTH, SURFACE & WIDTH:
0.4 mile; boardwalk, hardpacked dirt and gravel; 5' wide.

INCLINES & ALERTS:
There are no inclines over 10°, but there are a total of 100 steps. They are non-continuous throughout the trail with many offering benches and/or resting platforms. All steps on this trail are composed of wood, have double handrails and were in excellent shape at time of writing (summer 2004). Alert: No swimming or wading in river—swift currents, dangerous undertows and slippery rocks. Stay on trail.

CONTACT:
Porcupine Mountain Wilderness State Park: (906) 885-5275

MILEAGE & DESCRIPTION

0.0 Trailhead begins at end of paved parking area near sign on 5'-wide dirt trail. In 150', turn left at intersection following sign indicating "Footbridge to Island." This section of the forest is simply spectacular!

0.1 Find a bench that afforded a unique view of the hollowed base of a fallen tree at

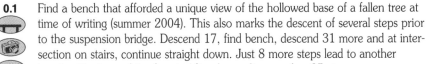
time of writing (summer 2004). This also marks the descent of several steps prior to the suspension bridge. Descend 17, find bench, descend 31 more and at intersection on stairs, continue straight down. Just 8 more steps lead to another bench with views of the forest. After descending another 35 steps, one more bench will provide a commanding view of the suspension bridge. Just 9 more

steps down bring you onto the bridge with a breathtaking view of the beautiful Presque Isle River. Hold that camera steady as the entire bridge is sensitive to any movement. Alert: Swift currents, dangerous undertows and slippery rocks off trail. Stay on trail for your safety.

0.2 At the end of this bridge is an island with no marked trails. The park service permits the public to explore the area carefully, taking heed to stay away from the river. The forest is simply stunning here. When ready, return to the suspension bridge and retrace path to trailhead.

0.4 Trailhead.

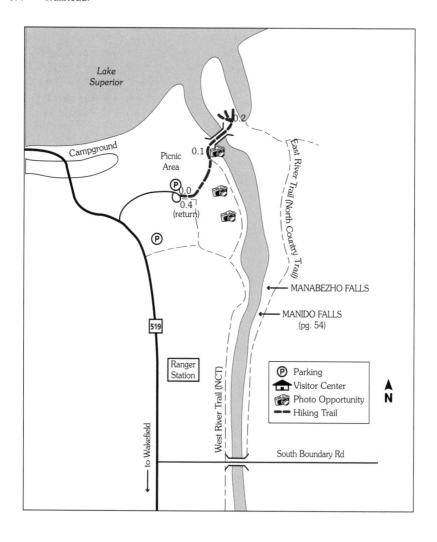

Porcupine Mountains Wilderness State Park • Off County Road 519, 28.1 miles from Silver City • *Gentle Hikes name

- **Lovely Manabezho Falls and highly scenic area of Presque Isle River.**
- **See the Midwest's largest remaining old-growth hardwood and hemlock forest!**
- **Unique opportunity to experience a suspension bridge and explore an island on Lake Superior.**

TRAILHEAD DIRECTIONS & PARKING:

From MI 28 in Bergland, turn north on MI 64 and drive 17.7 miles to the junction of MI 64 and MI 107 in Silver City. Turn left (west) on MI 107, drive for 2.7 miles to the intersection of MI 107 and South Boundary Road (notice sign that indicates Visitor Center). Turn left and drive along South Boundary Road for 24.4 miles and turn right (north) at County Road 519. Proceeding north you will pass the ranger station and the first parking area and come to a Y intersection in 0.9 mile. Go right and follow signs to paved picnic area parking lot.

TRAILHEAD FACILITIES & FEES:

Vault toilets (wheelchair accessible), beautiful wooded picnic area (see Presque Isle River Picnic Area pg. 204) information kiosk. Annual or day use state park permit is required and available at Presque Isle Ranger Station, Wilderness Visitor Center and Park Headquarters.

TOTAL TRAIL LENGTH, SURFACE & WIDTH:

0.7 mile; boardwalk, hardpacked dirt and gravel; 5' wide.

INCLINES & ALERTS:

There are no inclines over 10°, but there are a total of 332 steps. They are non-continuous throughout the trail and interspersed with benches and/or resting platforms. All steps on this trail are composed of wood, have double handrails and were in excellent shape at time of writing (summer 2004). Alert: No swimming or wading in river—swift currents, dangerous undertows and slippery rocks. Stay on trail.

CONTACT:

Porcupine Mountain Wilderness State Park: (906) 885-5275

MILEAGE & DESCRIPTION

0.0 Trailhead begins at end of paved parking area near sign on 5'-wide dirt trail. In
 150', turn right at intersection following sign indicating "Falls." Soon you will descend 13 steps onto a bridge overlooking fern glade and small creek. Shortly, ascend 17 steps.

0.1 At intersection, veer left (right leads to parking area for Manido Falls, see pg. 56)
 and follow sign indicating "Waterfall 100 yards." The next 350' proceeds through a somewhat open area filled with wildflowers during summer and leads to another intersection with two benches and views of beautiful hemlocks. Turn left,

following sign indicating "Manabezho Falls" (to the right is trail to Manido Falls).

0.2 Another bench marks the descent to Manabezho Falls. Take the 25 steps to a bench that provides a lovely wooded view of the forest before descending the remaining 22 steps to the falls. The falls are very nice and this vantage point should yield a good photo. In 150', descend 33 steps. This section of trail provides glorious river views to the right and views of the ancient forest to the left. Read the information marker and learn that some of these trees are four centuries old, making them part of the largest remaining old-growth hardwood and hemlock forest in the Midwest!

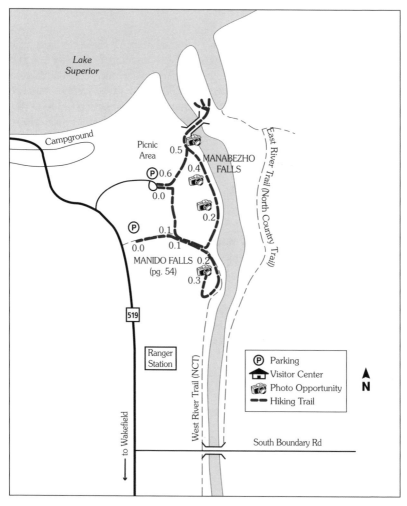

0.3 Shortly, 11 more steps lead to a bench with views of the ancient forest to the left and Presque Isle River to the right. Notice the various patterns of water flow guided by beautiful rock formations. Isn't it ironic that the very formations that the water made now guide it? Continue on, ascending 11 steps, and in 200', descend 49.

0.4   A "must sit" bench beckons with a view that is stunning. Gorgeous finely terraced rock hosts smaller falls that intriguingly flow over them—definitely worth stopping for a photo op! Ascend 19 more steps, descend 3, then ascend 3 more while noting the incredible continuous views of the river. Distinct potholes create interest in water patterns below. Read the info marker about Nonesuch Shale, which is that terraced rock you have been seeing. It is composed of sand and clay. The marker also tells how the potholes were formed; 26 steps take you up to more wonderful views of these sculptural creations.

Soon you will come to an intersection on the stairs. A right will take you to the suspension bridge; a left will take you back to the parking area in 0.1 mile. We recommend seeing the suspension bridge. Descend 8 steps, find a bench (views of the forest), descend 35 more and look up for a commanding view of this bridge! Another bench affords extended viewing pleasure and just 9 steps down puts you onto the bridge with a breathtaking view of the beautiful Presque Isle River. Hold that camera steady as the entire bridge is sensitive to any movement. Alert: Swift currents, dangerous undertows and slippery rocks off trail. Stay on trail for your safety.

At the end of this bridge is an island with no marked trails. The forest is simply stunning here. The park service permits the public to explore the area carefully, taking heed to stay away from the river.

0.5 Turn around from the suspension bridge and ascend the 52 steps back to the same intersection located on the stairs. At this intersection, continue straight up 31 more steps, to a bench, then up 17 more and another bench. This bench afforded a unique view of the hollowed base of a fallen tree at time of writing (summer 2004).

0.6 This section of the forest is simply spectacular. At intersection, turn right to return to parking area and trailhead.

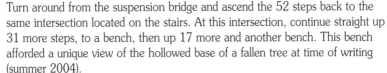

 Foot Note:

Manabezho Falls is the largest waterfall on the Presque Isle River.

MANIDO FALLS

Porcupine Mountains Wilderness State Park • Off County Road 519, 27.8 miles from
Silver City

- **Gorgeous Manido Falls and terraced rock sections contribute to the sheer beauty of this area!**
- **Nawadaha Falls can be seen in the distance.**
- **Trek along a section of the North Country National Scenic Trail.**

TRAILHEAD DIRECTIONS & PARKING:

From MI 28 in Bergland, turn north on MI 64 and drive 17.7 miles to the junction of MI 64 and MI 107 in Silver City. Turn left (west) on MI 107 and drive for 2.7 miles to the intersection of MI 107 and South Boundary Road (notice sign for Visitor Center). Turn left and drive along South Boundary Road for 24.4 miles and turn right (north) at County Road 519. Proceeding north for 0.7 miles you will pass the ranger station and turn right into the first paved parking area.

TRAILHEAD FACILITIES & FEES:

Vault toilet (wheelchair accessible), information kiosk, unique porcupine wood cutout showcases info on Presque Isle River Scenic Area. Annual or day use state park permit is required and available at Presque Isle Ranger Station, Wilderness Visitor Center and Park Headquarters.

TOTAL TRAIL LENGTH, SURFACE & WIDTH:

0.6 mile; boardwalk, hardpacked dirt and gravel; 5' wide.

INCLINES & ALERTS:

There are no inclines over 10°, but there are a total of 227 steps. They are non-continuous throughout the trail with many offering benches and/or resting platforms. All steps and bridges on this trail are composed of wood, have double handrails and were in excellent shape at time of writing (summer 2004). Alert: No swimming or wading in river—swirling currents, whirlpools, dangerous undertows and slippery rocks. Stay on trail.

CONTACT:

Porcupine Mountain Wilderness State Park: (906) 885-5275

MILEAGE & DESCRIPTION

0.0 Trailhead begins from parking area near information kiosk on 5'-wide hardpacked
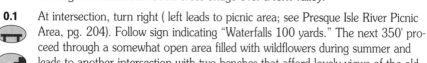 dirt and gravel trail. Almost immediately you are immersed in the forest's beauty
of old-growth hemlock. Soon cross bridge over a fern valley.

0.1 At intersection, turn right (left leads to picnic area; see Presque Isle River Picnic
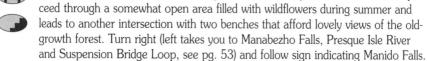 Area, pg. 204). Follow sign indicating "Waterfalls 100 yards." The next 350' proceed through a somewhat open area filled with wildflowers during summer and leads to another intersection with two benches that afford lovely views of the old-growth forest. Turn right (left takes you to Manabezho Falls, Presque Isle River and Suspension Bridge Loop, see pg. 53) and follow sign indicating Manido Falls.

Two steps up lead to another bench offering a foliage-dependent glimpse of the Presque Isle River below. Descend 30 steps to another bench that offers a better view of the river. After descending 41 more steps, find a bench that affords the beginning of views overlooking the top of Manabezho Falls. To the right will be a dirt trail (this is your return loop); continue straight on boardwalk.

0.2 Descend 29 steps and find the first viewing deck above Manabezho Falls. Down

another 8 steps leads to another bench with views of very interesting and beautiful terraced rock formations. They resemble rock-like shelves which elegantly display the river's waters. This section leads along the river and to another bench where foliage dependent views of both falls can be seen. About 20' farther, there is a better view of Manido Falls. This entire area is very picturesque, especially during high water levels. Not only are the falls themselves photo worthy, but they are well positioned to serve as an excellent backdrop for family photos. Bring the tripod and give the camera's automatic timer a workout!

Alert: Do not wade into river—dangerous undertow.

Ascend 37 steps and continue to the left on boardwalk (to the right is the dirt return trail). Ascend 2 steps, descend 2 steps and find another bench that provides a spectacular overlook over the top of Manido Falls and the Presque Isle River. Ascend 5 more steps to a taller platform, a bench, and views of Nawadaha Falls in the distance. A complimentary viewing scope brings them closer. From this platform you can also read about the Bald Eagle.

The trail does continue as part of the West River Trail, but the cliff ascent is extremely steep. We recommend turning around and retracing the boardwalk until you see a sign indicating "Trail return to stairs." This leads onto a 3'-wide dirt path and creates a 200' loop through the forest. This loop and two steps up lead back to the first set of stairs from which you entered this trail.

Ascend 41 steps to a bench and finally, ascend the last 30 steps to another bench. Follow sign back to parking area and trailhead.

0.6 Trailhead.

See map on page 54.

 Foot Note:

The Presque Isle River is the largest in the Porcupine Mountains.

REGION THREE: KEWEENAW PENINSULA AREA

Welcome to the "place of passage." This Ojibwe translation of Keweenaw can be interpreted today as a passage into a world where life is lived unhurried. It is also a passage into a place of sheer beauty. Referred to by *National Geographic Adventure Magazine* (2002) as "Lake Superior perfected and a whole lot of solitude," we invite you to this place of passage. The Peninsula has multiple access points and we have defined this region as far south as Bond Falls, and as far east as Canyon Falls. We highly recommend a visit to Bond Falls either en route or upon return from the Keweenaw as it has been deemed one of the most scenic natural places in the world! www.westernup.com/bondfalls/

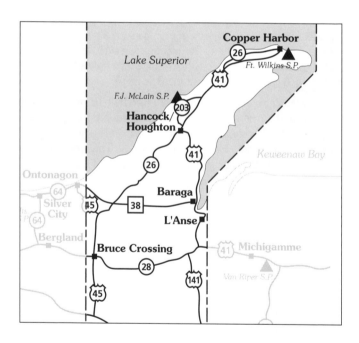

# BOND FALLS

Bond Falls Scenic Site • Off U.S. 45, 12.8 miles from Bruce Crossing, 3.2 miles from Paulding

- **Stunningly beautiful falls drop 50 feet as they divide into two sections, making it one of the most spectacular in the Upper Peninsula!**
- **Gorgeous views of the Bond River with drops over flat sections of rock.**
- **Bond Falls viewing area is wheelchair accessible!**

Note: Lighter Side of Gentle rating pertains to trail portion without steps.

TRAILHEAD DIRECTIONS & PARKING:
From MI 28 in Bruce Crossing, turn south on U.S. 45 and drive 9.5 miles into Paulding. Turn left onto Bond Falls Road and drive 3.2 miles to sign on left indicating "Bond Falls Scenic Site." Turn left into paved area. Wheelchair accessible parking.

TRAILHEAD FACILITIES & FEES:
Vault toilet (wheelchair accessible), picnic table, grill, information kiosk. No fees for trail use.

TOTAL TRAIL LENGTH, SURFACE & WIDTH:
0.5 mile; paved, boardwalk and gravel; 3–8' wide. Minimal rock and root.

INCLINES & ALERTS:
There are no inclines greater than 10°. No swimming or wading as this river is hazardous with fast moving water and slippery rocks. Certain stair access areas to the falls can be very slippery at any time or icy in spring and late fall.

CONTACT:
Baraga State Park: (906) 353-6558

MILEAGE & DESCRIPTION

0.0   Trailhead begins near information kiosk on 6'–8'-wide paved path.

    Continue on path for 500' to boardwalk area and viewing of falls. Spectacular! There are several viewing areas of Bond Falls along this boardwalk that are equipped with fencing and rails. A picturesque pond with stair access serves as the base of this incredible set of falls.

0.1   As you face the falls, trail continues to the right but wheelchair accessibility ends. If

 you desire to continue, the area is beautiful but use caution as steps are steep and

 so close to falls that you almost touch them! Consequently they can be very slippery or icy in spring and late fall. Ascend these 45 steps (cement, single handrail, non-continuous). In 100' cross bridge (wood, double handrail), then ascend five steps (stone, no handrail). Expect some gorgeous views of the river! There is plenty to explore as the path eventually leads to the campground area, gift shop and a larger picnic area (See Bond Falls Picnic and Day Use Area, pg. 206).

0.2   When finished exploring, retrace path to trailhead.

0.5   Trailhead.

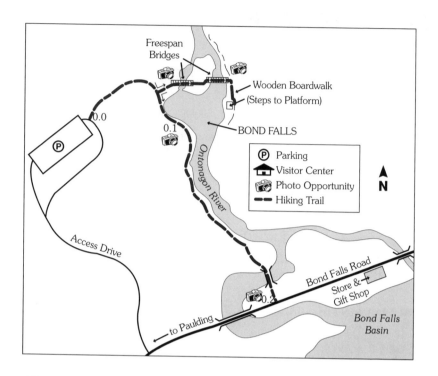

Freespan Bridges

Wooden Boardwalk (Steps to Platform)

BOND FALLS

Ontonagon River

0.0

0.1

Access Drive

P Parking
Visitor Center
Photo Opportunity
Hiking Trail

N

Bond Falls Road

Store & Gift Shop

to Paulding

0.2

Bond Falls Basin

Foot Note:

If you are a waterfall enthusiast, we highly recommend *A Guide to 199 Michigan Waterfalls* (see Appendix A, pg. 246)

AGATE FALLS

Agate Falls Park • Off MI 28, 8 miles from Bruce Crossing

- **See Agate Falls from two completely different viewing areas; lovely side view and over top from trestle.**
- **Agate Falls is wheelchair accessible (see pg. 230).**

Note: Lighter Side of Gentle rating pertains to side view.

TRAILHEAD DIRECTIONS & PARKING:
From the junction of MI 28 and U.S. 45 in Bruce Crossing, drive 7.6 east on MI 28. Closest access point is via gift shop parking on left side (north) near gravel parking area. Wayside (Agate Falls Roadside Park) is on the right side [south]).

TRAILHEAD FACILITIES & FEES:
Gift shop. Vault toilets (wheelchair accessible) at Agate Falls Roadside Park (pg. 186). No fees for trail use.

TOTAL TRAIL LENGTH, SURFACE & WIDTH:
0.2 mile to side view of falls, 0.4 mile to trestle; gravel, dirt and paved; 6–12' wide.

INCLINES & ALERTS:
There is one incline of 15° for 70' en route to trestle. Section of path to trestle is shared with ATV trail. No vehicles on other parts of trail.

CONTACT:
Agate Falls Gift Shop: (906) 852-3666, open May 31–October 15

MILEAGE & DESCRIPTION

For Agate Falls (side view)

0.0   Trailhead begins on 6'-wide gravel trail left of gift shop at sign indicating "Trail to Falls." Just 80' in takes you to a log hewn picnic table with sounds of the Ontonagon River in range. Shortly the trail splits—turn left and descend small decline. In 100' find paved path to Agate Falls.

0.1   Agate Falls viewing platform offers a wonderful side view of this 80'-wide falls. Nice. Retrace path to trailhead.

0.2   Trailhead.

For Agate Falls (top view from trestle)

0.0   Trailhead begins on 6'-wide gravel trail left of gift shop at sign indicating "Trail to Falls." Just 80' in takes you to a log hewn picnic table with sounds of the Ontonagon River in range. Shortly the trail splits—turn right, following sign indicating "Trestle." In 300', find 15° incline for 70', which leads to a trail intersection (unmarked at time of writing). Turn left onto dirt ATV trail. Alert: This portion of trail is shared with ATV riders.

0.1   A 12'-wide dirt path leads straight to trestle bridge (wood, double handrail).

0.2 Scenery abounds on both sides of trestle—highlight is the bird's-eye view of Agate Falls. This vantage point offers a wonderful view of the pine forest while looking down on the tree tops. Retrace path to trailhead.

0.4 Trailhead.

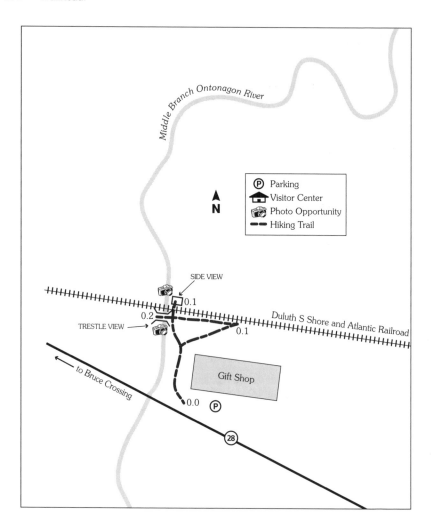

 **CANYON FALLS**

On U.S. 41, 40.5 miles from Bruce Crossing, 9.5 miles from L'Anse

- **Gorgeous hike along the Sturgeon River culminating at Canyon Falls.**

TRAILHEAD DIRECTIONS & PARKING:
From Bruce Crossing drive east on MI 28 for 38 miles until reaching intersection at U.S. 41. At intersection, turn north on U.S. 41 toward L'Anse/Houghton and drive about 2.5 miles. Look for sign for Canyon Falls Roadside Park and turn left (west) into wayside and park in paved lot (designated wheelchair accessible and RV parking).

TRAILHEAD FACILITIES & FEES:
Vault toilets (wheelchair accessible), water, picnic tables, grills, information kiosk. No fees for trail use.

TOTAL TRAIL LENGTH, SURFACE & WIDTH:
0.9 mile; gravel, mulch; 5' wide. Minimal rock and root.

INCLINES & ALERTS:
There are no inclines over 10°. Overgrowth possible on bridge.

CONTACT:
Baraga County Tourist and Recreation Association: (906) 524-7444

MILEAGE & DESCRIPTION

0.0   Trailhead begins at travel kiosk on 5–8' gravel path. Expect some washout for about 40'. In another 300', intermittent sections of boardwalk begin.

0.1   Cross over Bacco Creek on bridge (wood, double handrail). Overgrowth possible on bridge.

0.2   Views of Sturgeon River begin as the area turns photo worthy! Trail is lined with mulch in this section and another bench offers scenic views.

0.3   Trail changes back to gravel, more boardwalk and some rock in this section.

0.4   Another bench offers lovely scenic river views as Canyon Falls drops about 15'. There is a guardrail here at trail's end. Retrace path to trailhead.

0.9   Trailhead.

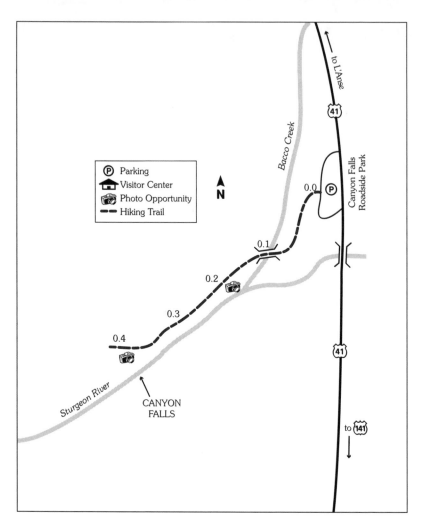

Map Legend

- **P** Parking
- Visitor Center
- Photo Opportunity
- Hiking Trail

N

to L'Anse

41

Bacco Creek

Canyon Falls Roadside Park

0.0 P

0.1

0.2

0.3

0.4

Sturgeon River

CANYON FALLS

41

to 141

🦉 SAYS WHO?

The heart will go on: Walking briskly on a regular basis offers considerable protection against heart disease.

New England Journal of Medicine [8, 9]

 FALLS RIVER FALLS

L'Anse • Off U.S. 41, 33.9 miles from Houghton

• **Lovely river views and splendid view of falls—bring camera.**

TRAILHEAD DIRECTIONS & PARKING:
From Houghton, turn south on U.S. 41 toward L'Anse. Drive 33.1 miles (from MI 28 turn north on U.S. 41). Turn left (north) on Broad Street into downtown L'Anse under the Welcome sign and travel 0.6 miles. At Main Street, turn left and continue to stop sign just before bridge. Paved parking available at extension of Waterfront Park across from power plant.

TRAILHEAD FACILITIES & FEES:
Nearby at L'Anse Waterfront Park Picnic Area (pg. 211). No fees for trail use.

TOTAL TRAIL LENGTH, SURFACE & WIDTH:
0.4 mile; hardpacked dirt and gravel; 2–5' wide. Minimal rock and root.

INCLINES & ALERTS:
There are no inclines greater than 10°. Use caution when walking on bridge as it may be used by motorized vehicles.

CONTACT:
Baraga County Tourist and Recreation Association: (906) 524-7444

MILEAGE & DESCRIPTION

0.0 Trailhead begins at sign indicating "Falls River Falls" near river's edge along power plant. Path may be quite narrow from overgrowth. You will encounter several sections of boardwalk with guardrail as you walk along the river.

0.1 Follow spur to bridge (steel girders with wood deck, double handrail) for views of Lower Falls. There will be another spur, which takes you closer to the river's edge in this area.

Back on the main trail you will find several spurs, which lead to views of the river.

0.2 The final spur provides a bench where you can enjoy a view of Middle Falls as it flows under a railroad trestle. The area under the trestle is a favorite fishing spot for the locals.

Turn around and retrace path to trailhead.

0.4 Trailhead.

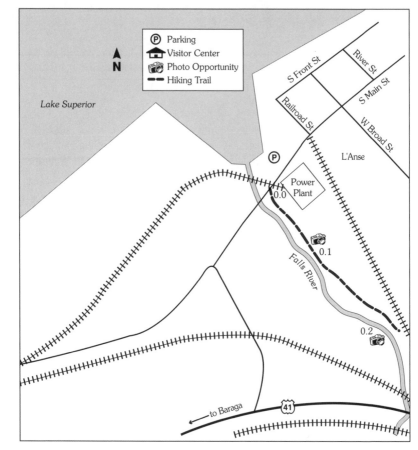

Feeling down? Walk around!

Hundreds of studies show that exercise done on a regular basis or even in a single bout can significantly reduce depression.

PCPFS Research Digest [20]

DEVRIENDT NATURE TRAIL

On U.S. 41, 11.5 miles from Houghton, 22.6 miles from L'Anse

- **This wildlife refuge and slough is home to over 50 birds, mammals, amphibians and reptiles!**
- **Interpretive trail signs throughout enrich the visit.**
- **Historic Quincy Mine Hoist can be seen in the distance from observation deck near parking area.**

TRAILHEAD DIRECTIONS & PARKING:
From MI 28, turn north on U.S. 45 at Bruce Crossing and drive 14.1 miles. At intersection, turn northeast on MI 26 toward Houghton–Hancock and drive about 57 miles. Look for signs for U.S. 41 south in Houghton and proceed straight (don't cross lift bridge) for 11.3 miles. Turn left at sign indicating Sturgeon Sloughs Wildlife Area and park in gravel lot.

TRAILHEAD FACILITIES & FEES:
Information kiosk and open-sided picnic shelter with table. No fees for trail use.

TOTAL TRAIL LENGTH, SURFACE & WIDTH:
1.4 miles; grass and dirt; 1–10' wide (contingent on mowing). Minimal rock; small sections of moderate root.

INCLINES & ALERTS:
There are no inclines over 10°. Danger—deep water, stay on trail at all times. Uneven boardwalk and overgrowth in sections.

CONTACT:
Keweenaw Peninsula Chamber of Commerce: (866) 304-5722

MILEAGE & DESCRIPTION

0.0 Before heading to the trailhead, which is just beyond gate, ascend 23 steps (wood, double handrail, non-continuous) to observation deck. Here find a "Great Blue Heron Marker" containing information about this magnificent bird. Look for them in this area. Also of great interest is the "Quincy Mine Shaft House Marker" that gives an overview of the No. 2 mine shaft. The house can be seen on the northern horizon and serves as a prominent reminder of the Keweenaw mining era, which provided the raw material that spurred the American Industrial Revolution. The No. 2 mine shaft drops an amazing 9,260' at a 55° angle and has 92 levels! The amount of copper produced is astonishing—nearly 11 billion pounds!

The "Common Wildlife Species Marker" describes over 50 wildlife inhabitants present on the refuge.

After descending the observation deck, find trailhead just beyond gate at sign indicating "trail." The "Old Homestead Marker" is atop this sign but you need to walk right up to it to see it. This area was once comprised of three farms with open fields or pastureland.

As you begin the trail it parallels the slough for a few hundred feet.

Alert: Stay on trail as water is deep.

0.3 "Osprey Marker." Did you know that the Osprey feeds solely on fresh fish? Read more about this large bird of prey, its nesting sites and young.

Trail soon narrows to 1–2' as you approach a section of boardwalk.

0.4 "Tag Alder Marker." Tag Alder commonly occupy poorly drained soils. Read more about why this is so at this marker. Also, discover just how well used this plant is by over 10 different species of wildlife!

Alert: Boardwalk in this area is wide but very slanted and uneven in places.

"Broad-Leaved Cattail Marker." Muskrats use the cattail for lodge construction and meals, but are not the only wildlife that fancy its supplies. Read about the variety of wildlife who depend on the cattail.

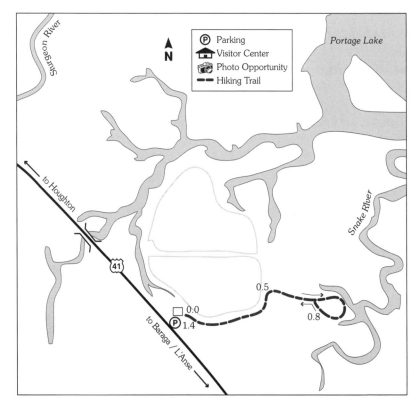

0.5 End of wide boardwalk. Soon you will encounter a moderate section of root followed by a small section of uneven and loose narrower boardwalk.

"Northern Red Oak." Learn to differentiate between the red oak and white oak and discover which trees' acorns animals love the most.

Trail narrows to 2' and becomes dirt as you enter a heavily forested area.

"Club Moss Marker." Learn how to differentiate between the two types and test your knowledge throughout this hike.

As you finish a very small boardwalk section, expect much overgrowth. Overgrowth continues for the next 1,000'.

0.6 "Snags Marker." In nature nothing is wasted. Snags are important food sources and shelters for over 85 bird species and 49 mammals. Read about the role of the Pileated Woodpecker and cavity formation.

Significant overgrowth throughout this section. Shortly you will see a deck and bench overlooking the water. Although damaged by the elements at time of writing (summer 2005), these markers were still somewhat readable: "Water Lilies," "Muskrat," "Pickerelweed" and "Wood Duck."

Use caution as trail surface becomes uneven in 50'.

"Beaked Hazelnut Marker." Yes, this is the same hazelnut that humans enjoy but it may be best to purchase yours because these are highly coveted by many birds and mammals.

"Bunchberry Marker" whose berries are eaten by many wild animals. They are also delightful blooming flowers in May and June.

0.7 "Spring Peeper Marker." Listen! When a pond is teeming with an all-male choir it could rival your stereo system! We're joking, of course, but they can be incredibly loud.

"Wood Duck Marker." Learn how to identify them. Did you know that after her eggs hatch, mom waits 24 hours before leaving her nest?

"Balsam Fir Marker." You may recognize it because of its popularity as a Christmas tree. This is because it has a very symmetrical shape, holds its needles well, retains its dark green color and is very aromatic!

"Quaking Aspen Marker." This is one of the first trees to leaf out and one of the last trees to drop its golden yellow leaves. Read more about it at this site.

0.8 Trail intersection; turn left. You are now back on the main trail from which you came. Cross boardwalk and return to trailhead.

1.4 Trailhead.

🌹 Foot Note:

Quincy Mine Hoist and Underground Mine Tours are available. Call (906) 482-3101.

HOUGHTON WATERFRONT TRAIL

Houghton • Off MI 26, 70.6 miles from Bruce Crossing

- **Paved, wheelchair accessible, award winning trail parallels the lovely Portage Waterway**
- **Unsurpassed views of Portage Lake Lift Bridge**
- **Isle Royale National Park Headquarters is located on this trail, which offers voyages to its absolutely spectacular roadless island (see Foot Note).**

TRAILHEAD DIRECTIONS & PARKING:
From MI 28, turn north on U.S. 45 at Bruce Crossing and drive 14.1 miles. At intersection, turn northeast on MI 26 toward Houghton–Hancock and drive about 56.5 miles. Before coming down the hill into Houghton, look to your left for City RV Park–Lakeshore Drive sign and turn left into the paved area. Wheelchair accessible and RV parking available.

TRAILHEAD FACILITIES & FEES:
Flush toilets (wheelchair accessible), water, picnic tables, bench, playground and concessions. See Houghton Waterfront Park Picnic Area (pg. 207). No fees for trail use.

TOTAL TRAIL LENGTH, SURFACE & WIDTH:
2.9 miles; paved; 5–10' wide.

INCLINES & ALERTS:
There are no inclines over 10°. Multi-use non-motorized path. There are four entrance crossings—use caution.

CONTACT:
Keweenaw Peninsula Chamber of Commerce: (866) 304-5722

MILEAGE & DESCRIPTION

0.0 Trailhead begins at parking area for the recreational hub of Houghton—Waterfront
 Park. Find wooden bridge near pavilion, pass restrooms, bench, playground and beach area as you head toward Waterway. The entire Portage Shipping Canal (Waterway) is 22 miles long before its entrance into Lake Superior!

0.1 Great views of the Portage Lake Lift Bridge begin and improve throughout trail.

0.3 As you approach road, do not cross but turn left onto blacktop (10' wide) and continue past dock area.

0.4 A couple of benches overlook a residential area as you draw closer to historical downtown Houghton.

0.5 Several picnic tables, grills and benches in this section, serving up terrific views of
 the Portage Lake Lift Bridge and Waterway!

0.7 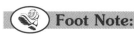 Boardwalk runs parallel to blacktop with great Waterway and bridge views with many benches throughout. Boardwalk ends at boat ramp but trail continues on blacktop.

Alert: Cross two entrances to parking areas in this section.

0.8 Restrooms (wheelchair accessible).

0.9 Picnic areas with grills, benches and nice views of bridge and Waterway in this section. As you enter Bridgeview Park, take time to read about Houghton Waterfront, the Portage Shipping Canal, Portage Bridge and Copper Boom. See actual photos from an era gone by.

1.0 Gazebo with picnic area, benches and pit. Views of Waterway continue.

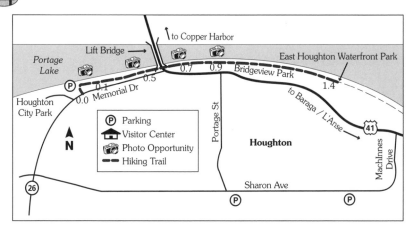

1.2 Alert: Cross two entrances to parking areas in this section. One is to the Isle Royale National Park Headquarters where you can board a voyage to the island (see Foot Note).

1.4 East Houghton Waterfront Park. Turn around here and retrace path to trailhead. Across the Waterway is the Quincy Smelting Works. Tours are available of the Quincy mine (see Foot Note on pg. 69).

2.9 Trailhead.

 **Foot Note:**

Isle Royale National Park Headquarters offers voyages to its absolutely spectacular roadless island! Accommodations or camping are available on Isle Royale. For more information call (906) 482-0984 or visit www.nps.gov/isro or email ISRO_ParkInfo@nps.gov

Foot Note:

"Houghton is one of the best 100 places to live" (*The 100 Best Small Towns in America*) by Norman Crampton

PEEPSOCK TRAIL

Houghton • Off U.S. 41 south, 73.4 miles from Bruce Crossing

- **Trail parallels Waterway for 2,000'—very nice!**
- **Excellent place to view wildlife and seasonal wildflowers.**

TRAILHEAD DIRECTIONS & PARKING:

From MI 28, turn north on U.S. 45 at Bruce Crossing and drive 14.1 miles. At intersection, turn northeast on MI 26 toward Houghton–Hancock and drive about 57 miles. Look for U.S. 41 south in Houghton and proceed straight (don't cross lift bridge) for 2.8 miles. Turn left at sign indicating Nara Nature Center and park in mulch parking area.

Note: Peepsock trailhead is 930' NW of Nara Nature Trailhead and can be accessed from paved bike path.

TRAILHEAD FACILITIES & FEES:

None. No fees for trail use.

TOTAL TRAIL LENGTH, SURFACE & WIDTH:

1.4 miles; mulch, gravel; 10' wide.

INCLINES & ALERTS:

There are no inclines over 10°. No motorized vehicles; please stay on trail. Dogs must be leashed.

CONTACT:

Keweenaw Peninsula Chamber of Commerce: (866) 304-5722

MILEAGE & DESCRIPTION

0.0 Peepsock trailhead is 930' NW of Nara Nature Trailhead and can be accessed from paved bike path. Peepsock trailhead begins at sign indicating such on a 10' mulched path. There are numerous paths in this area. For Peepsock trail, continue straight through what appears to be an old RV park and locate a steel-ribbed cement cylindrical pillar and follow that trail.

0.1 An almost 300'-long bridge (wood, double handrail) takes you across a pond. This is an ideal place to look for water lilies and wildlife, not to mention some really pretty scenery!

0.3 Path turns to gravel and travels through fields. Look for wildflowers.

0.5 Great views of Waterway begin with a bench perfectly placed for optimal viewing pleasure! Great photo ops as geese and ducks are prolific in this area.

0.7 Beautiful views continue from bench to bench as do the geese. Watch your step! Trail ends at this point. Retrace path to trailhead.

1.4 Trailhead.

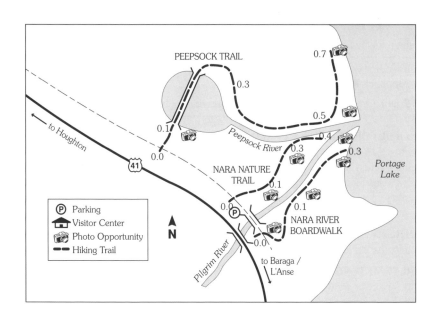

PEEPSOCK TRAIL

0.7

0.3

0.5

0.1

0.4

Peepsock River

0.3

0.0

0.3

NARA NATURE
TRAIL

Portage
Lake

0.1

0.0

0.1

Ⓟ Parking
🏠 Visitor Center
📷 Photo Opportunity
▬ ▬ Hiking Trail

▲
N

Ⓟ

NARA RIVER
BOARDWALK

to Houghton

41

0.0

Pilgrim River

0.0

to Baraga /
L'Anse

 Foot Note:

Keweenaw in the Ojibwe language means place where one crosses.

NARA NATURE TRAIL

Houghton • Off U.S. 41 south, 73.4 miles from Bruce Crossing

- **Barrier-free access through beautiful marshlands overlooking Pilgrim and Peepsock Rivers.**
- **Excellent place to view wildlife and seasonal wildflowers.**

TRAILHEAD DIRECTIONS & PARKING:
From MI 28, turn north on U.S. 45 at Bruce Crossing and drive 14.1 miles. At intersection, turn northeast on MI 26 toward Houghton–Hancock and drive about 57 miles. Look for U.S. 41 south in Houghton and proceed straight (don't cross lift bridge) for 2.8 miles. Turn left at sign indicating Nara Nature Center and park in mulch parking area.

TRAILHEAD FACILITIES & FEES:
Information kiosk. No fees for trail use.

TOTAL TRAIL LENGTH, SURFACE & WIDTH:
0.9 mile; boardwalk; 6' wide.

INCLINES & ALERTS:
There are no inclines over 10°. Boardwalk has "buckled" in places over the years yielding uneven sloping—use caution, especially if traveling by wheelchair. Expect some overgrowth in sections.

CONTACT:
Keweenaw Peninsula Chamber of Commerce: (866) 304-5722

MILEAGE & DESCRIPTION

0.0 Trailhead begins at sign indicating "Nara Nature Trail" on 6'-wide boardwalk (wood, double handrail) down slight decline to more boardwalk (no handrail). Prior to hiking, spend some time reading about the Nara family who made this trail possible. Also provided is wonderful information about marshlands and their importance to our ecosystem.

"Beaver Marker." Read about North America's largest rodent and look for its artwork along the trail.

0.1 At trail intersection, turn right onto spur. Find benches and overlooks of Pilgrim River. This area along the river is very nice. Return to main trail and continue through lovely marshlands to next viewing platform.

0.3 This viewing platform provides benches and an overlook of the Peepsock River.

0.4 The final viewing platform provides benches and an overlook of Peepsock and Pilgrim Rivers and Portage Lake. It also marks the end of this trail. Retrace path to trailhead.

0.9 Trailhead.

See map on page 73.

See map on page 73.

 Foot Note:

Nara Nature Park is made possible through the generosity of Dr. Robert O. Nara who dedicated the property to the City of Houghton in honor of his grandfather, father and brother. When visiting, spend some time reading the information kiosk about these four Copper Country pioneers whose legacy has always been one of community involvement and service.

A sign on the Nara Nature Trail. Photo by Lisa Vogelsang

NARA RIVER BOARDWALK

Houghton • Off U.S. 41 south, 73.4 miles from Bruce Crossing

- **Barrier-free access through beautiful marshlands along Pilgrim River.**
- **Excellent place to view wildlife and seasonal wildflowers.**

TRAILHEAD DIRECTIONS & PARKING:
From MI 28, turn north on U.S. 45 at Bruce Crossing and drive 14.1 miles. At intersection, turn northeast on MI 26 toward Houghton–Hancock and drive about 57 miles. Look for U.S. 41 south in Houghton and proceed straight (don't cross lift bridge) for 2.8 miles. Turn left at sign indicating Nara Nature Center and park in mulch parking area.

TRAILHEAD FACILITIES & FEES:
None, but trail was still under construction at time of writing (summer 2005). No fees for trail use.

TOTAL TRAIL LENGTH, SURFACE & WIDTH:
0.5 mile; boardwalk; 6' wide.

INCLINES & ALERTS:
There are no inclines over 10°. Boardwalk may be uneven in places and some overgrowth may be present in sections.

CONTACT:
Keeweenaw Peninsula Chamber of Commerce: (866) 304-5722

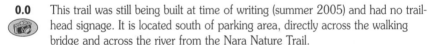

MILEAGE & DESCRIPTION

0.0 This trail was still being built at time of writing (summer 2005) and had no trail-head signage. It is located south of parking area, directly across the walking bridge and across the river from the Nara Nature Trail.

Trail begins on 4'-wide boardwalk (wood, double handrail) down slight decline and widens to 6' boardwalk (no handrail). This entire trail is one giant photo op beginning at the trailhead! Look for wildlife and wildflowers throughout.

0.1 Approximately every 300', find benches with beautiful views of Pilgrim River. This is a marvelous trail through the marshland, ending at Portage Lake. Enjoy!

0.3 End of trail, overlooking Portage Lake. Retrace path to trailhead.

0.5 Trailhead.

See map on page 73.

BEAR LAKE TRAIL

F.J. McLain State Park • Off MI 203, 10.8 miles from lift bridge in Hancock

- **Interpretive signs identify many trees through this beautiful wooded hike.**
- **Views of Bear Lake and sweeping vistas of Lake Superior!**

TRAILHEAD DIRECTIONS & PARKING:

From MI 28, turn north on U.S. 45 at Bruce Crossing and drive 14.1 miles. At intersection, turn northeast on MI 26 toward Houghton–Hancock and drive about 57 miles. Follow signs for U.S. 41 north in Houghton and cross Lift Bridge to Hancock. Stay on U.S. 41 until the intersection of MI 203. Turn left (north) on MI 203 and drive 9.8 miles to entrance of F.J. McLain State Park. Park on right side of road across from state park entrance in gravel area.

TRAILHEAD FACILITIES & FEES:

No facilities at trailhead but nearby find flush toilet (wheelchair accessible) in state park office. Fees are only required if you take your vehicle into the state park in which case you would need to obtain a permit from park office.

TOTAL TRAIL LENGTH, SURFACE & WIDTH:

2.1 miles; mulch, hardpacked dirt, grass; 2–5' wide. Minimal rock and root.

INCLINES & ALERTS:

There are two inclines ranging from 12–16°. The steepest incline is 16° for 15' at 0.1 mile. Multi-use, non-motorized path that may be used by cyclists. No pets allowed on portion of trail that crosses MI 203 or in cabin areas. After MI 203, trail becomes loosely defined as it parallels campground road and the steep cliffs (no guardrail) over Lake Superior. Watch for vehicles. Although there are grassy areas to keep hikers off the road, avoid cliff edges due to erosion.

CONTACT:

F.J. McLain State Park: (906) 482-0278

MILEAGE & DESCRIPTION

0.0 Trailhead begins across the street (MI 203) from park entrance at sign indicating "Bear Lake Trail" on 5' mulched path. About 10' into this trail, descend a 30' decline. Shortly, cross bridge (wood, double handrail), then encounter area of steepest incline (16° for 15'). To the right is a marker that gives information about the 1991 burn.

Throughout this trail various signs are posted to help you identify the following trees: Red oak, red maple, black spruce, red pine, white pine, white spruce, balsam fir, white cedar, hemlock, aspen and white birch.

0.3 Find black spruce marker across from bench. In 500', cross two bridges (wood, double handrail). Here is where the cover of this book was taken.

0.4 Logging information from 1993–94 slash where selective logging took place. Regeneration is well underway. Throughout this section look for a beautiful stand of pines.

0.5 Views of Bear Lake begin through the trees to your right. A small spur trail leads to bench with better views of the Lake. Look for water lilies. Note: White spruce marker is 100' farther up the trail on far left.

0.6 Another spur to bench overlooking Bear Lake. Photo worthy view!

0.8 To right find spur to observation platform (wood, double handrail). Note cattail bed and patch of water lilies. Bench in this area.

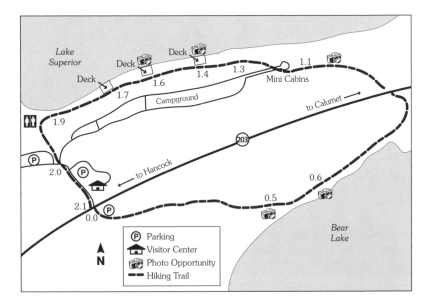

0.9 Trail continues across the road (MI 203) at sign indicating "No hunting/trapping" on 2'-wide dirt path (slightly to the south [left] of where you crossed the street).

1.0 Now entering a pet-free area. Enter at green gate. In 200', encounter an area of loose sand for 40'.

1.1 Path technically ends at Lake Superior but we recommend continuing alongside campground road or grassy area opposite bluff for continuous lake views. Alert: Danger. Steep Cliffs. No guardrail. Be careful not to get too close to the cliff edges due to erosion. Several benches throughout with sweeping vistas of Lake Superior! To the left are mini cabins. Please be respectful of others' privacy.

1.3 As you enter campground, walk along the paved road. Use caution and be respectful of campers.

1.4 Deck overlooking Lake Superior with benches. You can access the sandy beach by descending 16 steps (wood, double handrail, non-continuous).

1.6 Big observation deck and info kiosk about Keweenaw National Historic Sites and F.J. McLain State Park. You can access the sandy beach by descending 18 steps (wood, double handrail, non-continuous).

1.7 Another observation deck with benches and sweeping vista of Lake Superior!

1.9 When road curves out of campground, continue along lake on grass bluff. Alert: Steep cliffs. Continue through picnic area and turn left at restrooms.

2.0 Cross road to campground and head toward park office, then cross MI 203 at park entrance.

2.1 Trailhead.

Overlook of Superior on Bear Lake Trail. Photo by Lisa Vogelsang

BREAKWATER & FITNESS TRAIL

F.J. McLain State Park • Off MI 203, 11.1 miles from Lift Bridge in Hancock

• **Wonderfully wooded trail with peek-a-boo views of Lake Superior.**

TRAILHEAD DIRECTIONS & PARKING:

From MI 28, turn north on U.S. 45 at Bruce Crossing and drive 14.1 miles. At intersection, turn northeast on MI 26 toward Houghton–Hancock and drive about 57 miles. Follow signs for U.S. 41 north in Houghton and cross Lift Bridge to Hancock. Stay on U.S. 41 until the intersection of MI 203. Turn left (north) on MI 203 and drive 9.8 miles to entrance of F.J. McLain State Park. Once in park follow road toward left to large paved area (wheelchair accessible parking available).

TRAILHEAD FACILITIES & FEES:

Vault toilet (wheelchair accessible), grills, open-sided shelter, playground, benches, volleyball, horseshoe pit, water nearby, picnic area nearby (see Breakwater Beach House Picnic Area pg 208). Annual or day use state park permit is required and available at park office.

TOTAL TRAIL LENGTH, SURFACE & WIDTH:

1.2 miles; hardpacked dirt and loose sand; 5' wide.

INCLINES & ALERTS:

There are two inclines ranging from 11–18°. The steepest incline is 18° for 30' at 0.3 miles. Several sections of loose sand on trail.

CONTACT:

F.J. McLain State Park: (906) 482-0278

MILEAGE & DESCRIPTION

0.0 Trailhead begins at the very west end of parking lot near wheelchair accessible parking at small brown "Trail" sign on 8' mulched path. Views of Lake Superior begin early through lush forest of towering pines. There are several small intersections—stay on wider main trail. Soon encounter an incline (16° for 40').

0.3 In this section you will encounter the area of steepest incline (18° for 30'). Bench with great views of the North Entry Light.

At Y, veer left. There is a significant amount of loose sand here.

0.5 At Y in trail, veer left and follow path to basketball hoop near parking lot. As you near the parking lot you have a choice: Either turn around and retrace path to trailhead or take the Fitness Trail as your return path.

To follow the Fitness Trail, bear left about 300' past the basketball hoop and horseshoe pit toward two split rail fences. Start at the second fence, which is closest to park road, and turn left. There are several intersections. Continue straight on main path.

0.7 Chin-up bars.

1.0 Bench. In 250', veer right at Y. Descend two sections of decline prior to sit-up bench. A few more declines lead you to the parking area.

1.2 Parking lot and trailhead.

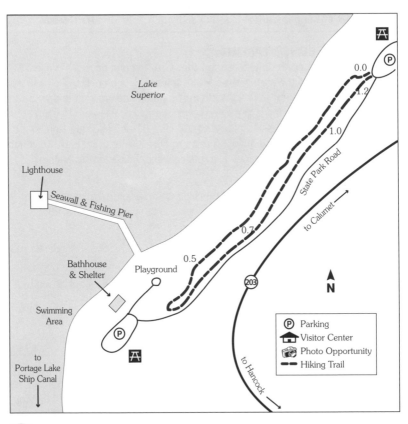

FORT WILKINS STATE PARK
LAKE SUPERIOR TRAIL

Copper Harbor • Off MI 26, 49.5 miles from Hancock

• **Nice views of Copper Harbor Lighthouse from across Copper Harbor.**

TRAILHEAD DIRECTIONS & PARKING:

From MI 28, turn north on U.S. 45 at Bruce Crossing and drive 14.1 miles. At intersection, turn to the northeast on MI 26 toward Houghton–Hancock and drive about 57 miles. Look for U.S. 41 north in Houghton and cross lift bridge to Hancock. Follow signs in Hancock and continue on U.S. 41 north to Copper Harbor for about 48 miles. At intersection of U.S. 41 and MI 26 in Copper Harbor, turn right (east) and drive 1.5 miles to Fort Wilkins State Park. Turn right into the large paved parking area. Designated wheelchair and RV parking.

TRAILHEAD FACILITIES & FEES:

Flush and vault toilets (wheelchair accessible), water, picnic area, visitor center. Annual or day use state park permit is required and available at park office.

TOTAL TRAIL LENGTH, SURFACE & WIDTH:

0.8 mile; hardpacked dirt and gravel; 1–6' wide. Minimal rock and moderate root.

INCLINES & ALERTS:

There are no inclines greater than 10°. Use caution when crossing U.S. 41 and park roads.

CONTACT:

Fort Wilkins State Park: (906) 289-4215

MILEAGE & DESCRIPTION

0.0　Trailhead begins from parking lot near playground area to the right of vault toilet on 4' gravel path. Continue past flush toilets and find sign for "Lake Superior Trail" near 3'-wide hardpacked dirt path. Alert: Cross park road and follow sign indicating "Nature Trail."

0.1　At Y in trail turn left following sign indicating "Lake Superior Trail." Trail turns to gravel for a short time. In 300', cross U.S. 41. Please use caution as vehicles travel fast on this road and it is curvy. Pick up trail near sign for "Nature Trail."

0.2　Continue toward Lake Superior. At next intersection turn left. You will begin to catch glimpses of Copper Harbor through the trees, but they get much better! In 300', a spur leads to a rocky outcrop with photo-worthy views of the lighthouse across the harbor. Continue to follow trail along the shoreline. There are several short spurs that offer photo ops of the lighthouse.

0.3　Find an unobstructed view of Copper Harbor Lighthouse. In this section, spur trails to the left lead back to U.S. 41 and main road entrance to park. Continue on trail.

0.5　More spurs to the right lead to water's edge where the lighthouse can be viewed from across the harbor. This section also provides unobstructed views of Lake Superior. Watch for ships. Trail narrows to 1' in places.

0.6 Area of decking with benches and a kiosk that tells about the shipwreck of the *John Jacob Astor*, Copper Harbor Lighthouse and settlement. Take some time to read some of the history of this interesting area. A viewing platform is just a few steps away. There you'll find benches on which to view the lighthouse and harbor, plus a picnic table. If you desire access to Superior's pebble beach, descend 9 steps (wood, double handrail) to shore for further exploration. Just opposite these steps is a 6'-wide gravel path that leads to a paved parking area. Follow this trail through the parking area and cross U.S. 41 again—use caution.

0.7 Once across road, turn left onto 6'-wide gravel path paralleling the outside fort wall.

0.8 At the intersection with a gravel park road go straight across—do not follow the "Trail" sign. In 200' begin looking left for brown fenced areas. These were the old mine shafts! Interpretive signs tell more about that era. Trail ends shortly near park store.

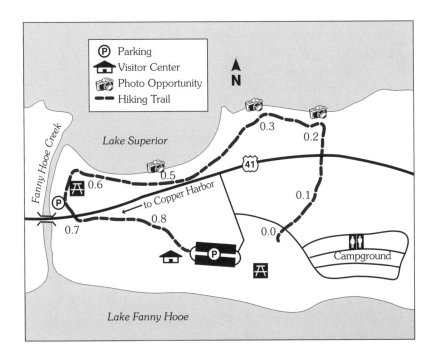

Foot Note:

If you would like to get a much closer view of Copper Harbor Lighthouse, take the Lighthouse Tour via water taxi. Contact (906) 289-4966 or www.copperharborlighthouse.com

LAKE FANNY HOOE VIEW TRAIL*

Fort Wilkins State Park, Copper Harbor • Off MI 26, 49.5 miles from Hancock • *Gentle Hikes name

---

- **Trail passes the Fort Wilkins Historic Site (see Almost Hike, pg. 168, for full description as it is a destination in and of itself).**
- **Nice views of Lake Fanny Hooe and lovely wooded sections.**

TRAILHEAD DIRECTIONS & PARKING:

From MI 28, turn north on U.S. 45 at Bruce Crossing and drive 14.1 miles. At intersection, turn northeast on MI 26 toward Houghton–Hancock and drive about 57 miles. Look for U.S. 41 north in Houghton and cross lift bridge to Hancock. Follow signs in Hancock and continue on U.S. 41 north to Copper Harbor for about 48 miles. At intersection of U.S. 41 and MI 26 in Copper Harbor, turn right (east) and drive 1.5 miles to Fort Wilkins State Park. Turn right into the large paved parking area. Designated wheelchair and RV parking.

TRAILHEAD FACILITIES & FEES:

Flush toilets (wheelchair accessible), water, picnic area (see Fort Wilkins State Park Picnic Area, pg. 210), bench, playground, info kiosk, and gift shop. Annual or day use state park permit is required and available at park office.

TOTAL TRAIL LENGTH, SURFACE & WIDTH:

2.4 miles; paved, grass, dirt and hardpacked gravel; 1–7' wide. Minimum rock and root (both moderate in sections).

INCLINES & ALERTS:

There are no inclines over 10°. No bikes or pets in buildings. A portion of the trail requires walking on a gravel road shared with vehicles entering boat launch. Another portion of trail requires walking through a paved parking area.

CONTACT:

Fort Wilkins State Park: (906) 289-4215

MILEAGE & DESCRIPTION

0.0 Trailhead begins in front of park store on 7'-wide cement path with double rail. The information marker at the trailhead reveals information about the copper discovery in 1844. Look for mineshaft in brown fenced area.

The entire first 0.1 mile of this trail passes through the Fort Wilkins Historic Site and Parade Grounds. The Site is wheelchair accessible. A more detailed description of the fort can be found in the Fort Wilkins Historic Site Almost Hike (pg. 168).

0.1 After Parade Grounds, trail turns to hardpacked gravel. Cross bridge (wood, double handrail) over Fanny Hooe Creek. This is a very picturesque creek with nice views of Lake Fanny Hooe as well.

0.2 At gravel road turn left. Use caution, as you will be walking along the road that is shared with vehicles en route to boat launch. Throughout this walk you will see glimpses of Lake Fanny Hooe.

0.3 Bench overlooking beautiful Lake Fanny Hooe! You are at the boat launch. Campground is to the right; continue straight along Lake Fanny Hooe on 12'-wide dirt path. Several spurs to the right lead to campground. Path turns to grass with some small rocks in this section. In 1,000', trail turns back to dirt (5' wide). Find picnic table and nice view of Lake Fanny Hooe.

0.5 Trail narrows to 4' as it showcases glorious views of Lake Fanny Hooe! Views continue throughout this section. Soon the trail narrows to 3' as it parallels the campground road in close proximity. In 500' you will reach a paved parking area and larger boat ramp facilities. Use caution when traveling through lot. There is also a vault toilet (wheelchair accessible) here.

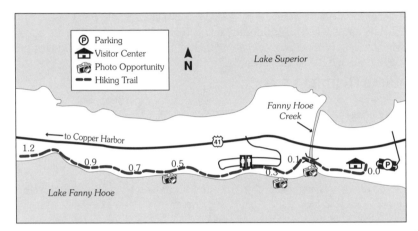

0.7 Continue through play area near lake and find trail marked by two posts with yellow reflectors. Trail narrows to 12'. In this section you will find moderate rock and root.

0.8 Enter a beautiful section of woods.

0.9 At intersection, continue straight through this glorious section of forest. Trail ends in 1,200' at Lake Fanny Hooe resort.

1.2 Lake Fanny Hooe resort. Retrace path to trailhead.

2.4 Trailhead.

HUNTER'S POINT TRAIL

Copper Harbor • Off MI 26, 48.4 miles from Hancock

- **Rugged but beautiful!**
- **Great views of Copper Harbor, Lake Superior and Porter's Island.**

TRAILHEAD DIRECTIONS & PARKING:

From MI 28, turn north on U.S. 45 at Bruce Crossing and drive 14.1 miles. At intersection, turn northeast on MI 26 toward Houghton–Hancock and drive about 57 miles. Look for signs for U.S. 41 north in Houghton and cross lift bridge to Hancock. Follow signs in Hancock and continue to follow U.S. 41 north to Copper Harbor for about 48 miles. At intersection of U.S. 41 and MI 26 in Copper Harbor, turn left (west) and drive 0.4 miles. Turn right at sign indicating "Copper Harbor State Harbor/Copper Harbor Marina." Park in paved lot. Designated wheelchair and RV parking available.

TRAILHEAD FACILITIES & FEES:

Seasonal flush toilet (wheelchair accessible), water and gift shop; vault toilet (wheelchair accessible), small picnic area. No fees for trail use.

TOTAL TRAIL LENGTH, SURFACE & WIDTH:

1.7 miles; hardpacked dirt; 1–4' wide. Moderate rock and root, significant in sections.

INCLINES & ALERTS:

There are no inclines greater than 10°. Trail could be seasonally wet. Possible overgrowth. Rock surface at the Point is very uneven.

CONTACT:

Hunter's Point Project at www.hunters-point.org

MILEAGE & DESCRIPTION

0.0   Trailhead begins at NW corner of parking area at sign indicating Hunter's Point. Enter on 4'-wide gravel trail changing to hardpacked dirt. In 100', the first intersection showcases two paths that lead to the same destination. Path to the right connects back to the main trail in a few hundred feet but is directly along the harbor—very scenic but much root. The main path continues straight ahead and has a short bout of significant rock. Either path will lead to a bridge (wood, double handrail). After bridge is a nice view of the marina.

0.1   More root leads to sections of boardwalk, which take you through a small grove of cedar. Soon cross a low-lying bridge (uneven, wood, no handrail). Boards may be loose—use caution. Throughout the next few sections there may be standing water and muddy areas.

0.2   This area contains significant root.

0.3   Two downed trees in this area at time of writing (summer 2005), but they are small and can easily be stepped over. Expect significant root in this section just prior to an open space for unobstructed harbor viewing.

0.4   Expect moderate to significant rock and root in this section.

0.5   Expect some overgrowth as trail surface turns to small pebbles ushering you to veer left and enjoy a glorious view of Lake Superior and her rocky coast! You can explore this area as you wish and can even follow the pebble beach all the way to Hunter's Point. Or for a bit easier surface upon which to walk, return to main trail and pick up trail to left. It is 0.3 mile to Hunter's Point on a dirt trail with minimal rock and root. Expect overgrowth, muddy areas and trail to narrow to 1' at times.

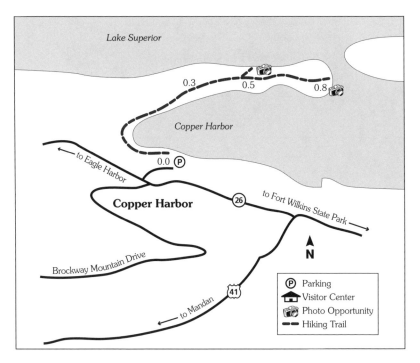

0.8   Hunter's Point! From here you will be looking directly at Porter's Island. For a complete history about the point, visit the website listed under contact information for this trail. This is a very scenic location with Lake Superior to the left and Copper Harbor to the right. It is also a popular fishing spot. Be careful as you explore because rocky surface on the Point is very uneven. When ready, retrace path to trailhead.

1.7   Trailhead.

REGION FOUR: MARQUETTE AREA

Spectacular vistas, beautiful waterfalls, sandy beaches and rugged Lake Superior shoreline are just a few descriptors of this area. Known throughout the United States for its natural beauty, Presque Isle Park serves as Marquette's recreational crown jewel. This 323-acre forested "almost" island juts into Lake Superior at the northern tip of the City and closes its road to motorized use during certain times—giving walkers and cyclists free rein! And if anyone in the family is seeking biking trails, *Bike* magazine (2001) declared Marquette the number two city in America for biking and living! In addition to its scenic beauty, Marquette is the largest city in the Upper Peninsula, making it easy to access what you need and equally as easy to retreat from what you don't.

www.mqtcty.org/departments/parksrec/presque.htm

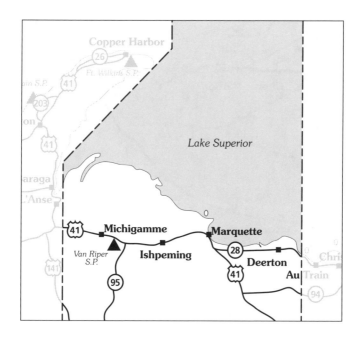

PRESQUE ISLE BOG WALK

Presque Isle Park, Marquette • Off U.S. 41/MI 28 bypass

- **Interpretive trail—a great opportunity to learn about life in the bog!**
- **Nice views of Lake Superior and Islands.**

TRAILHEAD DIRECTIONS & PARKING:
From U.S. 41/MI 28 bypass driving east into Marquette, turn left (north) on E. Lake Shore Blvd. followed by another left on N. Lake Shore Blvd. until you reach Presque Isle Park. Once past the park entrance you will find a small gravel parking area to the left directly across from the boat launching facility. No designated wheelchair accessible parking.

TRAILHEAD FACILITIES & FEES:
Nearby are flush toilets (wheelchair accessible) at MooseWood Nature Center. No fees for trail use.

TOTAL TRAIL LENGTH, SURFACE & WIDTH:
0.6 mile; paved, boardwalk, grass, gravel; 3–4' wide.

INCLINES & ALERTS:
There are no inclines greater than 10°. Do not walk out on bog or take samples. Grass trail width contingent on mowing.

CONTACT:
MooseWood Nature Center, Presque Isle Park: (906) 228-6250

MILEAGE & DESCRIPTION

0.0 Trailhead begins at sign indicating "Bog Walk and Nature Trail" on 4'-wide paved path that turns to boardwalk (wood, double handrail) in 200'. Just prior to boardwalk is "Station 1" sign that provides an overview of the trail. On boardwalk are "Stations 2 and 3" where you can read about bog formation and the impact of humans on wetlands. Soon find "Stations 4 and 5" that give details about bog plants and shrubs.

0.1 Surface becomes grass. In 300' find bench. Take boardwalk (no handrail) to "Stations 6 and 7" where you can read about beavers (look left for lodge), duckweed, birch, tamarack and birds of the bog.

0.2 "Station 8" tells how the bog achieves its color. In 200' trail becomes mulch. "Station 9" was missing at time of writing (summer 2005).

0.3 Find "Stations 10 and 11" showcasing how the dunes were formed and plants that grow on them as well as intriguing facts about dragonflies. Read about how the female lays her eggs. The spur to the left leads to Lake Superior. Soon find "Station 12" with interesting information about this region's formation. Bench nearby affords beautiful views of Lake Superior and distant views of Partridge Island, Sugarloaf Mountain and Hogback Mountain. Definitely worth a sit!

0.4 At intersection turn right and retrace path to trailhead.

0.6   Trailhead.

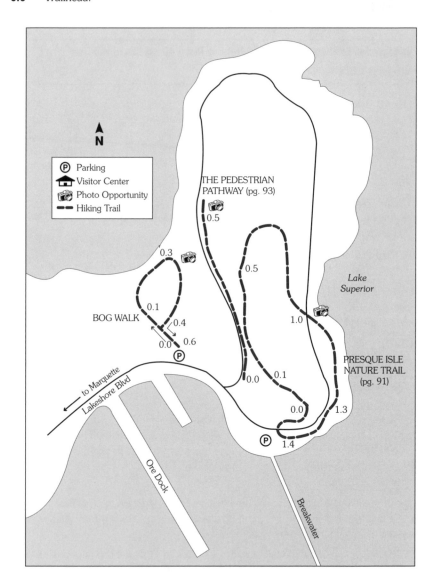

PRESQUE ISLE NATURE TRAIL

Presque Isle Park, Marquette • Off U.S. 41/MI 28 bypass

- **Lovely wooded hike through the heart of Presque Isle.**
- **Rugged cliff faces of Lake Superior.**
- **Memorial to last chief of the Chippewa Indians.**

TRAILHEAD DIRECTIONS & PARKING:
From U.S. 41/MI 28 bypass driving east into Marquette, turn left (north) on E. Lake Shore Blvd. followed by another left on N. Lake Shore Blvd. until you reach Presque Isle Park. Continue on the road around to the right beyond the park entrance, past the marina and boat launch. Park in paved circular parking area. Wheelchair accessible parking available.

TRAILHEAD FACILITIES & FEES:
Picnic area (see Presque Isle River Picnic Area pg. 204) and water. Nearby are flush toilets (wheelchair accessible), playground, concession stand and MooseWood Nature Center.

TOTAL TRAIL LENGTH, SURFACE & WIDTH:
1.4 miles; dirt, grass, paved; 3–6' wide.

INCLINES & ALERTS:
There are no inclines greater than 10°. No bikes. Must cross and walk along road for 0.1 of mile to trailhead. Another road crossing at 1.0 mile, then rough pavement, steep cliffs and area of major erosion—do not cross barricades due to unstable ground below. Also, there's an abundance of geese in this area. Watch your step.

CONTACT:
MooseWood Nature Center, Presque Isle Park: (906) 228-6250

MILEAGE & DESCRIPTION

0.0   Trailhead begins across and up the road 0.1 mile at sign indicating "Presque Isle Nature Trail" on 6–8'-wide dirt path. Immediately enter into a beautiful forest of pines and maple.

0.1   At Y, veer right.

0.2   Trail enters from left; continue straight.

0.5   At Y, veer right.

0.6   Surface turns to grass as trail widens. Shortly you will enter a lovely hemlock grove.

1.0   Alert: Cross road and find paved trail to scenic overlook of rugged cliff face.
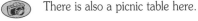   There is also a picnic table here.

1.1   Trail continues on ridge above Lake Superior. Alert: Rough pavement, steep cliffs and area of major erosion—do not cross barricades due to unstable ground below.

1.2   In this section there are two benches with wonderful views of Lake Superior.

1.3   View from bench is of the Presque Isle Light. Also in this area is a memorial to the last chief of the Chippewa Indians, Charley Kawbawgan (1799–1902), and his wife, Charlotte, who lived on Presque Isle for many years. Their spirit lives on.

Where pavement and road intersect, look toward end of guardrail to locate steps. Descend 25 steps (wood, double handrail) toward parking area. This area is inhabited by many geese so watch your step.

1.4   Parking area.

See map on page 90.

Lake Superior shoreline on the Presque Isle Nature Trail. Photo by Ladona Tornabene

THE PEDESTRIAN PATHWAY (WHEELCHAIR ACCESSIBLE ROUTE)*

Presque Isle Park, Marquette • Off U.S. 41/MI 28 bypass • *Gentle Hikes name

- **Nice, flat gravel trail that skirts around the island with wooded and Lake Superior views.**

TRAILHEAD DIRECTIONS & PARKING:

From U.S. 41/MI 28 bypass driving east into Marquette, turn left (north) on East Lake Shore Blvd, followed by another left on North Lake Shore Blvd until you reach Presque Isle Park. Continue on the road around to the right beyond the park entrance, past the marina and boat launch. Park in paved circular parking area. Wheelchair accessible parking available.

TRAILHEAD FACILITIES & FEES:

Picnic area (see Presque Isle River Picnic Area pg. 204) and water. Nearby are flush toilets (wheelchair accessible), playground, concession stand and MooseWood Nature Center.

TOTAL TRAIL LENGTH, SURFACE & WIDTH:

1 mile; gravel; 10' wide.

INCLINES & ALERTS:

There are no inclines greater than 10°. Must cross road if parked in Presque Isle Picnic Area.

CONTACT:

MooseWood Nature Center, Presque Isle Park: (906) 228-6250

MILEAGE & DESCRIPTION

0.0 Trailhead begins across the road on 10'-wide gravel path or can be accessed from lot near band shell. This trail curves around the perimeter of the island and parallels the road for the most part. It offers nice views of Lake Superior and wooded areas.

0.5 At time of writing (Summer 2005) this trail ended at the Pavilion, overlooking Lake Superior, but plans are to continue it around the island. (For more information, see Foot Note.) Retrace path to trailhead.

1.0 Trailhead.

See map on page 90.

 Foot Note:

The Presque Isle Park Advisory Committee City of Marquette invites you to become a "Friend of Presque Isle." Donations are used to help complete this trail. See Appendix A, pg. 246 under Additional Resources for address.

SUGARLOAF MOUNTAIN

Marquette area • Off County Road 550, about 5.4 miles north of Marquette

---

• **Stroll beneath a glorious canopy of forest culminating at the knob of Sugarloaf Mountain with stunning views of Partridge Island, Presque Isle and Lake Superior.**

TRAILHEAD DIRECTIONS & PARKING:
From U.S. 41/MI 28 just west of Marquette, turn left (north) on Wright Street and follow to Sugarloaf Ave (County Road 550). Turn left (north) on County Road 550 (Sugarloaf Ave), which becomes Big Bay Road, and drive about 3.6 miles until you see the large sign for Sugarloaf on the east side of the road. Park in paved area.

TRAILHEAD FACILITIES & FEES:
No amenities. No fees for trail use.

TOTAL TRAIL LENGTH, SURFACE & WIDTH:
1.2 miles; dirt, gravel; 3–6' wide. Minimal rock and root (moderate at times).

INCLINES & ALERTS:
There are no inclines over 10°, but there are a total of 322 steps. They are spread throughout the trail with many providing benches and/or resting platforms. Steps are composed of wood (with few exceptions) and have double handrails. Boardwalk uneven in places. Steep cliffs atop mountain (guardrail at overlooks only).

CONTACT:
Marquette Country Convention and Visitors Bureau: (800) 544-4321

MILEAGE & DESCRIPTION

0.0   Trailhead begins on a 4–6'-wide dirt and gravel path through lovely forest.

0.2   Find bench just prior to ascending 26 steps (non-continuous). A section of uneven boardwalk begins. Ascend 29 steps.

End of boardwalk. Path continues on dirt and gravel surface with some moderate rock and root.

0.4   Bench with cliff view. In this section, ascend the following series of steps: 11, 19, 9, 16, 6. At top of platform, turn right. Continue to the next bench as you enjoy this lovely forested area.

0.5   In this section expect some moderate to significant rock and root interspersed with steps as you begin the trek atop Sugarloaf Mountain. Ascend the following series of steps: 10, 20 (non-continuous), 26 (non-continuous), 15, 27. Find bench, ascend 30 steps. In 200', ascend 23 more steps, then 31 (non-continuous), then 9.

0.6 Glorious views and worth the steps! The top of Sugarloaf treats you to some spectacular vistas as far as the eye can see: waters of Superior, Little Presque Isle, Partridge Island and Presque Isle Point. Ample benches here spell lunch! Alert: Steep cliffs. Guardrail at overlooks only. Be sure to read the monument in memory of A. Bartlett King placed by Troop 1 of the Boy Scouts of Marquette. When finished, retrace path to trailhead.

1.2 Trailhead.

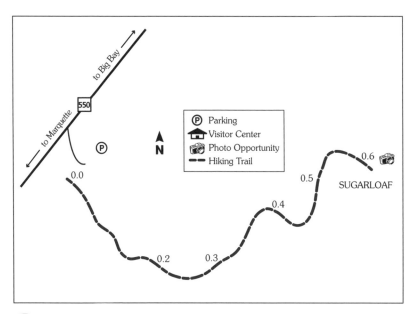

🦉 SAYS WHO?

Blood pressure high? Walk on by.

Regular physical activity helps lower the risk of developing high blood pressure or lowering it if you already have it. Note: If you do have high blood pressure, see your doctor prior to beginning an exercise program.

Agency for Healthcare Research and Quality & The Centers for Disease Control [31]

LITTLE PRESQUE ISLE SONG BIRD TRAIL

Marquette area • Off CR-550, about 7.3 miles north of Marquette

- **Beautiful wooded hike with access to Lake Superior's sandy beaches.**
- **To help identify bird calls, audio tapes that correspond with numbered trail markers can be checked out from the main DNR office.**
- **Look for Pink Lady's Slippers throughout this trail in mid to late June!**

TRAILHEAD DIRECTIONS & PARKING:
From U.S. 41/MI 28 just west of Marquette, turn left (north) on Wright Street and follow to Sugarloaf Ave (CR-550). Turn left (north) on CR-550 (Sugarloaf Ave), which becomes Big Bay Road and drive about 6.8 miles (you will pass Sugarloaf Mountain and Wetmore Pond). Take turnoff on right to Little Presque Isle Point and follow road to first gravel parking area on the left for Little Presque Isle Song Bird Trail.

TRAILHEAD FACILITIES & FEES:
No amenities. No fees for trail use.

TOTAL TRAIL LENGTH, SURFACE & WIDTH:
1.1 miles; dirt; 2–6' wide. Minimal rock and root (one moderate section).

INCLINES & ALERTS:
There is one incline (14° for 25') 400' into trail. Erosion and steep cliffs at 0.4 mile and loose sand in sections.

CONTACT:
Michigan DNR: (906) 228-6561

MILEAGE & DESCRIPTION

0.0 Trailhead begins on a 3–4'-wide dirt path near sign indicating LPI Song Bird Trail through lovely forest. In 150', turn left at intersection. Soon you will cross bridge (wood, double handrail) as you come to "Marker # 1, Song Bird Trail" just prior to incline (14° for 25').

0.1 Turn right at trail intersection. Soon find "Marker #2, Wet Thicket Habitat." Look and listen for the premier songster of the sparrow family as well as the American Redstart here.

0.2 Trail merges with North Country Trail. In 300' find "Marker #3, Dead Wood Habitat." Look for the Tree Swallow, Pileated Woodpecker (crow-sized) and Hairy Woodpecker. Loose sand for next 300'.

0.3 "Marker #4, Layered Habitat." Look for the following warblers: Yellow (found along edges of alder thickets), Yellow-rumped (mid-level limbs of pines and deciduous trees) and Blackburnian (upper canopy). Trail narrows to 2'. In 200', turn right at intersection to locate "Marker #5, Wetland Habitat." This is a good place to spot Common Yellowthroat Warblers.

0.4 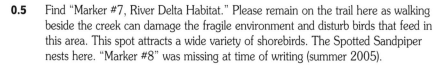 Beautiful overlook of Harlow Creek and the dense alder swamp. Alert: Erosion in this area with steep cliff. Backtrack to previous sign and continue to "Marker #6, Raptor Habitat." The Merlin has been observed near this spot.

0.5 Find "Marker #7, River Delta Habitat." Please remain on the trail here as walking beside the creek can damage the fragile environment and disturb birds that feed in this area. This spot attracts a wide variety of shorebirds. The Spotted Sandpiper nests here. "Marker #8" was missing at time of writing (summer 2005).

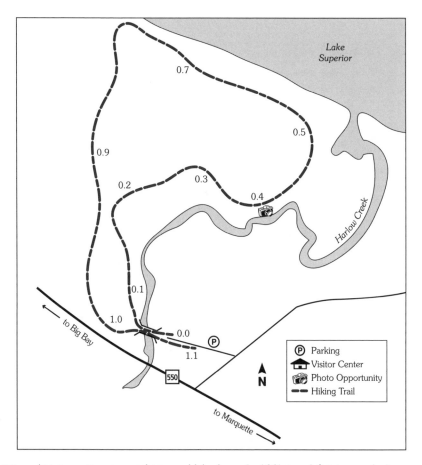

0.6 At intersection, turn right toward lakeshore. In 100', turn left into woods. Loose sand for the next 60'.

0.7 "Marker #9, Conifer Forest Habitat." Keep an eye out for the Black-throated Green Warbler and Dark-eyed Junco. In 200', find intersection and map; follow Song Bird Trail signs into woods. Spur trail leads to Lake Superior. "Marker #10" was missing at time of writing (summer 2005).

0.9 At intersection, stay left. You are making a loop that will soon return you to the first intersection encountered on this trail.

1.0   Now you are at the first intersection encountered on this trail. Turn left and return to parking lot.

1.1   Trailhead.

 Foot Note:

Enjoy identifying birds and birds calls? Check out Stan Tekiela's *Birds of Michigan Field Guide* and *Audio CDs* (see Appendix A, pg. 246).

 Foot Note:

Many trails in this book showcase beautiful seasonal wildflowers. A great guide for identification is *Wildflowers of Michigan Field Guide* by Stan Tekiela (see Appendix A, pg. 246).

Pink Lady's Slipper on the Little Presque Isle Song Bird Trail. Photo by Melanie Morgan

LITTLE PRESQUE ISLE POINT

Marquette area • Off County Road 550, about 7.3 miles north of Marquette

---

- **Stroll beneath a glorious canopy of towering pines culminating at the beaches of Lake Superior with stunning views of Little Presque Isle**

TRAILHEAD DIRECTIONS & PARKING:

From U.S. 41/MI 28 just west of Marquette, turn left (north) on Wright Street and follow to Sugarloaf Ave (County Road 550). Turn left (north) on County Road 550 (Sugarloaf Ave), which becomes Big Bay Road, and drive about 6.8 miles (you will pass Sugarloaf Mountain and Wetmore Pond). Take turnoff on right to Little Presque Isle Point and follow road to second gravel parking area on the right for Little Presque Isle Point.

TRAILHEAD FACILITIES & FEES:

Vault toilet (wheelchair accessible); information kiosk. No fees for trail use.

TOTAL TRAIL LENGTH, SURFACE & WIDTH:

0.6 miles; dirt; width varies due to layout of area.

INCLINES & ALERTS:

There are no inclines greater than 10°. Animals must be on 6' leash.

CONTACT:

Marquette Country Convention and Visitors Bureau: (800) 544-4321

MILEAGE & DESCRIPTION

0.0 Trailhead begins at yellow steel gate. Immediately enter through a beautiful stand of pines. Several spur trails lead to beach area from this path and views of Lake Superior can be caught through the trees.

0.1 At intersection, veer left and continue to end of point.

0.3 End of point and glorious views of Lake Superior with stunning views of Little Presque Isle! Beach areas abound on this sandy coast; however, use caution as sandstone underlay can be sharp in some places. Many photo ops. When ready, retrace path to trailhead.

0.6 Trailhead.

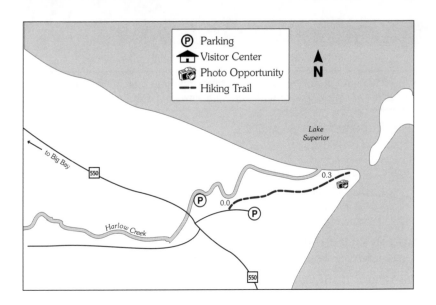

Parking
Visitor Center
Photo Opportunity
Hiking Trail

N

Lake
Superior

to Big Bay

550

0.3

P

0.0

P

Harlow Creek

550

LAUGHING WHITEFISH FALLS

Laughing Whitefish Falls State Park • Off MI 94, 24.5 miles from Marquette

- **See the water fall gently down 100' of sandstone.**
- **Picturesque scenery from various viewing areas affords marvelous photo ops.**

TRAILHEAD DIRECTIONS & PARKING:
From MI 41/MI 28 at intersection of Front Street, continue southeast on MI 41 for 15.9 miles and turn left (east) on MI 94. Continue on MI 94 for 6.3 miles and turn left (north) on N. Sundell Road (County Road 327) and drive 2.3 miles. Road surface changes from paved to gravel. Turn right to Laughing Whitefish Falls State Park on Dorsey Road. Park in gravel area.

TRAILHEAD FACILITIES & FEES:
Vault toilet (wheelchair accessible), information kiosk. Bring your own water as it did not appear that pump worked at time of writing (summer 2005).

TOTAL TRAIL LENGTH, SURFACE & WIDTH:
1 mile; gravel; 6' wide.

INCLINES & ALERTS:
There are no inclines greater than 10°, but the trail is not completely flat.

CONTACT:
None.

MILEAGE & DESCRIPTION

0.0   Trailhead begins near kiosk on 6'-wide gravel path.

0.1   Bench with wooded view. In this section, cross a bridge (wood, double handrail)
 as you travel through a mixed forest.

0.3   Encounter two more benches in this section with wooded views.

0.4   First viewing platform and bench overlooking the Laughing Whitefish River and a
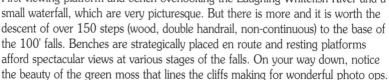 small waterfall, which are very picturesque. But there is more and it is worth the descent of over 150 steps (wood, double handrail, non-continuous) to the base of the 100' falls. Benches are strategically placed en route and resting platforms afford spectacular views at various stages of the falls. On your way down, notice the beauty of the green moss that lines the cliffs making for wonderful photo ops.

0.5   Base of Laughing Whitefish Falls with two benches for your viewing pleasure!
 Enjoy, then retrace path to trailhead. If you love photography, allow plenty of time in this area, as creative shots are abundant. It has been rumored that one of the authors spent an entire hour photographing (starting at the first platform) and still wanted more!

1.0   Trailhead.

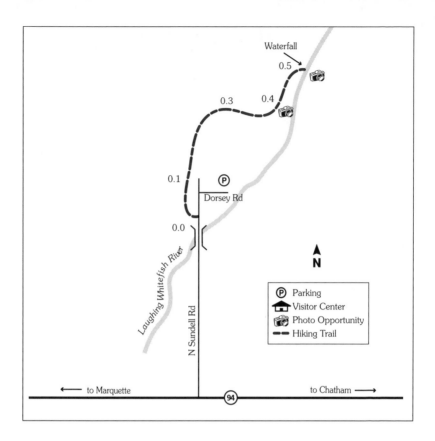

Foot Note:

If you are waterfall enthusiast, we highly recommend *A Guide to 199 Michigan Waterfalls* (see Appendix A, pg. 246)

SAYS WHO?

Walk away from type 2 diabetes.

Regular physical activity helps lower the risk of developing adult onset (type 2) diabetes.

Agency for Healthcare Research and Quality & The Centers for Disease Control [31]

REGION FIVE: MUNISING/PICTURED ROCKS NATIONAL LAKESHORE AREA

Towering, 200-foot-tall mineral-stained sandstone cliffs in shades of brown, tan and green rise dramatically from Lake Superior. These prominent features comprise a significant portion of the 73,000-acre-plus Pictured Rocks National Lakeshore, making them a top attraction in the Upper Peninsula! Its most famous formation, Miners Castle, is featured on pg. 118. Farther east lie some of the largest and most rugged sand dunes in the United States. Between cliffs and dunes are some absolutely spectacular waterfalls and Grand Sable Lighthouse.

Although not part of the park, south of it is 95,000-plus acres of marsh, field and forest known as Seney National Wildlife Refuge! The serenity here is astounding and wildlife is incredible. Seney hosts over 200 bird species and 50 mammals as it protects habitat for threatened/endangered species. We take you straight to its heart via a drive (pg. 175).

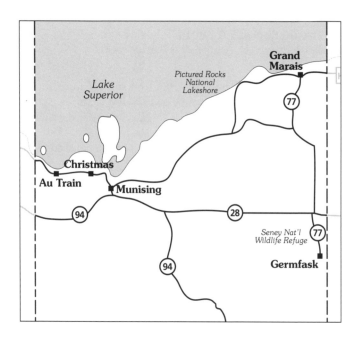

AU TRAIN SONGBIRD TRAIL

Au Train, Hiawatha National Forest • Off MI 28 on H-03, 19 miles from Munising

- **Interpretive trail—listen and look for a variety of bird species.**

TRAILHEAD DIRECTIONS & PARKING:
From MI 28 turn south on H-03 (also called Forrest Lake Road). Drive 4.3 miles to FR-2276 (also called BuckBay Road). Turn left onto FR-2276 (Alert: Road is paved but can be rough with potholes) and drive 0.6 mile. Turn left on Campground Road and stay on pavement until you reach the campground in another 1.2 miles. Once in campground turn right for the Songbird Trail Parking area. Park in gravel lot just past campsite #11 on the left side of the road near vault toilets.

TRAILHEAD FACILITIES & FEES:
Vault toilet, water, info kiosk. No fees for trail use; however, if you decide to rent the self-guiding audio kit, the fee is $10.00 ($8.00 refundable upon return). The kit contains a hefty cassette player, an instructional bird song tape, field guide and binoculars. It is available from either of the two grocery stores in Au Train.

TOTAL TRAIL LENGTH, SURFACE & WIDTH:
2.2 miles; dirt; 1–3' wide. Moderate root, minimum rock.

INCLINES & ALERTS:
There are five inclines ranging from 12–18°. Steepest is 18° for 20' at 0.6 mile. Trail surface uneven at times. Muddy areas and standing water necessitate sturdy footwear. Expect overgrowth in sections. Entire trail was marked with blue diamonds at time of writing (summer 2004). This was helpful as the trail is less defined in a few areas. Please be respectful of campers en route to trailhead as you drive through campground.

CONTACT:
Hiawatha National Forest Visitor Center: (906) 387-2512

MILEAGE & DESCRIPTION

0.0 Trailhead begins at sign for "Wildlife Viewing Area" near information kiosk on 3' dirt path. Follow "Songbird Trail" sign. First marker is only 20' into the trail and describes the song of Michigan's state bird, the American Robin. Another marker tells you where to look for the Red-winged Blackbird. In 200' find intersection. Since this is a loop hike, you can go either way; however, if you have checked out a tape, veer left onto the wider path. This is how we wrote the trail. In 70', a marker features one of the most abundant warblers, the Common Yellowthroat.

0.1 Marker showcases the Black-capped Chickadee. Did you know that their young are raised in tree holes? In 300', cross a single board (10" wide) over a small wet area. Expect mud in this section. Soon find info on the Winter Wren, just prior to crossing boardwalk over another wet area.

0.2 More muddy area prior to marker on White-throated Sparrow. Listen for his beautiful song! In another 350', find info on the Black-throated Green Warbler whose home is among the conifers.

0.3 Bench with forest views. In 200', cross old sand road and continue straight on trail.

0.6 Trail narrows to 2' en route to marker on the large Pileated Woodpecker—as large as a crow! In another 200' expect to get your feet wet as you negotiate a very wet and muddy area. The trail narrows to 1' and you can expect overgrowth before reaching info on the Black-throated Blue Warbler. Soon encounter the steepest incline (18° for 20').

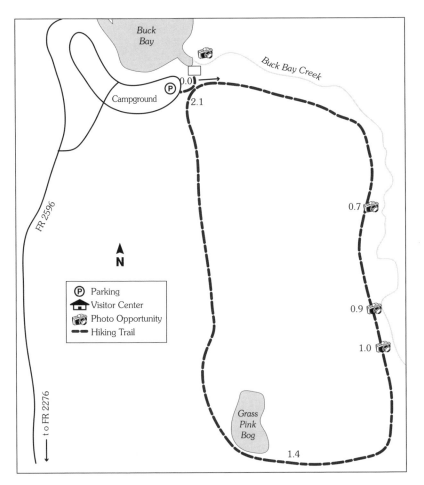

0.7 Enjoy the nice views of the creek as you walk along the ridgeline. Shortly, find a bench that overlooks a stream, which marks the descent off the ridgeline. Find info about the Veery. Expect overgrowth as trail narrows to 1'. This area is very picturesque as trail parallels Buck Bay Creek.

0.8 An incline (17° for 25') welcomes you back to the ridgeline as you continue to follow the creek and find out about the Hairy Woodpecker.

0.9 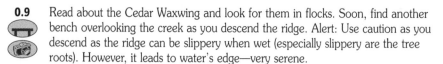 Read about the Cedar Waxwing and look for them in flocks. Soon, find another bench overlooking the creek as you descend the ridge. Alert: Use caution as you descend as the ridge can be slippery when wet (especially slippery are the tree roots). However, it leads to water's edge—very serene.

1.0 This section of trail passes along an especially scenic area of Buck Bay Creek. Find marker about the White-breasted Nuthatch. Watch how he spirals down a tree trunk headfirst! In 300', find incline (15° for 20'). Shortly the trail turns away from the creek at a field. Continue right following sign indicating "Songbird Trail." Read about the Rose-breasted Grosbeak—the most beautiful songster in the forest! Alert: After this marker, the trail becomes loosely defined in the field. Look to the right for about 100' and spot a post with a blue arrow near woods. Pick up narrow trail here. Root becomes minimal after field.

1.1 Continue on the narrow path and in 200', find information about the Ovenbird who is hard to see but easy to recognize by song.

1.2 Trail narrows as you cross a very wet and muddy area.

1.3 Alert: Trail crosses what appears to be an ATV trail. In 400' you come to the Grass Pink Bog where a nice view awaits 80' farther down the trail.

1.4 Find bench with partial view of bog.

1.5 Read about the Eastern Wood-Pewee and in 250', the Red-eyed Vireo.

1.6 There is one incline (15° for 6') in this section.

1.7 Find marker about the Least Flycatcher.

1.8 Cross a section of boardwalk over a muddy area en route to the last incline (12° for 35') on the trail. Look for the Indian Pipe wildflower in this area. Soon trail begins to narrow. Expect overgrowth.

2.0 Read about the Blue Jay. Shortly, trail crosses what appears to be an ATV trail. The last marker is 150' farther and has information on the Yellow-rumped Warbler who is the earliest to arrive in spring.

2.1 This intersection marks the completion of the loop. Continue straight (right returns to the trail you just exited; left leads to a campsite). Instead of returning to parking area, we suggest turning right at trailhead toward the observation platform overlooking Buck Bay in Au Train Lake. In 90' encounter boardwalk that is slippery when wet, uneven in places and lined with overgrowth. To access platform, ascend 25 steps (wood, double handrail, non-continuous). The view is spectacular. This is a great place to spot birds and other wildlife! Look for Red-winged Blackbirds and Cedar Waxwings. Read the signs about birds, wetlands, geology and vegetation. When finished, follow this short portion back to parking area.

2.2. Trailhead.

 **Foot Note:**

If you enjoy identifying birds, pick up a copy of *Birds of Michigan* by Stan Tekiela (see Appendix A, pg. 246). This field guide also comes with audio CDs. If you like simply relaxing to birdsongs, the *Bird Songs of the Northwoods* CD delivers.

BAY FURNACE HISTORIC SITE

Christmas, Hiawatha National Forest • On MI 28, 3 miles from Munising.

- **Of historical significance: See remains of the 1870s furnace that still dominates this site with arches of stone.**
- **Beautiful views of Lake Superior.**

TRAILHEAD DIRECTIONS & PARKING:
From MI 28 in Munising drive 3 miles west to Christmas. Turn right (north) at sign indicating "Bay Furnace Historic Site." Park in gravel lot.

TRAILHEAD FACILITIES & FEES:
Vault toilet, information kiosk. No fee for trail use.

TOTAL TRAIL LENGTH, SURFACE & WIDTH:
0.1 mile; gravel, boardwalk; 5–6' wide.

INCLINES & ALERTS:
There are no inclines greater than 10°. Please do not disturb historic site.

CONTACT:
Hiawatha National Forest Visitor Center: (906) 387-2512

MILEAGE & DESCRIPTION

0.0 Trailhead begins on 5'-wide gravel path to left of vault toilet. Take some time to
 read the info markers about this historic site and how fire was used to make iron. At 200' boardwalk begins as you approach the furnace. Learn about hot pigs in a sand bed! Several benches in this area provide views of the furnace and Lake Superior. A couple of spur trails, which involve 10 steps, lead to a very small beach area and more benches overlooking Lake Superior. As the boardwalk ends, another marker sports photos of how this furnace looked originally. Compare that to what you see now.

0.1 Bay Furnace Ruins marker and another bench brings the trail full circle to the parking area.

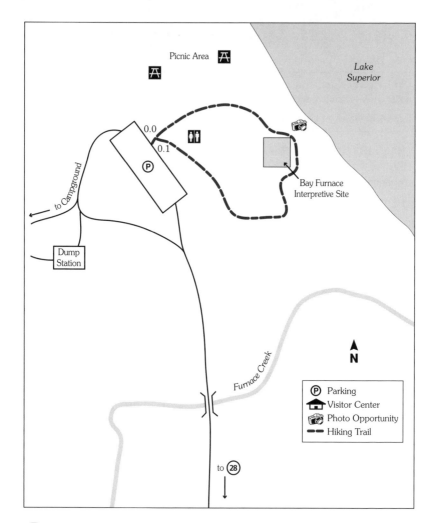

Picnic Area

Lake Superior

0.0
0.1

to Campground

Dump Station

Bay Furnace Interpretive Site

Furnace Creek

N

P Parking
Visitor Center
Photo Opportunity
Hiking Trail

to 28

 SAYS WHO?

Did you know that more women die from heart disease than breast cancer?

Regular physical activity can help prevent both.

New England Journal of Medicine [8, 9, 13]

Munising • Off MI 28 on MI 94, 1.5 miles from Munising, 33 miles from Seney

- **Gorgeous Wagner Falls!**

TRAILHEAD DIRECTIONS & PARKING:
From the Visitor Center in Munising, drive 1.2 miles southeast on MI 28 and turn right on MI 94 West. Drive another 0.3 miles and take a left into the Wagner Falls Scenic Site. Park in gravel area.

TRAILHEAD FACILITIES & FEES:
Information kiosk, which lists sites of all waterfalls in Michigan's Upper Peninsula. No fees for trail use.

TOTAL TRAIL LENGTH, SURFACE & WIDTH:
0.2 mile; gravel; 5' wide.

INCLINES & ALERTS:
There are no inclines greater than 10°. Bridge is slippery when wet.

CONTACT:
Women's National Farm and Garden Association: www.wnfga.org

MILEAGE & DESCRIPTION

0.0 Trailhead begins at sign indicating "Wagner Falls" on 5'-wide gravel path through
 a glorious stand of cattails. In 300' find a bench with another in 100'. Cross bridge (wood, double handrail). Alert: Slippery when wet.

0.1 Descend 10 steps (wood, double handrail). Find bench that provides a glorious
 view of the falls. This one is a must see!

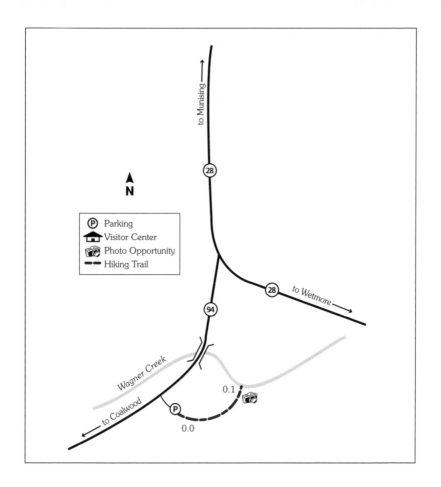

🌹 Foot Note:

If you are a waterfall enthusiast, we highly recommend *A Guide to 199 Michigan Waterfalls* (see Appendix A, pg. 246)

MUNISING FALLS

Pictured Rocks National Lakeshore • Off H-58, 2 miles from MI 28 in Munising

---

- **See beautiful, picturesque Munising Falls drop 50' over sandstone cliff into its horseshoe-shaped valley.**
- **Picturesque Munising Creek en route to falls.**

Note: Lighter Side of Gentle rating pertains to trail portion without steps.

TRAILHEAD DIRECTIONS & PARKING:

From MI 28, go east on H-58 (East Munising Avenue) for 1.3 miles to Washington Street. Turn left and drive 0.5 miles to Sand Point Road. Turn right and follow for 0.2 miles to Visitor Center paved parking area. Designated wheelchair and RV parking. Alert: Use caution when traveling through residential area.

TRAILHEAD FACILITIES & FEES:

Flush toilets (wheelchair accessible), water, picnic tables (see Munising Falls Picnic Area pg. 215), nature center, bench. No fees for trail use.

TOTAL TRAIL LENGTH, SURFACE & WIDTH:

0.5 mile; paved; 4' wide.

INCLINES & ALERTS:

No inclines over 10°. Fragile slopes, please stay on trail. Do not go beyond rails in falls area as rock is unstable and poses danger.

CONTACT:

Pictured Rocks National Lakeshore: (906) 387-3700

MILEAGE & DESCRIPTION

0.0

Trailhead begins at sign indicating "Munising Falls 800'" on 4'-wide paved path. A bench waits as you approach the nature center. Soon find info on the Munising Blast Furnace that produced thousands of tons of pig iron. Vintage photos give insight into an era gone by. This site is listed on the National Register of Historic Places. As you continue on the trail, expect lovely views of Munising Creek. A bench offers lingering view time. When you see steps, continue on main trail as we will revisit the steps later. Cross bridge (wood, double handrail) over creek.

0.1

Cross another bridge (wood, double handrail) over the creek, find a bench. Crossing one more bridge (wood, double handrail) brings you to a gorgeous view of Munising Falls! This is the center viewing platform with a commanding view. A bench is provided. If you desire to see the falls a bit closer, ascend 47 steps (wood, single and double handrail, non-continuous) closest to you. Alert: Do not veer from platform. Danger of rock fall beyond this point. Notice info marker about the horseshoe-shaped valley that has been partially carved by this creek. When finished, turn right back onto main trail and proceed to next set of steps that you encountered earlier.

0.2

Ascend 93 steps (wood, double and single handrails, non-continuous). Atop steps is a dirt path alongside the massive sandstone cliffs!

0.3 Another overlook of Munising Falls from a different perspective. Alert: Danger of rock fall beyond this point. Do not veer from platform. When finished, retrace path to trailhead.

0.5 Trailhead.

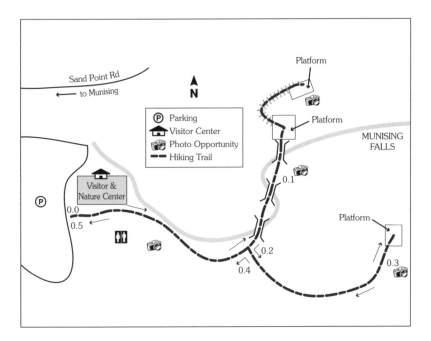

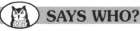

🦉 SAYS WHO?

More is better—when it comes to brains, that is!

Individuals who improved aerobic fitness have been shown to maintain more brain tissue density as they age.

Journals of Gerontology Series A: Biological Sciences & Medical Sciences [32]

SAND POINT MARSH TRAIL

Pictured Rocks National Lakeshore • Off H-58, 4 miles from MI 28 in Munising

- **Wheelchair accessible boardwalk through a marsh experience!**
- **Interpretive trail (pick up guide book at trailhead).**

TRAILHEAD DIRECTIONS & PARKING:

From MI 28, go east on H-58 (East Munising Avenue) for 1.3 miles to Washington Street. Turn left and drive 0.5 miles to Sand Point Road. Turn right and follow for 2.2 miles to the Sand Point Marsh Trail and Sand Point Beach/Picnic Area paved parking area. Designated wheelchair and RV parking. Alert: Use caution when traveling through residential area.

TRAILHEAD FACILITIES & FEES:

Picnic area (see Sand Point Picnic Area, pg. 216), bench, and info kiosk. No fees for trail use.

TOTAL TRAIL LENGTH, SURFACE & WIDTH:

0.6 mile; paved, boardwalk; 3–5' wide.

INCLINES & ALERTS:

There are no inclines over 10°. Loose sand and overgrowth in sections.

CONTACT:

Pictured Rocks National Lakeshore: (906) 387-3700

MILEAGE & DESCRIPTION

0.0   Trailhead begins at sign indicating "Sand Point Marsh Trail" on 3' paved trail. May be loose sand on path in this section. Turn right onto boardwalk (wood, double handrail) and pick up a trail guide from box as you enter. If you have no further use for the guide when done, please return it to the box.

"A Marsh Experience Marker" welcomes you to Sand Point Marsh Trail and its 16 wayside exhibits found along the path, which reflect a rich biological diversity. Allow approximately 45 minutes to explore leisurely.

"What's Going On Here?" Read about how Sand Point was formed.

"Wetland Communities Marker" tells about the forested swamp and aquatic communities. A good place to spot animal tracks.

0.1 "Forest Interdependence Marker" invites you to listen for call of the red squirrel and read about its habitat and habits. Take a right to the viewing platform, then return to boardwalk. Find bench with view of "A Wilderness Clearing." This marker tells how this wetland is regulated by a beaver dam and of its domination by moisture-dependent sedges, leatherleaf, and sweetgale. A good place to see White-throated Sparrows.

"Similar But Different!" Read about the different plant combinations and watch for short-tailed shrews and frogs.

"Just Another Ridge?" This marker informs us of the role of fire in this area. Look for the Pine Marten.

0.2 "The Sand Point Marsh Trail Marker" showcases those who made it possible.

"Winter Wonderland Marker" has sketches of animal tracks and features the Snowshoe Hare. There may be overgrowth in this section.

"Early Residents Marker" provides a brief history of the Anishinabe people and their use of wetland materials.

0.3 Several benches in this and following sections with views of marshland.

"Sand Point's Life Stream." Find out where the wetland water comes from and about its amazing ability to retain enormous quantities of water.

"Look, A Beaver!" Look for the beaver lodge and read about how well it is adapted to an aquatic environment. Also, learn why it is not safe to drink untreated surface water.

"Life of the Pond Marker" gives an overview of several aquatic species.

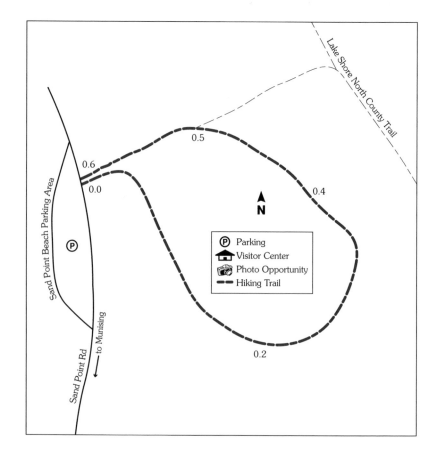

0.4 "A Northern Forest Marker" brings you to drier conditions. Look for blueberries.

 "Seasonal Sounds Marker" provides an overview of the various sounds that are present in the wetlands throughout the year.

0.5 At intersection, turn left to return to parking lot on paved trail. "Legacy of the Marsh" is the last marker and urges us to put a higher value on wetlands as it explains their importance.

0.6 Trailhead.

Foot Note:

Interested in identifying animal tracks? Pick up a copy of *Mammals of Michigan* by Stan Tekiela (see Appendix A, pg. 246).

Sand Point Marsh Trail. Photo by Lisa Vogelsang

 **MINERS FALLS**

Pictured Rocks National Lakeshore • Off H-58, 9.6 miles from MI 28 in Munising

- **See Miners Falls as it plummets 60'—greatest volume of waterflow in the park!**
- **Self-guided interpretive trail (pick up pamphlet at trailhead).**

TRAILHEAD DIRECTIONS & PARKING:
From MI 28 in Munising, turn east on H-58 and drive 5.3 miles to Miners Castle Road. Turn left and drive 3.8 miles to Miners Falls Trail turnoff. Turn right and continue for 0.5 miles to gravel lot. Wheelchair accessible and RV parking available.

TRAILHEAD FACILITIES & FEES:
Vault toilet (wheelchair accessible), picnic tables, grills, bench. No fees for trail use.

TOTAL TRAIL LENGTH, SURFACE & WIDTH:
1.2 miles; gravel; 5' wide. Minimal rock and root.

INCLINES & ALERTS:
No inclines over 10°. Trail surface can be uneven at times. Surface to waterfall viewing platform may be slippery.

CONTACT:
Pictured Rocks National Lakeshore: (906) 387-3700

MILEAGE & DESCRIPTION

0.0 Trailhead begins at sign indicating "Miners Falls 1.2 miles" on 5'-wide gravel path. This is an interpretive trail so check the box for free guides. Marker # 1 begins just 150' into the trail and states how the Miner name became associated with this trail. In another 150', Marker #2 gives information on the beech and maple trees.

0.1 Find bench. Marker #3 reveals the reason behind the large leaves of the saplings and more information about the forest floor. Alert: Watch for uneven trail surface in this area. Marker # 4 describes why the landscape here is so lumpy!

0.2 Find bench with a forest view. In 200', Marker #5 tells the story of how life is brought forth from death during seasons of the forest.

0.3 Find bench and Marker #6, which tells of the forest's hidden critters. Find another bench shortly before Marker #7, which explains how this area looks in mid-May—a perfumed banquet of wildflowers!

0.4 Marker #8 discusses the formation of the ridge on which you are now standing.

0.5 Find two more benches prior to Marker #9, which takes you back in time to Miners Lake. Listen! You can hear the falls. At the overlook there is a partial view of the falls, but the best view is down the steps. Descend 64 steps (wood, double handrail, non-continuous). Alert: Slippery surfaces from fall spray. Find two more benches en route to this wonderful waterfall. Marker #10 is behind the last bench. It describes this area as indicative of a northern climate.

0.6 At the base of the steps you are treated to Miners Falls. Expect the area to be wet and slippery, but beautiful. It will be challenging to snap a photo as mist gravitates toward the lens very quickly. But use it as an opportunity to be creative because the scene is photo worthy! Marker #11 provides information on why the water is tea-colored and other info about this site. When finished, retrace path to trailhead as you listen to the sounds of the forest.

1.2 Trailhead.

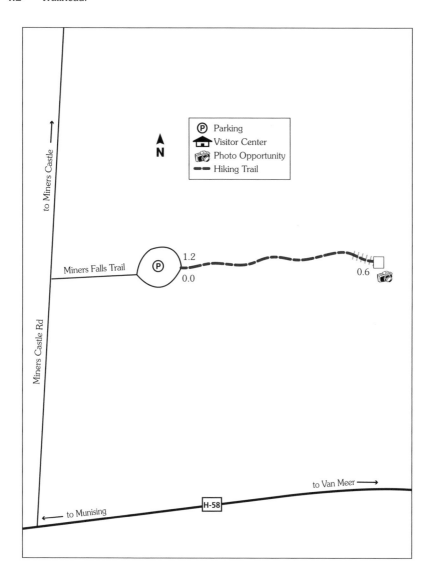

Pictured Rocks National Lakeshore • Off H-58, 10.7 miles from MI 28 in Munising

- **Spectacular overlooks of Miners Castle and Lake Superior (wheelchair accessible)!**
- **Stand directly on top of Miners Castle on a safe, spacious viewing platform for wonderful photo op at sunset!**

Note: Lighter Side of Gentle rating pertains to trail portion without steps.

TRAILHEAD DIRECTIONS & PARKING:
From MI 28 in Munising, turn east on H-58 and drive 5.3 miles to Miners Castle Road. Turn left and drive 5.1 miles to Y intersection. Turn left and continue 0.3 miles into paved parking area. Wheelchair accessible and RV parking available.

TRAILHEAD FACILITIES & FEES:
Flush toilets (wheelchair accessible), water, picnic tables (see Miners Castle Picnic Area, pg. 217), grills, visitor center, gift shop, bench. No fees for trail use.

TOTAL TRAIL LENGTH, SURFACE & WIDTH:
0.6 mile; paved; 5' wide.

INCLINES & ALERTS:
No inclines over 10°. Do not veer from designated trail for your safety as this area has very steep cliffs.

CONTACT:
Pictured Rocks National Lakeshore: (906) 387-3700

MILEAGE & DESCRIPTION

0.0 Trailhead begins at sign indicating "Miners Castle Overlook 265'" on 5'-wide paved path that is west of the information center. This overlook is wheelchair accessible and simply gorgeous! Bring the camera. A bench and lower viewing window for children or persons using wheelchairs make this a truly barrier-free overlook. Continue along paved path.

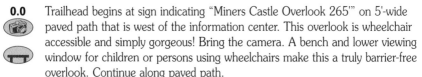

0.1 Info marker on "Lake Superior Basin Geology" as well as lovely Lake Superior views. Wheelchair accessibility ends here as the trail leads to a platform directly atop Miners Castle. Find bench prior to descending 17 steps (wood, double handrail). At intersection, turn left and follow sign indicating "Miners Castle." Continue down a series of paved switchbacks on a slight decline. Find two more benches over the next 300'.

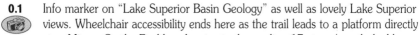

0.2 Ascend two steps to platform with info marker "Crumbling Into Time and A Layered Past." Find one more bench before descending 29 steps (wood, double handrail, non-continuous).

0.3 You are now on a platform literally over Miners Castle! Please do not veer from designated trail as this area is very steep beyond guardrails. This is a great place to catch the sun setting over the tip of the castle. Also, look for more picturesque cliffs in the distance. Retrace path to trailhead.

0.6   Trailhead.

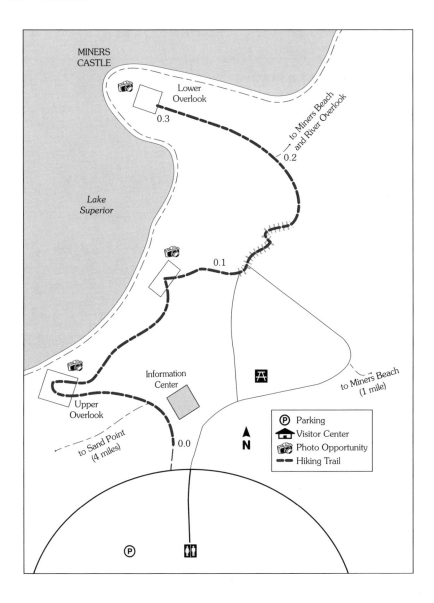

CHAPEL FALLS

Pictured Rocks National Lakeshore • Off H-58, 19.4 miles from MI 28 in Munising

- **See Chapel Falls at the end of a beautiful wooded hike!**
- **Drive through the spectacular Lake Superior State Forest of hardwoods en route to trailhead.**

TRAILHEAD DIRECTIONS & PARKING:
From MI 28 in Munising, turn west on H-58 and drive 14.1 miles to Chapel Road in Melstrand. (Alert: Chapel Road is a seasonal dirt road and is not plowed in winter; sections may be rough.) Turn left on Chapel Road and continue for 5.3 miles to Chapel Falls dirt parking area.

TRAILHEAD FACILITIES & FEES:
Vault toilet (wheelchair accessible), info kiosk, bench. No fees for trail use.

TOTAL TRAIL LENGTH, SURFACE & WIDTH:
2.8 miles; dirt; 3–5' wide. Moderate root near overlook to falls. Minimum rock.

INCLINES & ALERTS:
One incline of 11° for 20' at 0.6 mile. No pets or bicycles (potential $100 fine). This area includes 200' cliffs, loose sand and soft undercut rock. Stay on designated trails and back from cliff edges. May be areas of standing water.

CONTACT:
Pictured Rocks National Lakeshore: (906) 387-3700

MILEAGE & DESCRIPTION

0.0 Trailhead begins near vault toilets at sign indicating "Chapel Falls 1.4 miles" on 5'-wide dirt path. You will be treated to a beautiful mixed hardwood forest en route to the falls.

0.6 One incline (11° for 20') in this section.

0.8 Spur to left leads to a foliage-dependent view of Chapel Lake Overlook in 180'. Continue straight on main trail.

1.0 Expect standing water in this section for the next 40'.

1.2 Note sign to the left indicating "Chapel Falls Overlook." While this is a nice view, the best is yet to come! Descend 15 steps (wood, single handrail) as you continue on main trail.

1.3 Cross bridge (wood, double handrail) across river. Descend two steps (no handrail) to exit bridge and turn left. You will encounter moderate root up to the overlook.

1.4 Ascend two steps (no handrail) to falls overlook for the best view of Chapel Falls! A bench is provided for your viewing pleasure.

Retrace path to trailhead.

2.8 Trailhead.

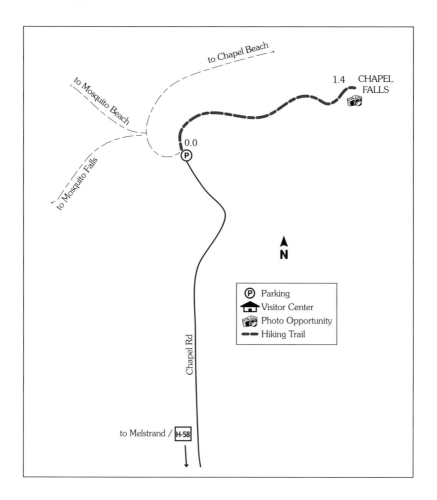

to Chapel Beach

to Mosquito Beach

to Mosquito Falls

1.4 CHAPEL FALLS

0.0

N

Chapel Rd

Ⓟ Parking
🏠 Visitor Center
📷 Photo Opportunity
●━● Hiking Trail

to Melstrand / H-58

 Foot Note:

All of H-58 should be paved by the year 2009. It is currently paved to Log Slide from east and Little Beaver Lake from west. In spring/summer of 2006, from Log Slide to Hurricane River will be paved.

WHITE PINE SELF-GUIDING NATURE TRAIL

Pictured Rocks National Lakeshore • Off H-58, 22.2 miles from MI 28 in Munising

- **Interpretive trail in the Beaver Basin area (pick up a brochure at trailhead)**
- **See 300-year-old white pine!**
- **Picturesque views of Little Beaver Creek**

TRAILHEAD DIRECTIONS & PARKING:
From MI 28 in Munising, turn west on H-58 and drive 19.2 miles to Little Beaver Lake turnoff. (Alert: The road to Little Beaver Lake is a seasonal dirt road and is not plowed in winter.) Turn left and continue for about 3 miles into the Little Beaver Campground. Park in gravel area near trailhead close to HCA vault toilet. Parking is very limited and often shared with campers.

TRAILHEAD FACILITIES & FEES:
Vault toilet (wheelchair accessible). No fees for trail use.

TOTAL TRAIL LENGTH, SURFACE & WIDTH:
0.7 mile; dirt; 2–3' wide. Minimum rock, moderate root (significant in sections).

INCLINES & ALERTS:
One incline (20° for 13') at 0.4 mile. Uneven trail surface and boardwalk loose at times. Overgrowth in sections.

CONTACT:
Pictured Rocks National Lakeshore: (906) 387-3700

MILEAGE & DESCRIPTION

0.0   Trailhead begins at sign indicating "White Pine Self-Guiding Nature Trail" on 3'-wide dirt path. You will need a brochure for interpretive markers, as there is no signage on the trail, only numbers that correspond to the brochure.

A few big rocks are at the entry, but can be sidestepped. Look for sandstone cave in this area. In 200', DO NOT take the steps to the left. This is a loop trail and you will return via these steps. "Marker #1." Read about the Eastern Hemlock and its many uses over the years.

0.1   "Marker #2" gives interesting information about the Black Bear.

"Marker #3" showcases an exposed layer of sandstone—the very same rock formation found in the Pictured Rocks cliffs! Boardwalk and uneven ground ahead. "Marker #4" provides information about the wetlands and those who benefit from them.

0.2   Boardwalk ends. In 300', turn left at the intersection toward sign indicating "White Pine Trail." You are now along Little Beaver Creek. "Marker #5" reveals some interesting facts about water. Did you know that Americans use approximately 200 gallons per day? Expect moderate root. Shortly you will encounter more boardwalk directly along the creek prior to ascending seven steps (wood and dirt, no handrail) as you climb onto ridge. "Marker #6" welcomes you to the "Gardens of Lilliput," but you must look closely to enter this miniature world.

0.3 Ascend 9 steps (wood, no handrails, non-continuous) to boardwalk, which is non-continuous for the next 300'. Expect moderate root in this section. "Marker #7" showcases the Balsam Fir, a popular Christmas tree due to its robust, spicy fragrance. Read more about this wonderful conifer in your brochure. "Marker #8" encourages you to look for animal tracks; we encourage you to look at the creek as well for photo ops! In 150', ascend 2 steps (wood, no handrail) to more boardwalk. Alert: Boardwalk was uneven at time of writing (summer 2005). In another 150', ascend 4 steps (dirt and log, no handrail) and look for many wonderful photo ops along the creek, as this area is very scenic.

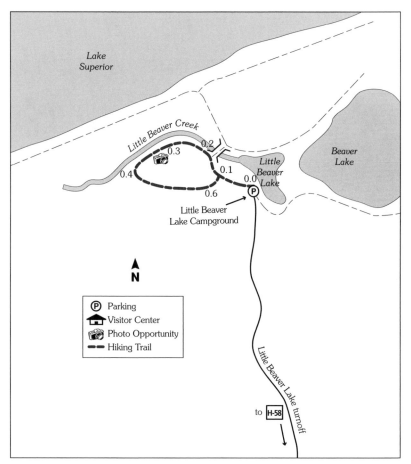

0.4 Ascend 2 steps (dirt and log, no handrail) as trail turns away from the creek. Expect moderate to significant root in this section. "Marker #9" showcases the "king" of trees that played a great role in the Midwest's development—the White Pine. Please stay on the trail when viewing the 300-year-old giants! In 400', find

"Marker #10," which features the Yellow Birch. Did you know that Yellow Birch can be tapped for sap just like the Sugar Maple? Boardwalk is loose in places; use caution.

0.5 Ascend 18 steps (dirt and log, no handrail, non-continuous). Turn left and follow sign indicating "White Pine Nature Trail." Alert: Trail may be hard to find, but veer left immediately after sign. There were many fallen leaves in August that obscured the trail. "Marker #11" invites you to look at the former "dining hall" of the now extinct Passenger Pigeons: the American Beech. Marker #12 beckons you to stroll among the thick stands of Sugar Maple. If you happen to visit in fall, you're in for a real treat!

0.6 Descend 34 steps (wood, double handrail, non-continuous) and turn right. You are now back to the trail on which you began your hike. Follow it to the trailhead.

0.7 Trailhead.

Along the White Pine Self-Guiding Nature Trail. Photo by Lisa Vogelsang

⬤ SABLE FALLS

Pictured Rocks National Lakeshore • On H-58, 26.6 miles from Seney

---

• **Gorgeous Sable Falls!**

TRAILHEAD DIRECTIONS & PARKING:
From MI 28 in Seney, turn north on MI 77 and drive 25 miles toward Grand Marais. In Grand Marais, turn left on H-58 and drive 1.4 miles to turnoff for Sable Falls and Dunes area. Park in paved lot (designated wheelchair accessible and RV parking available).

TRAILHEAD FACILITIES & FEES:
Flush toilets (wheelchair accessible), water, grills, info kiosk, bench. No fees for trail use.

TOTAL TRAIL LENGTH, SURFACE & WIDTH:
0.6 mile; paved, dirt; 3–5' wide.

INCLINES & ALERTS:
There are no inclines, but there are a total of 166 steps. They are non-continuous with some benches and/or resting platforms. Alert: Steps and walk may be slippery with some muddy areas. Watch for uneven surfaces and areas of erosion. Trail was under construction at time of writing (summer 2005).

CONTACT:
Pictured Rocks National Lakeshore: (906) 387-3700

MILEAGE & DESCRIPTION

0.0 Trailhead begins from parking area at sign indicating "Sable Falls 500'" on 5'-wide paved path. Pass a bench and restrooms prior to the trail turning to dirt. At intersection, turn right. In 100', descend 19 steps (wood, double and single handrails, non-continuous) to partial view of falls. Continue down for much better views. Two more benches in this area.

0.1 Descend 166 steps (wood, double and single handrails, non-continuous) to base of Sable Falls. This is a commanding view and well worth the trip down. Descend 10 more steps (wood, no handrail) onto elevated boardwalk as you follow along the creek.

0.3 Encounter loose sand as you approach Lake Superior. Shortly you will see the mouth of the creek and beautiful Lake Superior! Look west for a view of the dunes in the distance and if you look closely, you can also see Au Sable Lighthouse off Au Sable Point to the west. Grand Marais Breakwater is to the east. There is much beach area to explore here. When you're ready, retrace path to trailhead.

0.6 Trailhead.

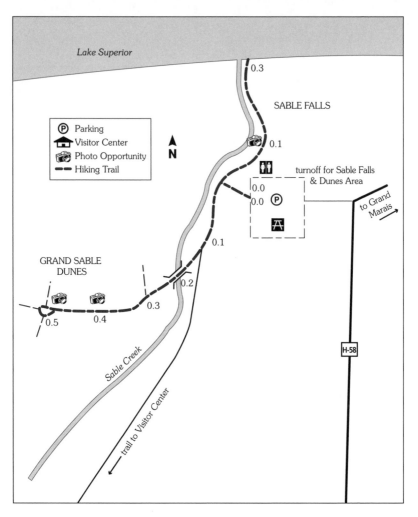

Lake Superior

SABLE FALLS

0.3

Parking
Visitor Center
Photo Opportunity
Hiking Trail

N

0.1

turnoff for Sable Falls
& Dunes Area

0.0
0.0 P

to Grand
Marais

0.1

GRAND SABLE
DUNES

0.2

0.3

0.5   0.4

Sable Creek

trail to Visitor Center

H-58

SAYS WHO?

Want to lose a few pounds or more? Get out-of-doors!

Walking 45-60 minutes a day was shown to improve fitness and reduce weight without dieting in overweight men, as well as to reduce the incidence of heart disease and type 2 diabetes.

Exercise and Sports Science Reviews [35]

Pictured Rocks National Lakeshore • On H-58, 26.6 miles from Seney

- **Grand Sable Dunes are spectacular, as is the view of Lake Superior from them!**

TRAILHEAD DIRECTIONS & PARKING:
From MI 28 in Seney, turn north on MI 77 and drive 25 miles toward Grand Marais. In Grand Marais, turn left on H-58 and drive 1.4 miles to turnoff for Sable Falls and Dunes area. Park in paved lot. Wheelchair accessible and RV parking available.

TRAILHEAD FACILITIES & FEES:
Flush toilets (wheelchair accessible), water, grills, info kiosk, bench. No fees for trail use.

TOTAL TRAIL LENGTH, SURFACE & WIDTH:
0.5 mile; paved, dirt, loose sand; 1–5' wide.

INCLINES & ALERTS:
There are five inclines ranging from 18°–20°. Steepest incline is 20° for 50' at 0.4 mile. Loose sand can be very challenging for walking. No bikes. Bring plenty of water. On hot days, the sun's reflection off the dunes is very intense.

CONTACT:
Pictured Rocks National Lakeshore: (906) 387-3700

MILEAGE & DESCRIPTION

0.0 Trailhead begins from parking area at sign indicating "Dunes" on 5'-wide paved path. Pass a bench and restrooms prior to the trail turning to dirt. At intersection, turn left.

0.1 Pass through an apple orchard on a very narrow (1') path for the next 300'. Expect overgrowth.

0.2 Encounter a decline (18° for 30'), which will be an incline upon return. At intersection, turn right and follow sign indicating "Grand Sable Dunes 500'". Ascend two steps (wood, double handrail) across picturesque Sable Creek. Ascend 11 steps (wood and sand, no handrail).

0.3 At intersection turn left and follow sign indicating "Dunes Trail" for a beautiful walk through a Jack Pine forest. In 400' the forest yields to the dunes as trail takes on loose sand. Info marker, "From Forest to Dunes." Encounter incline (19° for 80') of loose sand. Another marker about "Sand Stopper" is in this area. Encounter another incline (18° for 35') of loose sand.

0.4 Info marker about "Plant Pioneers" just prior to another incline (18° for 80'). Immediately veer right and look for Lake Superior in the distance and the glorious sand dunes in front of you. This area is gorgeous, but absolutely stunning under deep blue skies! Encounter another decline (20° for 50') of loose sand and in another 250' you will see a marker about the "Ghost Forest."

0.5 More gorgeous views of Lake Superior and the Dunes! There are many dunes in this area, including a very steep descent in just 50'. We recommend turning around prior to the descent and retracing steps to trailhead. Alert: If you decide to descend, it is 20° for 99'—easy going down, but a sweat-producing calf workout coming back up. The view isn't much different from what you have already seen. If you do decide to explore this area, please use caution as walking in loose sand can be very challenging, especially on inclines and during hot weather.

1.0   Trailhead.

See map on page 126.

Grand Sable Dunes. Photo by Ladona Tornabene

LOG SLIDE OVERLOOK

Pictured Rocks National Lakeshore • Off H-58, 33.2 miles from Seney

- **Spectacular overlook of Grand Sable Banks and Dunes!**
- **Of historical significance: Site of former log chute and logging wheel display.**
- **Interpretive trail.**

TRAILHEAD DIRECTIONS & PARKING:
From MI 28 in Seney, turn north on MI 77 and drive 25 miles toward Grand Marais. In Grand Marais, turn left on H-58 and drive 7.4 miles to the stop sign and turnoff for Log Slide Overlook Area. It is 0.8 miles to gravel lot. Wheelchair accessible and RV parking available.

TRAILHEAD FACILITIES & FEES:
Vault toilet (wheelchair accessible), water, picnic tables, grills, info kiosk, bench. No fees for trail use.

TOTAL TRAIL LENGTH, SURFACE & WIDTH:
0.4 mile; hardpacked gravel; 10' wide.

INCLINES & ALERTS:
No inclines over 10°. No bicycles. Do not attempt to descend the former log slide. This is very dangerous and numerous warning signs are posted.

CONTACT:
Pictured Rocks National Lakeshore: (906) 387-3700

MILEAGE & DESCRIPTION

0.0 Trailhead begins near info kiosk on 8'-wide hardpacked gravel path. Find bench
 and info marker about the cabin in the clearing—Jones's Cabin. See replica of
 property deed from 1902. In 80', the first intersection leads to a picnic table semi-secluded in the woods.

In another 200', find info marker about "The Changing Forest." Path turns to hardpacked dirt. In 100', find another bench with lovely views of the forest.

0.1 Info marker about the "Tools of the Trade" containing great information on lum-
 berjack vernacular. To them, sand meant sugar! Look for historic logging wheels
 and sled on display under shed about 100' farther on trail. Impressive. Next find bench and actual site of the former log chute. It is a 300' vertical drop and we strongly caution against descent. Warning signs are strategically placed.

0.2 Spectacular overlook platform (grate, double guardrail) of Grand Sable Banks and Dunes! Truly a speechless moment for the most talkative author. Absolutely photo-worthy. Spend some time at this peaceful place and read the displays about Maritime Connection, Log Slide Overlook and Grand Sable Dunes. Retrace path to trailhead.

0.4 Trailhead.

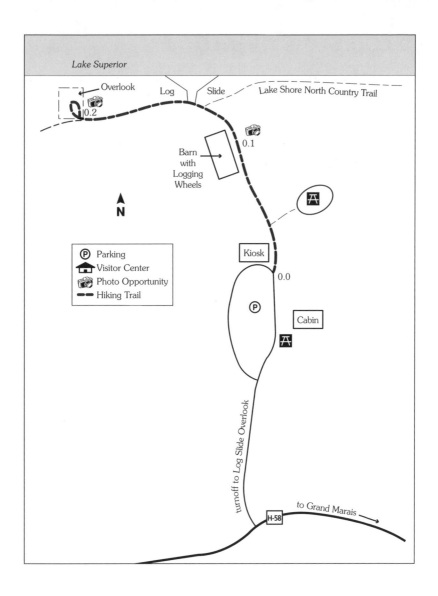

Lake Superior

Overlook

0.2

Log   Slide   Lake Shore North Country Trail

0.1

Barn
with
Logging
Wheels

N

Parking
Visitor Center
Photo Opportunity
Hiking Trail

Kiosk

0.0

P

Cabin

turnoff to Log Slide Overlook

to Grand Marais

H-58

AU SABLE LIGHT STATION

Pictured Rocks National Lakeshore • Off H-58, 37.1 miles from Seney

- **Tour Au Sable Lighthouse.**
- **See the Graveyard Coast of Lake Superior and view remnants of wreckages.**
- **Drive to trailhead travels through the spectacular Lake Superior State Forest of hardwoods.**

TRAILHEAD DIRECTIONS & PARKING:

From MI 28 in Seney, turn north on MI 77 and drive 25 miles toward Grand Marais. In Grand Marais, turn left on H-58 and drive 12.1 miles to turnoff for Lower Hurricane River Campground (comes after Upper Hurricane River Campground). Park in day use parking area immediately to left as you enter the campground. No parking permitted at trailhead.

Note: Parking area is 1,400' from trailhead. To access trailhead, turn left from day parking area and walk along hardpacked sand road (Alert: Road is shared with vehicles in campground) past picnic area. Turn left at Y intersection and continue to trailhead at gated service road.

TRAILHEAD FACILITIES & FEES:

Located 975' from the day parking area are vault toilets (wheelchair accessible), water (at info kiosk just past picnic area), picnic tables, info kiosk. No fees for trail use, but there is a small fee ($2.00 per person; summer 2004) to tour lighthouse.

TOTAL TRAIL LENGTH, SURFACE & WIDTH:

2.6 miles; hardpacked sand; 10' wide.

INCLINES & ALERTS:

No inclines over 10°. Foot traffic only. No bikes. May be standing water in some sections. Hardpacked sand road en route to trailhead is shared with vehicles. If you plan to tour the lighthouse, tours are generally available July 1st–Labor Day, but stop by the visitor center to ensure hours.

CONTACT:

Pictured Rocks National Lakeshore: (906) 387-3700

MILEAGE & DESCRIPTION

0.0 Trailhead begins at gated service road at the northeast end of Lower Hurricane
 River Campground loop. Look for sign indicating "Lakeshore Trail Au Sable Point 1.5 miles." Trail is 10'-wide hardpacked sand. Very soon, encounter a sign indicating "Shipwrecks"—follow a 100' spur to beach area for exploration. After this, the main trail continues relatively uneventful for quite awhile.

0.5 May be standing water in this area.

0.8 A bench and marker about the Graveyard Coast, which notes all of the wrecks
 near here. To explore traces of shipwrecks, descend 13 steps (wood, double
 handrail) to the beach area. Alert: Watch your footing along the beach near wreckages as hazards can be partially hidden in sand.

1.3 Behold beautiful Au Sable Lighthouse! Take some time to tour this area, then retrace path to trailhead.

Note: There is another route back to trailhead, but due to unevenness and height of steps leading to beach, it did not meet our Gentle Hikes criteria. However, if you can negotiate such steps, this route is right on the beach of Lake Superior and joins the main trail in 0.5 miles at the stairs, which were alluded to in the above section.

2.6 Trailhead.

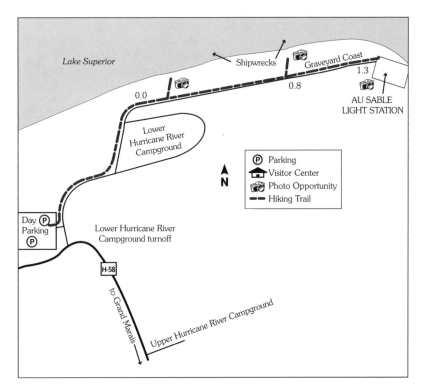

PINE RIDGE NATURE TRAIL

Seney National Wildlife Refuge • Off MI 77, 5.9 miles from MI 28 in Seney

• **Interpretive trail—listen and look for a variety of waterfowl and wildlife.**

TRAILHEAD DIRECTIONS & PARKING:

From MI 28 in Seney, turn south on MI 77 and drive 4.8 miles to the entrance of Seney National Wildlife Refuge. Turn right (west) into the entrance and drive 1.1 miles to Visitor Center paved parking area. Designated wheelchair parking.

TRAILHEAD FACILITIES & FEES:

Flush toilets (wheelchair accessible), water, info kiosk, bench, gift shop, exhibits and more (see Seney Visitor Center Stroll Almost Hike, pg. 174). No fees for trail use.

TOTAL TRAIL LENGTH, SURFACE & WIDTH:

1.4 miles; grass, dirt; 4' wide.

INCLINES & ALERTS:

There is one incline of 12° for 15' at 0.4 mile. No bicycles. Overgrowth in sections.

CONTACT:

Seney National Wildlife Refuge: (906) 586-9851 ext. 15

MILEAGE & DESCRIPTION

0.0 Trailhead begins at east side of visitor center at sign indicating "Pine Ridge Nature Trail" on 4' grassy path. The little white birdhouse just prior to the trailhead on left is home to the Purple Martin. Notice the information marker describing what you will see on your journey. After crossing a bridge (wood, double handrail), find info Marker #2 and learn about birds that feed on the Highbush Cranberry. Trail parallels pond affording wonderful marsh views. Soon find Marker #3 and information about the Tamarack. Did you know that it is the only conifer to lose its needles each fall?

0.1 Look right for a beaver dam. In 200', find Marker #4 about Juneberries, which can be eaten or used for baking.

0.2 Look for lovely marsh view to the right.

0.3 Bench with beautiful view of pond, an excellent place to view wildlife. Marker #5 informs us that some wildlife actually prefers the leaves of the blueberry to the fruit itself!

0.4 Marker #6 features the Paper Birch, which is very popular for two birds: Ruby-throated Hummingbird and Yellow-bellied Sapsucker. But a real surprise is what else you will find beneath this tree. Soon you will encounter the only incline on this trail (12° for 15').

0.5 As you cross a bridge (wood, double handrail) over a small pond, look for birds in shrubs. Expect overgrowth in this area. As boardwalk begins, look for wild roses in summer. In 500', Marker #7 tells us who loves Alder seeds.

0.6 Overgrowth in this area could be significant. Marker #8 informs us that cattails are important building materials for many inhabitants. Look among them for leaves that have been "tied down." These are homes that a spider has built in order to lay her eggs. Cross over two more bridges (wood, double handrail). In summer, numerous cattails are in this area.

0.7 End of boardwalk as you enter into a nice stand of pines, which are symphonic if it's windy. Marker #9 features Seney's neotropical migrants in lovely photos and legend of migration patterns. Marker #10 showcases the Quaking Aspen, which provides a year-round feast for some of Seney's inhabitants.

0.8 Bench overlooking cattails. In 400', find intersection. Turn left and find Marker #11. Did you know that a dead tree is prime real estate for woodpeckers, Black Bears, Great Horned Owls and more?

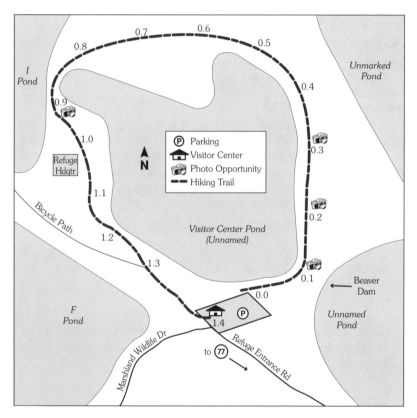

0.9 Marker #12 features information on Michigan's three native species: White, Red and Jack Pine. Read about wildlife that love them, but don't rush off just yet. Relax a bit on the bench and look around you. Save one lone bridge to the left, this location offers a wonderfully pristine view of the majestic and magnificent sites of Seney. As you continue in this section, views of a gorgeous pond abound to the right as trail parallels endless cattails to the left.

1.0 Marker #13—beyond water's edge lies an under-the-surface smorgasbord for Trumpeter Swans, Moose, coots and more!

1.1 At intersection, turn left and follow sign indicating "Nature Trail" as path narrows to 3' and turns to dirt. Cross bridge (wood, double handrail) for views of pond and cattail. Marker #14 is near a bench and showcases water lilies, which are popular pads for wildlife.

1.2 Cross bridge (wood, double handrail) with views of pond. Marker #15 features the Red-osier Dogwood.

1.3 Marker #16 invites you to read about how to create a refuge for wildlife in your own backyard using native plants in your area. In 100' the trail ends and you'll need to walk back to the parking area via a paved road. There is a bench strategically placed near a Purple Martin house in front of a pond. This is a great place to look for wildlife!

1.4 Parking area.

Trumpeter Swans on the Pine Ridge Nature Trail. Photo by Melanie Morgan

REGION SIX:
TAHQUAMENON FALLS AREA

This area showcases one of the largest waterfalls east of the Mississippi: Tahquamenon Falls! An impressive 50-foot drop of thunder spread over some 200 feet in width is a sight and sound to behold—more than 50,000 gallons of water per second rush from its cascade! The park encompasses close to 40,000 acres and features the smaller yet very picturesque Lower Falls, fantastic views of Lake Superior and Clark Lake, a pristine remote area.

Although it's not part of the park, we have included Oswald's Bear Ranch, a place to safely view the Black Bear, and a wonderful cliffside Lake Superior hike at Muskallonge State Park.

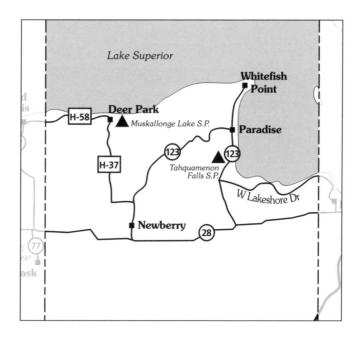

Off H-37, 10 miles from Newberry

- **Bears, bears, bears—close enough to get a decent photo with just about any camera!**
- **Bears are located within a secure enclosure, but have plenty of space and greenery in which to play.**
- **Family-friendly photo ops at bear statues where kids can ride the "cubs."**

TRAILHEAD DIRECTIONS & PARKING:

From MI 28, turn north on MI 123 toward Newberry and drive 7.9 miles to 4 Mile Corner (Deer Park Road, H-37, Muskallonge Lake, and County Road 407). Turn left and drive 4.5 miles to Oswald's Bear Ranch entrance (on right). Park in dirt lot. RV parking available though not designated.

TRAILHEAD FACILITIES & FEES:

Portable toilet, picnic tables, gift shop. There is a $10.00 entry fee per car/RV/cycle and rates for tour buses. Although the fee is per vehicle, the actual trail is a walk-about, not a drive through. Ranch is open Memorial Day Weekend through September 30; 10am–6pm.

TOTAL TRAIL LENGTH, SURFACE & WIDTH:

Loop one is 0.3 mile and loop two is 0.5 mile; sand; width difficult to determine due to nature of trail layout.

INCLINES & ALERTS:

There are no inclines greater than 10°. Do not reach inside enclosures. Trail may be shared with golf carts that the staff uses to accommodate visitors needing ambulatory assistance (see pg. 230 for more information).

CONTACT:

(906) 293-3147

MILEAGE & DESCRIPTION

Loop One

0.0 Trailhead for Loop One begins north of gift shop on 3' loose sand path. These enclosures are very photo-friendly as Oswald has equipped the fences with photo holes to allow unobstructed photography within mere feet of the bears! For safety, Oswald has an electrical fence inside the outer fence to keep the bears away from the photo holes. Do not reach inside enclosures. Also in this area is the first viewing platform where you can see over the fence for more photo ops of the bears! Look for bears in trees as well. To access this platform you must ascend 10 steps (wood, double handrail). As you continue on the trail, there is a sign about the history and facts of Oswald's Bear Ranch. Interesting information. In 100', as you turn the corner you will be treated to a gorgeous view of Oswald Lake. Over the next 1,000' there are three benches strategically placed for your bear viewing pleasure.

0.3   End of Loop One as you find yourself back at the gift shop, which is precisely where trailhead for Loop Two begins.

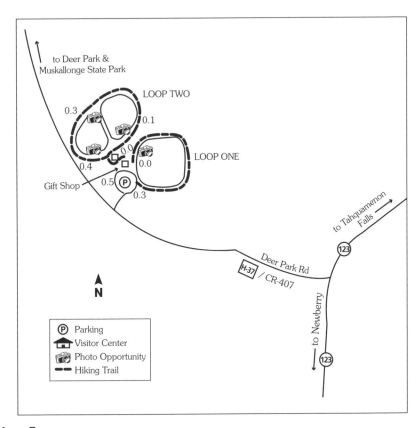

Loop Two

0.0   Trailhead begins through the gift shop (wise Oswald!). The cub habitat is immediately to the right and you will want to spend time here if there are cubs and especially if staff is feeding them! The cubs are absolutely adorable; however, there are no photo holes and the area is completely enclosed. Therefore, all photos must be taken with fences visible. Do not reach into enclosure.

From here, turn right and follow signs indicating "Waterfalls and Walk." In 200', although optional, we recommend ascending the 10 steps (wood, double handrail) to observation deck. Manmade waterfalls coupled with downed trees makes this a great bear habitat! Soon you will cross a bridge (wood, double handrail). At trail intersection, veer right and continue right.

0.1   Find bench with view of pond and bear enclosure. As you continue, this section affords a very nice view of Sugar Maple stand and is surrounded by woods. Stay on main trail around fenced enclosure.

0.3 Find two more benches in this area with views of the bear enclosures.

0.4 Although optional, we recommend ascending the 10 steps (wood, double handrail) to observation deck for more bear viewing. In 70', turn right at intersection to return to cub habitat and exit through gift shop.

0.5 Parking area.

 Foot Note:

Did you know that any time you take a photo of an animal in a captive setting, ethically you should declare this information when the photo is circulated or published?

Foot Note:

Oswald's Bear Ranch opened to the public in July of 1997.

Black Bear at Oswald's Bear Ranch. Photo by Lisa Vogelsang

Muskallonge Lake State Park, near Deer Park • Off H-37, 27.3 miles from Newberry

- **Beautiful views of Lake Superior along a lovely wooded trail.**

TRAILHEAD DIRECTIONS & PARKING:

From MI 28, turn north on MI 123 toward Newberry and drive 7.9 miles to 4 Mile Corner (Deer Park Road, H-37, Muskallonge Lake, and County Road 407). Turn left and drive 23.3 miles into Deer Park. Follow signs and turn left toward Muskallonge Lake State Park on H-58. Park entrance is on left side of street. Pull into paved lot just beyond contact station.

TRAILHEAD FACILITIES & FEES:

Nearby (see Muskallonge Lake Picnic Area, pg. 220). For wheelchair accessible toilet, please use facility in campground.

TOTAL TRAIL LENGTH, SURFACE & WIDTH:

1.3 mile; dirt and sand; 1–4' wide.

INCLINES & ALERTS:

There is one incline of 15° for 95' at 0.3 mile. Highway crossing en route to trail. Wash out area in some sections as well as erosion (significant at times). Steep cliffs in places along ridgeline. Stay on trail. Low-hanging branches in spots. Minimum rock and moderate root in sections.

CONTACT:

Muskallonge Lake State Park: (906) 658-3338

MILEAGE & DESCRIPTION

0.0 From parking area, locate post indicating a #1 and map. From this point, cross highway and veer left toward brown sign indicating "Chief Kawgayosh" and follow 1' dirt path.

0.1 Do not take the washout area, but veer left, then right toward Lake Superior. In 150', encounter loose sand and tree root-like steps.

In 100', take the spur trail as you will be treated to incredible views of Lake Superior! However, do not attempt to ascend to beach here due to erosion. There is an access point in about 800'. We recommend staying along fence line in order to pick up main trail again. There is some root in this section as well as erosion; use caution.

0.2 Lake Superior views through the trees as you come upon an area of soft sand.

0.3 Beach access with gorgeous views of the lake just prior to incline (15° for 95'). In 150' you will encounter the DNR working area. Stay toward Lake Superior on grass around parking area and pick up trail at sign indicating "North Country Trail." This puts you on a ridgeline with views of Lake Superior for about 3,000', until you see a sign indicating "Marker #4."

0.7 At Marker #4 we recommend turning around and retracing path to trailhead. The North Country Trail does continue straight ahead and another trail that is part of the park's system continues to the left. The park's trail eventually crosses the highway to the campground. However, there is a very steep decline en route to the highway of 29°, which exceeds Gentle Hikes criteria.

1.3 Trailhead.

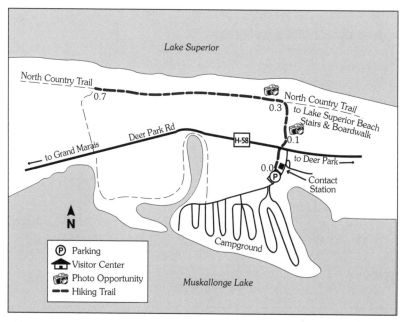

 SAYS WHO?

Want to improve your immunity? Walk briskly around your community!

Regular moderate exercise such as brisk walking can improve immunity by increasing white blood cells (WBC). Walking a short time can increase WBC for one to two hours and walking over 30 minutes can increase WBC production for over 24 hours!

The Physician and Sportsmedicine [33]

TAHQUAMENON FALLS (UPPER)

Tahquamenon Falls State Park, Paradise • Off MI 123, 24.2 miles from Newberry

- **See one of the biggest waterfalls west of Niagara, measuring in at 200' wide with a 50' drop!**
- **Wheelchair accessible up to the second viewing platform of falls.**

Note: Lighter Side of Gentle rating pertains to trail portion without steps.

TRAILHEAD DIRECTIONS & PARKING:
From MI 28, turn north on MI 123 toward Newberry. Drive 27.1 miles to Upper Falls entrance for Tahquamenon Falls State Park. Park in large paved lot. Wheelchair accessible and RV parking available.

TRAILHEAD FACILITIES & FEES:
Flush toilets (wheelchair accessible), water, grills, info kiosk, bench, gift shop and restaurant (privately owned and operated—not on state park property). Annual or day use state park permit is required and available at park office.

TOTAL TRAIL LENGTH, SURFACE & WIDTH:
1.5 miles; paved; 10–20' wide.

INCLINES & ALERTS:
No inclines over 10°. There are a total of 306 steps; however, they are non-continuous throughout the trail with many providing resting platforms. For your safety, do not veer from designated trail. Foot traffic only.

CONTACT:
Tahquamenon Falls State Park: (906) 492-3415

MILEAGE & DESCRIPTION

0.0 Trailhead begins near information kiosk that features Tahquamenon Falls State Park Upper Falls Area on 20'-wide paved path. Note Marker #1 about Michigan's state tree, the Eastern White Pine. Find bench and restrooms to the right as well as a seasonal naturalist tent. Soon you will pass an unpaved drive to the right—continue straight on pavement. Encounter Marker #2 featuring the American Beech and read about its nuts.

0.1 Marker #3 on Sugar Maple. Find out what other critters of the forest enjoy its sweetness. Find bench with views of the forest. In 250', Marker #4 tells us that the Yellow Birch's bark provides daytime roosting for the Little Brown Bat. Can you spot any?

0.2 At map kiosk, veer right. Do you hear the thunder of the falls yet?

Find bench and continue following sign indicating "Falls Brink Viewing Area." Marker #5 provides an opportunity to learn about the Eastern Hemlock. Its bark and tannin were once used by the leather industry to tan hides!

0.3 Here is the first viewing area of the falls. It is beautiful but it gets better in 100'.

Marker #6 features the Northern White Cedar and its importance to the deer in winter. A bench marks the second overlook of the falls and you can see more of its width. Read about the Tahquamenon River and find out why there is so much foam. There is always open water on the falls even deep into Michigan's winter! In 300', wheelchair accessible portion of the trail ends as stairs descend to the third viewing platform.

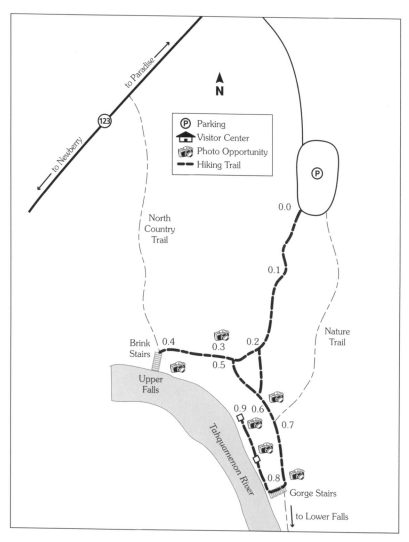

0.4 Descend 94 steps (iron grate, double handrail, non-continuous) to the third viewing area. You are now overlooking beautiful Tahquamenon Falls in all its glory! This overlook is directly on top of a portion of the falls and is a crowd favorite, so expect them in the summer (we had to wait in line to get a photo!). This area has several viewing points and we found it exceptionally scenic when the Fireweed was blooming in August. Benches beckon for company as Marker #7 showcases the Tahquamenon River and the plan to tame it. Alert: Do not travel beyond the fenced areas as it is dangerous. To access different views, ascend steps from which you came and turn right. Follow past the first two viewing areas until you reach the first intersection. A left leads back to the parking area, so veer right following sign indicating "Falls Gorge Viewing Area." In 300', there is another intersection. A left leads back to the parking area; continue straight.

0.6 Find bench and information kiosk about logging. Did you know that from 1870–1910 the Tahquamenon River was used to transport logs from the wilderness to sawmills? The observation platform in this area is wheelchair accessible and offers a more distant view of falls; however, you can now see the full width of the falls! Wheelchair accessibility ends in 600' and there are no more views without steps involved.

0.7 At intersection, continue straight. In 300', find another bench and turn right toward the steps. A left takes you on a primitive 8-mile trail to Lower Falls, but there is a much easier and shorter route (see Tahquamenon Falls [Lower], pg. 147).

0.8 Descend 115 steps (iron grate, double handrail, non-continuous) and note scenic cliffs on the way down. Ascend 3 steps (iron grate, double handrail), then descend 24 steps (iron grate, double handrail, non-continuous) to river bed for a nice view of part of the falls. Alert: Access beyond this point is prohibited. Go back up the steps and turn left; ascend 4, then 5 steps (wood, double handrail). Descend 12 steps (wood, double handrail, non-continuous). In 100', descend 5 steps (wood, double handrail) to a viewing platform and bench with an absolutely gorgeous full-length view of Tahquamenon Falls. However, the best is yet to come! Ascend 3 steps (wood, double handrail) and turn left.

0.9 Ascend 22 steps (wood, double handrail, non-continuous). In 100', descend 19 steps (wood, double handrail, non-continuous). In our opinion, this is the very best view of the fall's width and definitely merits the trek down here! Bench provided for your viewing pleasure. When ready, retrace path to trailhead.

1.5 Trailhead.

CLARK LAKE

Tahquamenon Falls State Park, Paradise • Off MI 123, 29.4 miles from Newberry

- **Very pristine Clark Lake.**

- **One of the remotest hikes whose trailhead is accessible by vehicle (see alert section below).**

TRAILHEAD DIRECTIONS & PARKING:
From MI 28, turn north on MI 123 toward Newberry. Drive 30.5 miles to the turnout for Clark Lake (0.4 miles before the entrance to Lower Falls) on the left (northwest). The road to the trailhead is one lane ("two-track") and very narrow with bumps and loose sand (State Park service recommends driving at your own risk). In 1.1 miles you will see signpost #6. Continue another 0.2 mile past it to main sand parking area.

TRAILHEAD FACILITIES & FEES:
None. Annual or day use state park permit is required and available at park office.

TOTAL TRAIL LENGTH, SURFACE & WIDTH:
0.8 mile; sand; 2–5' wide.

INCLINES & ALERTS:
No inclines over 10°. The one lane "two-track" road to trailhead is very narrow with its fair share of bumps, holes and loose sand. Park service advises driving at your own risk. Our average speed was 5 mph. Brush could be problematic—expect a few scratch souvenirs. Follow 1.3 mile road until it ends in sandy parking area. No wheeled motor vehicles allowed on trail. Expect overgrowth and loose sand.

CONTACT:
Tahquamenon Falls State Park: (906) 492-3415

MILEAGE & DESCRIPTION

0.0   Trailhead begins at sign for "Tahquamenon Falls Natural Area" on 2'-wide sand path. Immediately look right for Lily Pond just 25' into trail. Expect loose sand.

0.1   Spur trail leads to a pond in 200'. Expect overgrowth.

0.4   You are now on the ridgeline overlooking beautiful, pristine Clark Lake! Look for Osprey nest and waterfowl. The trail continues but exceeds Gentle Hikes distance criteria. Retrace path to trailhead.

0.8   Trailhead.

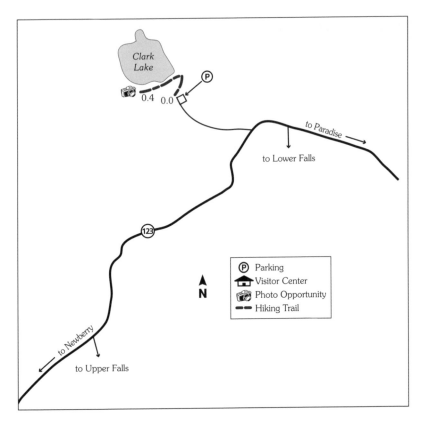

TAHQUAMENON FALLS (LOWER)

Tahquamenon Falls State Park, Paradise • Off MI 123, 29.3 miles from Newberry

- **Although not nearly as big as the upper falls, these falls still have plenty of beauty to offer!**

TRAILHEAD DIRECTIONS & PARKING:

From MI 28, turn north on MI 123 toward Newberry. Drive 30.9 miles to Lower Falls entrance for Tahquamenon Falls State Park. Once inside park, continue 0.8 miles past first campground entrance to large paved parking area. Wheelchair accessible and RV parking available.

TRAILHEAD FACILITIES & FEES:

Flush toilets (wheelchair accessible), grills, open-sided shelter, info kiosk, bench, gift shop, concession stand. Annual or day use state park permit is required and available at park office.

TOTAL TRAIL LENGTH, SURFACE & WIDTH:

1.2 miles; paved, boardwalk; 6–10' wide.

INCLINES & ALERTS:

No inclines over 10°. This area is beautiful but treacherous with whirlpools and undertows. Stay on boardwalk.

CONTACT:

Tahquamenon Falls State Park: (906) 492-3415

MILEAGE & DESCRIPTION

0.0 Trailhead begins from parking area on 10'-wide paved path near sign indicating
  "Lower Falls." In 300', veer left at intersection as you continue to follow sign indicating "Lower Falls." Soon you will see concessions, gift shop and picnic tables to the right. Look closely toward the left and Lower Falls is visible in the distance. But keep going as the best is yet to come! From the first viewing platform you can see three sets of falls. Bench provided for your viewing pleasure.

0.1 At information kiosk, veer right following sign indicating "River Trail Viewing Platform." Stairs to the left lead to boat rentals (see Foot Note for a different way to view Lower Falls Area). Soon you will see the second and third viewing platforms for the falls prior to boardwalk (wood, double handrail). Benches available. These offer nice views, but the best is yet to come!

0.2 Information kiosk explains why the boardwalk was built in order to protect and preserve the environment around you.

0.3 Find two benches throughout this section of boardwalk with views of forest.

0.4 Another bench near "Prayer of the Woods" sign. Soon you will pass a picturesque creek; as you reach the intersection with another trail, stay on boardwalk.

0.5 Here is the view we alluded to earlier. From this observation deck you are within about 50' of Lower Falls. This is simply beautiful! This platform has more than one viewing area with about 500' to explore—enjoy. When ready, retrace path to trailhead.

1.2 Trailhead.

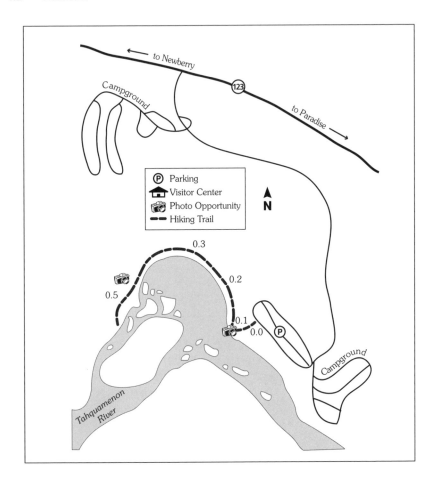

 **Foot Note:**

To see this area from a different perspective, rowboats and canoes can be rented on site through Tahquamenon Outfitters, which is open Memorial Day through the second weekend in October.

TAHQUAMENON RIVERMOUTH WALK*

Tahquamenon Falls State Park, Paradise • On MI 123, 46.4 miles from Newberry
*Gentle Hikes name

• **This entire little stroll is a photo op, especially when wildflowers are blooming.**

TRAILHEAD DIRECTIONS & PARKING:
From MI 28, turn north on MI 123 toward Newberry. Drive 41.4 miles to the stop
sign and continue right on MI 123 toward Tahquamenon Falls State Park Picnic
Area and Rivermouth Campground. Drive 5 miles (0.3 miles south of Picnic Area
and 0.2 miles north of Rivermouth Campground). Turn left into gravel pullout with
brown sign indicating "No Camping; No Groundfires."

TRAILHEAD FACILITIES & FEES:
Nearby at Tahquamenon Rivermouth Picnic Area (pg. 221). No fees for trail use.
Annual or day use state park permit is required and available at park office.

TOTAL TRAIL LENGTH, SURFACE & WIDTH:
0.3 mile; grass, sand; 1–15' wide (contingent on mowing and mood of Lake Superior!).

INCLINES & ALERTS:
No inclines over 10°. Some sections may be impassible depending on Lake
Superior's mood. Surfaces narrow and uneven in places.

CONTACT:
Tahquamenon Falls State Park: (906) 492-3415

MILEAGE & DESCRIPTION

0.0   Trailhead begins at wooden markers near sign indicating "No Camping; No
   Groundfires" on a 15'-wide grassy path. The first 300' are flat with gorgeous
view of evergreens and Lake Superior. After this the trail narrows to 12" with
uneven surfaces. Depending on Superior's mood, some sections may be impassible as path is at water's edge. Use common sense and caution.

0.1   Here you are treated to a two-sided bench with views of Lake Superior on one
   side and the rivermouth on the other. Fantastic! Enjoy exploring this area, which
   is especially picturesque when wildflowers are in bloom. When done, retrace path
to trailhead.

0.3   Trailhead.

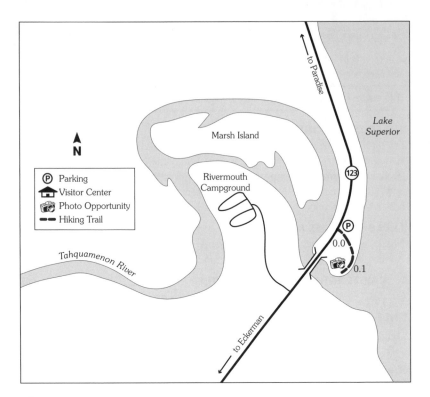

 SAYS WHO?

Do your energy levels need a spike? Take a hike!

Walking has been shown to result in a large increase in energy and vigor.

The Physician and Sports Medicine 2000 [36]

REGION SEVEN: SAULT STE. MARIE AREA

Visit the world-famous Soo Locks in the Upper Peninsula's most popular vacation destination! The Soo Locks are one of the busiest lock systems in the world.

Surrounded by fresh water, clean air and the four seasons of beauty, Sault Ste. Marie has been deemed the "Gathering Place" for hundreds of years, with something for the whole family to love. To the west is beautiful Point Iroquois Lighthouse perched on a magnificent stretch of Lake Superior beach. Not to be missed.

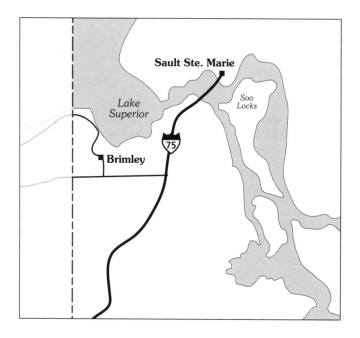

Sault Ste. Marie • Off I-75, 67.2 miles from Newberry • *Gentle Hikes name

- **Award-winning Soo Locks.**

- **World-class Soo Locks Visitor Center filled with demonstrations of how the locks work, nostalgic photos of portaging the falls, lock history, theater and many other exhibits.**

- **Interpretive signs throughout the grounds peppered with artifacts.**

Note: Lighter Side of Gentle rating pertains to trail portion without steps.

TRAILHEAD DIRECTIONS & PARKING:
From MI 28, turn north on I-75 and drive 8.8 miles to exit #394. Turn left off exit and follow signs to the Michigan Welcome Center. Turn right on W. Portage Ave and after passing the Welcome Center, follow signs to Soo Locks. At the curve, continue right onto E. Portage Ave and drive for about 1.3 miles and turn right on Magazine Street. Park in gravel parking area immediately to the right. Although there are many parking areas around Soo Locks Park, this one seemed the largest, so it is where we begin this urban hike. Note: International Bridge to Canada can be seen from this parking lot.

TRAILHEAD FACILITIES & FEES:
At Soo Locks Park are flush toilets (wheelchair accessible), water, and world class visitor center! There is no fee for park admittance.

TOTAL TRAIL LENGTH, SURFACE & WIDTH:
2.0 miles; paved; 6' wide.

INCLINES & ALERTS:
No inclines over 10°. Several street crossings en route to Soo Locks Park. Foot traffic only in park. Please be aware that all visitor packs, purses, coolers, bags and strollers must be searched prior to entry. No weapons. All persons entering this installation are liable to search upon entry or exit and while within confines of this installation. Do not play in fountain, as there is high voltage.

CONTACT:
U.S. Army Corps of Engineers at Soo Area Office: (800) 990-0231

MILEAGE & DESCRIPTION

0.0   Trailhead begins from Soo Locks Parking area. Cross Magazine Street and stay east on 6'-wide sidewalk along Portage Ave. In 250', look for Koi Carp as you pass the mini golf.

0.1   This will be a unique urban hike experience as you pass several gift shops and eateries en route to the Soo Locks Park.

0.2   Use caution when crossing Portage Ave (we chose Ferris Street) as you draw near to Soo Locks Park. Use crosswalks. Please see "Alert" section above for park rules as you will be searched upon entry for security reasons. Once inside the park, before exploring the grounds, we strongly recommend a stop at the visitor center. It is labeled world-class for a reason. Our highlights above should whet your appetite but this truly is a place that the entire family can enjoy. Allow plenty of time here. Staff can know of a ship's arrival up to two hours ahead of time so you can plan accordingly. But even if you do not get to see a ship, there is plenty to see. Once you return to the grounds, there are many artifacts in this area. Follow the "ship signs."

0.3 Find a model of the Poe Lock as you approach the first observational deck located right over the lock! Ascend 34 steps (iron, double handrail, non-continuous) to the fully enclosed viewing area for a bird's eye view of the ships. Note: For wheelchair accessibility, contact security for accommodations. As you continue to explore the grounds there are several benches along the locks.

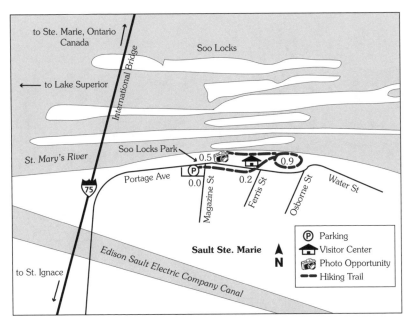

0.4 Ascend 24 narrow steps (cement, double handrail, non-continuous) to the second observation deck to an open-sided, covered viewing area, which is also directly above the locks.

0.5 Ascend 24 narrow steps (wood, double handrail) to the third observation deck, which overlooks the gate. From this point you can find your way back to the park's exit, or if you have time, we highly recommend a visit to the spectacular fountain located in the park adjacent to the lock complex. To get there, return to the first observation deck, but do not ascend the steps. Instead look near the lock model and take the ramp down. Continue to follow the "ship signs."

0.8 We found the Governor Chase S. Osborn Memorial to be very intriguing, as each section contains a plaque cast in copper depicting various aspects of Osborn's life. In 200', find a spectacular fountain and bench. Listen closely for soothing music. Alert: Danger—High voltage! Keep out of fountain.

0.9  Continue to follow the "ship signs" as this path brings you along the Soo Locks where you will find many benches. After ample exploration, return to park exit and then to parking area.

2.0 Parking area.

Foot Note:

Ride with the freighters! For information on the Soo Locks Boat Tours, contact (800) 432-6301 or www.soolocks.com

The Soo Locks. Photo by Ladona Tornabene

POINT IROQUOIS LIGHTHOUSE & BOARDWALK

Iroquois Point • Off West Lakeshore Drive, 28 miles from Sault Ste. Marie

---

- **This entire trail is a photo op with stunning Lake Superior views and quaint lighthouse and grounds.**

TRAILHEAD DIRECTIONS & PARKING:

Leaving Sault Ste. Marie on I-75 South, take the #392 exit and turn right on 3 Mile Road. Drive 1.2 miles and turn left on Baker Road toward Brimley. Drive 3.2 miles and turn right on 6 Mile Road. After passing Brimley State Park, 6 Mile Road becomes West Lakeshore Drive at junction of MI 221. Follow road and signs for Iroquois Point for about 9 miles and see sign for "Lighthouse 500 ft." prior to Lighthouse entrance on the right. Park in paved lot with wheelchair accessible and RV parking available.

TRAILHEAD FACILITIES & FEES:

Flush toilet (wheelchair accessible), water, small museum. No fees for trail use.

TOTAL TRAIL LENGTH, SURFACE & WIDTH:

0.3 mile; boardwalk; 4' wide.

INCLINES & ALERTS:

No inclines over 10°. Boardwalk may be slippery if wet.

CONTACT:

(906) 437-5272

MILEAGE & DESCRIPTION

0.0   Trailhead begins near parking area on 4'-wide boardwalk. In 500', views of Lake
   Superior are beautiful.

0.1   At intersection, stay on boardwalk. A perfectly placed bench affords an opportu-
   nity to watch for ships as wonderful views of Superior continue.

0.2   Another bench with Lake Superior view as you approach the 1870 lighthouse. If
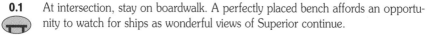   it is open, climb up the 72 steep stairs (loose rail at time of writing, summer
2004) but the view of Superior is stunning!

0.3   Parking lot.

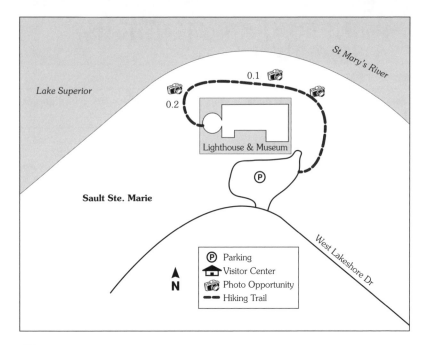

"Each time you go outside and walk, as long as you stay within your capabilities, you will come home feeling better than you did when you left."

American Hiking Society [37]

ALMOST HIKES
An Almost Hike is:

-a very short trail, ranging from 80' to 0.6 mile with spectacular scenery.

-typically not a trail per se, but a route to scenic beauty.

-usually has an original name as this concept is original to our book.

We hope you'll enjoy the following strolls. We give you highlights, total length/surface, safety concerns, amenities, applicable fees and a brief narrative of what you'll see while there.

Most Almost Hikes are very suitable for families travelling with small children. Great leg stretchers and highly scenic—but please heed safety concerns.

BLACK RIVER HARBOR

Black River Harbor Area • Off U.S. 2, 15.1 miles from Bessemer

- **Picturesque Black River and suspension bridge.**
- **Beaches of Lake Superior.**

DIRECTIONS & PARKING:
From U.S. 2 in Bessemer, turn north on CR-513 (Black River Road). Drive 15.1 miles to paved parking area for Black River Harbor. Designated wheelchair parking.

TRAILHEAD FACILITIES & FEES:
Flush & vault toilets (wheelchair accessible), water, picnic area (see Black River Harbor Picnic Area, pg. 202). information kiosk, bench, playground and small gift shop. No fees for trail use.

TOTAL LENGTH/SURFACE:
0.6 mile; paved, gravel, hardpacked dirt, sand.

ALERT:
Uneven surfaces on blacktop.

NARRATIVE:
Trailhead begins from parking area at information kiosk on 5' paved path. Journey through picnic area where you will find water and vault toilet (wheelchair accessible). At 400', find suspension bridge. Just prior to this bridge is an intersection. Right takes you down 17 steps (wood and dirt, single handrail) to dock area along boardwalk, which parallels the Black River. Left takes you to the concession stand and small gift shop. For now, cross bridge (wood, double handrail) for lovely views of the river, harbor area and Lake Superior. After bridge, a gentle slope leads down along river's edge as you approach trailhead for Rainbow Falls. Continue along river as we have chosen a different route for Rainbow Falls (pg. 24). At 800', find bench with river view. Trail turns to a mixture of gravel, hardpacked dirt and sand. At 1,210', find another bench with expansive Lake Superior views! At 0.3 mile, trail ends at beach area. Retrace path to trailhead.

 SAYS WHO?

Joint pain keeping you off the trail?

Jarring forces on knees and other joints can be reduced 12-25% by using hiking poles.

Harvard Women's Health Letter [38]

SUNDAY LAKE BOARDWALK

Wakefield • Off U.S. 2, 11.8 miles from Ironwood • *Gentle Hikes name

- **Beautiful Sunday Lake!**

DIRECTIONS & PARKING:
From U.S. 2 in Wakefield, turn north on Lakeshore Drive (west side of Sunday Lake). Park in paved lot.

TRAILHEAD FACILITIES & FEES:
Flush toilet (wheelchair accessible), bench and picnic tables.

TOTAL LENGTH/SURFACE:
0.5 mile; boardwalk.

ALERT:
Boardwalk uneven in sections.

NARRATIVE:
Trailhead begins to left of restrooms on boardwalk. In 100', there is a bench and soon, an intersection. Turn left and enjoy the lake views with benches spread approximately 300' apart. In 0.3 mile the boardwalk ends at roadway. Retrace path back to intersection and continue straight for another 730' where boardwalk ends at a fishing pier. Benches are spaced approximately 100' apart in this section. This entire Almost Hike is a nice stroll with continuous lake views on one side and mixed forest on the other.

SUNDAY STROLL AT SUNDAY LAKE*

Wakefield • 14 miles from Ironwood • *Gentle Hikes name

- **A lovely paved path located in Eddy Park along beautiful Sunday Lake.**
- **Several picnic areas along the way.**

DIRECTIONS & PARKING:
From U.S. 2 in Wakefield, turn left (northeast) on MI 28 (Chicago Mine Road) and drive 0.9 miles. Turn left (west) at park sign indicating Eddy Park. Park in gravel parking area along paved road.

AMENITIES & FEES:
Flush toilets (wheelchair accessible, except in area near swimming beach), water, grills, two enclosed shelters, playground, benches, beach, volleyball. No fees for trail use.

TOTAL LENGTH/SURFACE:
0.6 miles; paved.

ALERT:
No dogs, bicycles or motor vehicles permitted. No lifeguard at beach—swim at your own risk.

Trailhead begins on paved path near restrooms. Several benches throughout offer lovely views of Sunday Lake with an open-sided picnic shelter and swimming beach. When paved portion of trail ends, retrace path to trailhead.

BONANZA FALLS

Ontonagon County near Silver City • Off MI 64, 0.8 miles from Silver City

- **Small but picturesque and the intriguing rock formations are worth the visit regardless of water flow.**

DIRECTIONS & PARKING:
From MI 28 in Bergland, turn north on MI 64 and drive 16.9 miles and turn left (west) into the parking area for Bonanza Falls. Bonanza Falls is 0.8 miles south of the junction of MI 64 and MI 107 in Silver City.

TRAILHEAD FACILITIES & FEES:
None.

TOTAL LENGTH/SURFACE:
80', grass and dirt.

ALERT:
Steep trail beyond 80' if you decide to go to the base of the falls.

NARRATIVE:
Trailhead begins near cement pillars on grassy path to the left. In 80' you can view the falls.

UNION RIVER

Silver City • On MI 107, 2.3 miles from junction of MI 64 in Silver City

- **Easy stair access to Lake Superior's sandy beach at the foot of the Porcupine Mountains.**
- **Excellent location to take in a sunset (bring the camera).**

DIRECTIONS & PARKING:
From MI 28 in Bergland, turn north on MI 64 and drive 17.7 miles to the junction of MI 64 and MI 107 in Silver City. Turn left (west) on MI 107 drive for 2.3 miles until you see Silver Sands Motor Lodge and Union Bay Outpost on the left side of the road. Parking available alongside the road on the right.

TRAILHEAD FACILITIES & FEES:
No facilities. No fees for trail use.

TOTAL LENGTH/SURFACE:
Just 13 steps bring you down to the sandy beach with plenty of shoreline to stroll.

ALERT:

Uneven surfaces (as you might expect from sand).

NARRATIVE:

Trailhead begins from roadside across from Silver Sands Motor Lodge and Union Bay Outpost. Descend 13 steps (iron grate, double handrail) to the sandy beach front and beautiful Lake Superior shoreline! Great place to watch the sun set behind the Porcupine Mountains.

EN ROUTE TO LAKE OF THE CLOUDS

Porcupine Mountains Wilderness State Park • On MI 107, 8 miles from Silver City

• **Beautiful sweeping vista of Lake Superior.**

DIRECTIONS & PARKING:

From MI 28 in Bergland, turn north on MI 64 and drive 17.7 miles to the junction of MI 64 and MI 107 in Silver City. Turn left (west) on MI 107 and drive for 8.0 miles (1.6 miles past Government Peak Trail, pg. 32). Parking available alongside the road near picnic area.

TRAILHEAD FACILITIES & FEES:

Vault toilet, picnic area (see En Route to Lake of the Clouds Picnic Pullover, pg. 204). No fees for trail use.

TOTAL LENGTH/SURFACE:

0.1 mile; hardpacked gravel.

ALERT:

Use caution when descending steps as some are composed of gravel enclosed in wooden structure. None of the steps have handrails.

NARRATIVE:

Trailhead begins from roadside pull-off at steps. Descend 5 steps (gravel and wood), 4 more (cement), then 3 more to information sign. Read about how the Porcupine Mountains got their name and discover what businesses once occupied these mountains until the area was made a state park in 1945. A small pond will be to the left as you head out toward the lake on a 5'-wide hardpacked gravel path. It is 210' to the bench that provides a sweeping vista of Lake Superior.

OVERLOOKED FALLS

Porcupine Mountains Wilderness State Park • Off South Boundary Road, 19.6 miles from Silver City

• **Beautiful wooded drive on a dirt road culminating at Blowdown Creek. Exceptionally scenic short hike along the Little Carp River leads to the lovely Overlooked Falls.**

• **Bring the camera—the entire Almost Hike is one big photo op!**

DIRECTIONS & PARKING:

From MI 28 in Bergland, turn north on MI 64 and drive 17.7 miles to the junction of MI 64 and MI 107 in Silver City. Turn left (west) on MI 107 drive for 2.7 miles to the intersection of MI 107 and South Boundary Road (notice sign that indicates Visitor Center). Turn left and drive along South Boundary Road for 16.4 miles and turn right at the dirt road called Little Carp River Road. Notice a sign that says "Dead End No Trailers." Do not take trailers or RVs as there is not enough room to turn around. Continue straight on Little Carp River Road for 0.5 miles along a beautiful wooded drive until you reach the parking area (also dirt) just before wooden bridge.

TRAILHEAD FACILITIES & FEES:

Information kiosk, bench. Annual or day use state park permit is required and available at Wilderness Visitor Center, Park Headquarters and Presque Isle Ranger Station.

TOTAL LENGTH/SURFACE:

0.1 mile, dirt (width difficult to determine).

ALERT:

Uneven surface and some tree roots.

NARRATIVE:

Your journey begins at the sign indicating "Overlooked Falls." In 145', views begin and continue up to the natural bench (huge fallen tree) that Mother Nature placed at just the right spot for a beautiful view of the falls. The trail is closed beyond this point, but don't rush off. The Little Carp River is absolutely gorgeous and if time permits, we strongly recommend a hike to Greenstone Falls (see pg. 48), which is very close by.

ONTONAGON MARINA & BOARDWALK STROLL

Ontonagon • On MI 64, 12.3 miles from Silver City • *Gentle Hikes name

- **Picturesque stroll along the Ontonagon River.**
- **Small quaint marina.**
- **Home to many Canada Geese.**

DIRECTIONS & PARKING:

From MI 28 in Bergland, turn north on MI 64 and drive 17.7 miles to the junction of MI 64 and MI 107 in Silver City. Turn right to stay on MI 64 and drive 12.3 miles east until just before it meets the Ontonagon River prior to the town of Ontonagon. Turn right at sign indicating park and marina area. Park in paved lot near river (wheelchair designated parking).

TRAILHEAD FACILITIES & FEES:

Vault toilet (wheelchair accessible), picnic area, grills, tourist information, sand volleyball court and small playground. No fees for trail use.

TOTAL LENGTH/SURFACE:
0.2 miles; paved, boardwalk.

ALERT:
No skateboarding, bicycle riding, roller skating or motorized vehicles. No swimming. There may be an abundance of geese, so watch your step.

NARRATIVE:
Trailhead begins from paved parking area on 5' cement path. Just 100' takes you to the boardwalk (under construction, Summer 2004). This boardwalk parallels the river for 400'. Four benches strategically placed for your viewing pleasure.

Bonanza Falls (see pg. 160). Photo by Melanie Morgan

BISHOP BARAGA SHRINE & HISTORICAL SITE

L'Anse • Off U.S. 41, 33.2 miles from Houghton

- **Majestic 35' statue of Father Frederic Baraga holding cross and snowshoes.**
- **Arches representative of 5 major missions among the Great Lakes Indians.**

DIRECTIONS & PARKING:

From MI 28, turn north on U.S. 41 toward L'Anse. At Welcome sign to L'Anse continue to follow U.S. 41 toward the left (west). Watch for brown & white Bishop Baraga Shrine signs. One mile out of L'Anse, turn left on Lambert Road. At Y in road, turn right and go 0.4 mile to Baraga Shrine and paved parking area on the right.

AMENITIES & FEES:

Flush toilet, water in seasonal gift shop. Few picnic tables in grassy area. No fees for trail use.

TOTAL LENGTH/SURFACE:

645'; paved, grass and woodchips.

ALERT:

Must cross railroad tracks 88' from entrance.

NARRATIVE:

Trailhead begins between a pair of tepees under a Welcome sign. At 88' from entrance, cross railroad tracks—use caution. Information kiosks abound. Follow the path to left toward shrine. The statue is impressive and the afternoon sun compliments the rich hues, creating wonderful photo ops.

F.J. MCLAIN SCENIC BOARDWALK AND GAZEBO*

F.J. McLain State Park • Off MI 203, 11.1 miles from Lift Bridge in Hancock •
*Gentle Hikes name

- **Totally accessible scenic views from gazebo just 420' from your vehicle.**
- **Double-size gazebo—spectacular!**

DIRECTIONS & PARKING:

From MI 28, turn north on U.S. 45 at Bruce Crossing and drive 14.1 miles. At intersection, turn northeast on MI 26 toward Houghton-Hancock and drive about 57 miles. Follow signs for U.S. 41 north in Houghton and cross lift bridge to Hancock. Stay on U.S. 41 until the intersection of MI 203. Turn left (north) on MI 203 and drive 9.8 miles to entrance of F.J. McLain State Park. Once in park, follow road toward left to large paved area from which you can see the gazebo.

Wheelchair accessible parking available.

AMENITIES & FEES:
Vault toilet (wheelchair accessible), grills, open-sided shelter, playground, benches, volleyball, horseshoe pit, water nearby, picnic area nearby (see Breakwater Beach House Picnic Area pg. 208). Annual or day use state park permit is required and available at park office.

TOTAL LENGTH/SURFACE:
840'; paved, boardwalk.

ALERT:
No bikes or inline skates.

NARRATIVE:
Trailhead begins at designated wheelchair parking area near small open-sided shelter on 5'-wide cement path. Follow path through picnic area on pavement to boardwalk with double handrail (240' of pavement to boardwalk). Benches are conveniently located along boardwalk and at gazebo. Benches in gazebo allow expansive views of Lake Superior in three directions. Also views of North Entry Light and Keweenaw hills. Photo ops abound!

EAGLE RIVER FALLS AND HISTORIC BRIDGE

Eagle Harbor • Off MI 26, 27.4 miles from Hancock, 21.6 miles from Copper Harbor

- **Eagle River Falls.**

DIRECTIONS & PARKING:
From MI 28, turn north on U.S. 45 at Bruce Crossing and drive 14.1 miles. At intersection, turn northeast on MI 26 toward Houghton-Hancock and drive about 57 miles. Look for U.S. 41 north in Houghton and cross lift bridge to Hancock. Follow signs in Hancock and continue to follow U.S. 41 north for about 25 miles to Phoenix. Turn left (northwest) on MI 26 and continue 2.4 miles into Eagle River. Turn right on 4th Street and park in paved lot.

TRAILHEAD FACILITIES & FEES:
No facilities. No fees for trail use.

TOTAL LENGTH/SURFACE:
400'; paved.

ALERT:
No motorized vehicles.

NARRATIVE:
Trailhead begins near information kiosk. Take some time to read about the Lake Shore Drive Bridge and Eagle River. In just 50' onto bridge, views mount, showcasing Eagle River Falls. Views are nice on the other side of the bridge as well.

EAGLE HARBOR LIGHTHOUSE

Eagle Harbor • Off MI 26, 35.4 miles from Hancock, 13.6 miles from Copper Harbor

- **Eagle Harbor Lighthouse.**
- **Broken Thumb observation deck with spectacular, sweeping vista of Lake Superior!**

DIRECTIONS & PARKING:

From MI 28, turn north on U.S. 45 at Bruce Crossing and drive 14.1 miles. At intersection, turn northeast on MI 26 toward Houghton-Hancock and drive about 57 miles. Look for U.S. 41 north in Houghton and cross lift bridge to Hancock. Follow signs in Hancock and continue to follow U.S. 41 north for about 25 miles to Phoenix. Turn left (northwest) on MI 26 and continue past Eagle River toward Eagle Harbor for 10.4 miles. Turn left on North Road in Eagle Harbor. Turn left again at Lighthouse Road and continue straight past the lighthouse until road dead ends into gravel parking lot.

TRAILHEAD FACILITIES & FEES:

Portable toilet, information kiosk, open-sided shelter with picnic table. No fees for trail use, but fee required for lighthouse and museum tours.

TOTAL LENGTH/SURFACE:

Just 31 steps to deck.

ALERT:

Steps vary in height: Use caution. Please be respectful of private residence on site.

NARRATIVE:

Ascend 31 steps (wood, double handrail, non-continuous, height varies) to spectacular overlook of rocky coastline. Marker gives information about freighters, shipping lanes, cargoes, Lake Superior and Eagle Harbor Lighthouse.

COPPER HARBOR BOAT LAUNCH

Copper Harbor • Off MI 26, 48.4 miles from Hancock

- **Beautifully maintained harbor area with completely wheelchair accessible public boat landing and transient marina.**

DIRECTIONS & PARKING:

From MI 28, turn north on U.S. 45 at Bruce Crossing and drive 14.1 miles. At intersection, turn northeast on MI 26 toward Houghton-Hancock and drive about 57 miles. Look for U.S. 41 north in Houghton and cross lift bridge to Hancock. Follow signs in Hancock and continue on U.S. 41 north to Copper Harbor for about 48 miles. At intersection of U.S. 41 and MI 26 in Copper Harbor, turn left (west) and drive 0.4 miles and then turn right into the Copper Harbor State Harbor/Copper Harbor Marina at the sign. Park in paved lot with designated wheelchair and RV parking available.

AMENITIES & FEES:

Seasonal flush toilet (wheelchair accessible), water and gift shop. Vault toilet (wheelchair accessible), small picnic area. No fees for trail use.

TOTAL LENGTH/SURFACE:

0.2 mile; paved.

ALERT:

Boat launch area, shallow water, no swimming or diving. Open dock and pier—no fencing or guardrails.

NARRATIVE:

Trailhead begins at parking area to the left of the gift shop. Follow cement path down to pier for lovely views of Copper Harbor. At the end of pier, look in the distance for Copper Harbor Lighthouse.

 Foot Note:

If you would like a much closer view of Copper Harbor Lighthouse, take the Lighthouse Tour via water taxi. Contact (906) 289-4966 or www.copperharborlighthouse.com.

COPPER HARBOR LIGHTHOUSE OVERLOOK

Fort Wilkins State Park, Copper Harbor • 49.2 miles from Hancock

- **Lovely views of Copper Harbor and Copper Harbor Lighthouse.**

DIRECTIONS & PARKING:

From MI 28, turn north on U.S. 45 at Bruce Crossing and drive 14.1 miles. At intersection, turn northeast on MI 26 toward Houghton-Hancock and drive about 57 miles. Look for U.S. 41 north in Houghton and cross lift bridge to Hancock. Follow signs in Hancock and continue on U.S. 41 north to Copper Harbor for about 48 miles. At intersection of U.S. 41 and MI 26 in Copper Harbor, turn right (east) and drive 1.2 miles toward Fort Wilkins State Park. Immediately after crossing Fanny Hooe Creek, turn left into small paved parking area. Designated wheelchair parking.

TRAILHEAD FACILITIES & FEES:

Vault toilet (wheelchair accessible), information kiosk, bench. Water, picnic area and flush toilets nearby (see Fort Wilkins State Park Picnic Area, pg. 210). Annual or day use state park permit is required and available at park office.

TOTAL LENGTH/SURFACE:

300'; hardpacked gravel.

ALERT:

None

NARRATIVE:

From parking area, trailhead begins near designated wheelchair accessible parking sign at posts on 6' gravel path. In 150', you will reach the observation platform with views of Copper Harbor and Copper Harbor Lighthouse across the cove. Views of Lake Superior abound as well. All very nice!

FORT WILKINS HISTORIC SITE

Fort Wilkins State Park, Copper Harbor • 49.5 miles from Hancock

- **See historic Fort Wilkins—a well-preserved example of army life in 1844.**

- **Exhibits, audiovisual programs and seasonal living history interpretations invite the visitor to slow down and travel back in time.**

- **All buildings are wheelchair accessible and can be viewed at virtually any pace; however, the park service recommends 1-2 hours. We concur.**

DIRECTIONS & PARKING:

From MI 28, turn north on U.S. 45 at Bruce Crossing and drive 14.1 miles. At intersection, turn northeast on MI 26 toward Houghton-Hancock and drive about 57 miles. Look for U.S. 41 north in Houghton and cross lift bridge to Hancock. Follow signs in Hancock and continue on U.S. 41 north to Copper Harbor for about 48 miles. At intersection of U.S. 41 and MI 26 in Copper Harbor, turn right (east) and drive 1.5 miles to Fort Wilkins State Park. Turn right into large paved parking area. Designated wheelchair and RV parking.

TRAILHEAD FACILITIES & FEES:

Flush toilets (wheelchair accessible), water, picnic area (see Fort Wilkins State Park Picnic Area, pg. 210), bench, playground, info kiosk and gift shop. Annual or day use state park permit is required and available at park office.

TOTAL LENGTH/SURFACE:

0.2 mile, but will vary depending upon how grounds are explored. Paved, grass, hardpacked gravel.

ALERT:

No bikes or pets in buildings.

NARRATIVE:

Before heading to the Fort, pick up brochure from park office as it contains a lay-out of Fort Wilkins Historic Site. Trailhead begins in front of park store on 7'-wide cement path with double rail. Marker at trailhead reveals information about the cop-per discovery in 1844. Turn right at intersection onto blacktop and find partial views of Lake Fanny Hooe as you enter the world of 1870. The first buildings were the Married Soldiers Quarters. Building #1 now houses a wildflower exhibit; building #2 beckons a visit for an 8-minute video of the Fort Wilkins Story; building #3 invites you to discover what life was like at Fort Wilkins; building #4 houses a room decorated in authentic 1870s style! As you enter the actual Fort, check out the dis-tinctive fencing surrounding the complex. Then visit the bakery, carpenter and blacksmith shops that will be to the left. These buildings are furnished to showcase life as it was back then. As you enter the Parade Grounds, you may indeed believe time travel is possible as twelve of the nineteen buildings are original structures from the 1840s! We highly recommend spending some time here and exploring at your own pace. Throughout your visit you will find the kitchen and mess room, company and officer quarters, hospital, powder magazine, guardhouse, warehouse, ice house, sutler's building and storehouse. See incredible views of Lake Fanny Hooe and cannons that still work! Seasonally, there are living history interpretations and a Civil War Encampment.

Cabins at Fort Wilkins Historic Site (see pg. 168). Photo by Lisa Vogelsang

Cannon at Fort Wilkins Historic Site (see pg. 168). Photo by Ladona Tornabene

FORT CEMETERY

Fort Wilkins State Park, Copper Harbor • 49.5 miles from Hancock

- **Fort Cemetery.**
- **Nice views of Lake Fanny Hooe.**

DIRECTIONS & PARKING:

From MI 28, turn north on U.S. 45 at Bruce Crossing and drive 14.1 miles. At intersection, turn northeast on MI 26 toward Houghton-Hancock and drive about 57 miles. Look for U.S. 41 north in Houghton and cross lift bridge to Hancock. Follow signs in Hancock and continue on U.S. 41 north to Copper Harbor for about 48 miles. At intersection of U.S. 41 and MI 26 in Copper Harbor, turn right (east) and drive 1.5 miles to Fort Wilkins State Park. Turn right into large paved parking area. Designated wheelchair and RV parking.

TRAILHEAD FACILITIES & FEES:

Flush toilets (wheelchair accessible), water, picnic area (see Fort Wilkins State Park Picnic Area, pg. 210), bench, playground, info kiosk and gift shop. Annual or day use state park permit is required and available at park office.

TOTAL LENGTH/SURFACE:

0.3 mile, paved.

ALERT:

Blacktop uneven in places.

NARRATIVE:

Trailhead begins in front of park store on 7'-wide cement path with double rail. The marker at the trailhead reveals information about the copper discovery in 1844. Turn left at the intersection near bench onto blacktop and find partial views of Lake Fanny Hooe. In 150', find "Livestock for Food and Work" marker. Read about what used to be at this present site. In another 100', find bench with beautiful views of Lake Fanny Hooe. At intersection, turn left to Post Cemetery and read about burials at Fort Wilkins. In 100', find "Hard Work for Just Potatoes" marker. It tells of challenges soldiers faced simply to eat. Retrace path to trailhead or continue on blacktop to return to parking area.

PRESQUE ISLE BREAKWALL

Presque Isle Park, Marquette • Off U.S. 41/MI 28 bypass

- **Active ore dock with unobstructed views.**
- **Presque Isle Light and Lake Superior.**
- **Rugged cliffs of Presque Isle.**

DIRECTIONS & PARKING:

From U.S. 41/MI 28 bypass driving east into Marquette, turn left (north) on East Lake Shore Blvd. followed by another left on North Lake Shore Blvd. until you reach Presque Isle Park. Continue on the road around to the right beyond the park entrance, past the marina and boat launch. Park in paved circular parking area. Wheelchair accessible parking available.

TRAILHEAD FACILITIES & FEES:

Picnic area (see Presque Isle Picnic Area pg. 212) and water. Nearby are flush toilets (wheelchair accessible), playground, concession stand and MooseWood Nature Center. No fees for trail use.

TOTAL LENGTH/SURFACE:

0.5 mile; cement.

ALERT:

Keep off during storms or rough seas, violent waves, turbulent water. Do not walk on breakwall when waves are high. Cement uneven in places.

NARRATIVE:

Trailhead begins within the picnic area just prior to the curve in road at a memorial for those who lost their lives in high waves. This memorial also serves as a warning for others not to take such risks. Descend 14 steps (wood and hardpacked dirt, double handrail) onto breakwater. Width begins at 15' then narrows to 4'. Once you reach the end of the cement portion of the Breakwater, do not continue onto rocks. Turn around and retrace path to trailhead.

CINDER POND

Marquette • Off U.S. 41/MI 28 bypass, 41 miles from Munising

- **Barrier-free path with beautiful views of Lake Superior and a wheelchair accessible fishing area.**
- **Kids Cove Playground.**
- **See Marquette's Fire Bell—cast in bronze in 1882.**

DIRECTIONS & PARKING:

From U.S. 41/MI 28 bypass driving east into Marquette, turn left (north) on East Lake Shore Blvd. followed by another left on North Lake Shore Blvd., and a right turn into the Cinder Pond Marina paved parking lot (designated wheelchair accessible and RV parking).

TRAILHEAD FACILITIES & FEES:

Flush toilets (wheelchair accessible), water, picnic tables and open-sided shelter, playground, benches, concession stand and wheelchair accessible fishing area.

TOTAL LENGTH/SURFACE:

0.5 mile; paved.

ALERT:

Service vehicles and bikes share part of path. No pets in playground. No golfing or ball playing allowed.

NARRATIVE:

Trailhead begins on sidewalk toward Kids Cove Playground. Take some time to view the wood carvings done "in memory of" at the entrance of this playground. Also, each piece of equipment is sponsored by a different organization and some of the Cove is wheelchair accessible. In 300', turn left onto blacktop bike path and follow for 0.2 mile to fire bell. There are two access points to bell area. One is via ascending 16 steps, then 10 more (concrete, double handrail) and the other is via a paved path leading to the same location. There is also a Memory Garden as a tribute to those who lost their lives on 9-11 as well as information about Marquette's fire department. After leaving bell, trail offers lovely views of Lake Superior. Alert: Watch for service vehicles in this section. Multiple benches abound, and in another 0.1 mile, find a Vietnam POW-MIA memorial. Another 0.1 mile leads to the accessible fishing area with bench and picnic table offering beautiful views of the shoreline. In 20', trail returns to parking area to complete this loop.

Canada Geese near Presque Isle Nature Trail (see pg. 91). Photo by Ladona Tornabene

GRAND ISLAND OVERLOOK*

Hiawatha National Forest, Munising • Off MI 28, 1.8 miles from junction of MI 28 and East Munising Ave(H-58) near Visitor Center • *Gentle Hikes name

* **Sweeping vista of Grand Island and Lake Superior.**

DIRECTIONS & PARKING:

From junction of MI 28 and East Munising Ave (H-58) near Visitor Center, turn west on MI 28 and drive 1.8 miles, then turn left into driveway for Grand Island Harbor Scenic Turnout–Roadside Park. Park in paved lot (wheelchair accessible parking available).

TRAILHEAD FACILITIES & FEES:

Vault toilet (wheelchair accessible), water, information kiosk, grills, picnic tables. No fees for trail use.

TOTAL LENGTH/SURFACE:

370'; boardwalk.

ALERT:

Park closed 10pm–7am.

NARRATIVE:

Trailhead begins on boardwalk (wood, double handrail) near wheelchair accessible parking place and leads to sweeping vista of Grand Island and Lake Superior. Bench and information marker provided at the overlook.

MINERS BEACH

Pictured Rocks National Lakeshore • Off H-58, 11.7 miles from MI 28 in Munising

* **Cliffs of Pictured Rock National Lakeshore.**
* **Beach of Lake Superior.**

DIRECTIONS & PARKING:

From MI 28 in Munising, turn east on H-58 and drive 5.3 miles. Turn left on Miners Castle Road. Drive for 5.1 miles and turn right at Y intersection. Soon road changes from paved to gravel to dirt. In about 1 mile, turn left at intersection to Miners Beach and in 0.3 miles park in gravel lot.

TRAILHEAD FACILITIES & FEES:

Vault toilet (wheelchair accessible), information kiosk, grills, picnic tables and bench. No fees for trail use.

TOTAL LENGTH/SURFACE:

0.2 mile; boardwalk.

ALERT:

Walkway may be slippery. Step height higher than average.

Trailhead begins on boardwalk at sign indicating beach access. Find first bench at 75' as you continue on boardwalk. Pass several wooded picnic sites en route to the beach. In 430', descend 12 steps (wood and sand, single handrail) toward a beautiful beach with nice views of sand cliffs.

SENEY VISITOR CENTER STROLL*

Seney National Wildlife Refuge • Off MI 77, 5.9 miles from MI 28 in Seney •
*Gentle Hikes name

- **Abundance of seasonal water lilies can be viewed from parking area.**
- **Children's Touch Table (for kids of all ages) with touchable furs, fact sheets and track table!**
- **Exhibits of owls, Trumpeter Swan, cub, loon and others.**

DIRECTIONS & PARKING:

From MI 28 in Seney, turn south on MI 77 and drive 4.8 miles to the entrance of Seney National Wildlife Refuge. Turn right (west) into the entrance and drive 1.1 miles to Visitor Center paved parking area. Designated wheelchair accessible parking available.

TRAILHEAD FACILITIES & FEES:

Flush toilets (wheelchair accessible), water, info kiosk, bench, gift shop, exhibits and more. No fees for trail use or entry.

TOTAL LENGTH/SURFACE:

0.1 mile; paved.

ALERT:

Daylight use only.

NARRATIVE:

Trailhead begins from parking area for visitor center near info kiosk. Grab a free brochure and read about the various ways you can explore this refuge. Also at this kiosk are benches overlooking ponds of seasonal water lilies, viewing scopes (wheelchair accessible), and other interesting facts. The ponds are a good place to view wildlife, but don't forget to look up as you may see a Sandhill Crane or Trumpeter Swan flying through! Proceed toward visitor center, veering left on sidewalk toward benches and pond. Expect sidewalk to be lined with an abundance of wildflowers during summer. More benches by this pond beckon and the fire tower can be seen from this vantage point. Continue around to the back of the visitor center to the deck and viewing platform amply equipped with benches overlooking the pond. Viewing scopes (wheelchair accessible) are available here as well. Continue to circle around building and on east side, note the Purple Martin bird house. Some wildflowers in this area are labeled for your convenience. To the left is the Pine Ridge Nature Trail (pg. 133). For now, turn right and plan to spend some time at the visitor center. At time of writing (summer 2004) plans were being considered to revise the 14-minute slide show. However, if it is still there, we highly recommend a viewing as the photography is simply breathtaking, plus it provides an introduction to the natural and cultural history of Seney. Inquire of staff regarding availability.

The Children's Touch Table is fun for kids of all ages! Laminated fact sheets featuring photos of wildlife and descriptions make this a very educational "must-stop." After all, where else can you "pet" an exhibit of Michigan mammals? But the fun doesn't stop here because the Track Table allows you to create over a dozen animal tracks in the sand with track stamps! There are also a host of other non-touchable exhibits such as owls, Trumpeter Swan, cub, bobcat, loon, eagle, Sandhill Crane, and numerous interactive displays. You can also read about the Great Lakes ecosystem, managing wildlife, migration schedule and more. This site has been identified as being significant for world bird conservation.

 Foot Note:

Proceeds from the bookstore go to Seney Natural History Association (SNHA). SNHA has helped fund programs, provide viewing scopes, fund visitor center displays, support teacher workshops and many other activities. To become a Friend of Seney National Wildlife Refuge visit www.seneyfriends.org.

MARSHLAND WILDLIFE DRIVE—THE ALMOST HIKE THAT'S A DRIVE THROUGH!*

Seney National Wildlife Refuge • Off MI 77, 5.9 miles from MI 28 in Seney •
*Gentle Hikes name

- **A 7-mile, one-way auto tour route alongside beautiful wetlands and meadows with three observation decks equipped with viewing scopes (wheelchair accessible).**
- **See Trumpeter Swans, Common Loons, nesting Bald Eagles and Sandhill Cranes.**
- **One of the largest refuges east of the Mississippi River.**

DIRECTIONS & PARKING:
From MI 28 in Seney, turn south on MI 77 and drive 4.8 miles to the entrance of Seney National Wildlife Refuge. Turn right (west) into entrance and drive 1.1 miles to Visitor Center (VC) paved parking area. Maps available at VC. Marshland Drive begins directly across road from VC. Since this is a drive, parking is very limited around observation decks. Nothing is paved.

TRAILHEAD FACILITIES & FEES:
Nearby at visitor center are flush toilets (wheelchair accessible), water, info kiosk, bench, gift shop, exhibits and more (see Seney Visitor Center Stroll Almost Hike, pg. 174). No fees for Marshland Drive.

TOTAL LENGTH/SURFACE:
7 miles; gravel.

ALERT:

Speed limit is 15 mph for a reason—narrow (one-way), winding roads, bridges, sharp curves, pedestrians and frequently stopped vehicles necessitate a cautious drive. Allow at least one hour to complete the 7-mile loop. Daylight use only.

NARRATIVE:

Marshland Wildlife Drive begins on one-way gravel road directly across from visitor center parking area. Ponds begin immediately so start looking for wildlife. At about 2 miles is the first viewing platform (wood, double handrail). It is a 40' walk to the viewing scopes and there is an info marker about the Trumpeter Swans. These swans are the largest North American waterfowl and can weigh up to 30 lbs. with an 8' wingspan. In another 1.5 miles, find second viewing platform (wood, double handrail). It is a 40' walk to the viewing scopes and there is an info marker about the Common Loon. If you see a loon dancing while you are boating or canoeing it signals that you are much too close to its nest or offspring. In about another 1.5 miles is the third and last viewing platform (wood, double handrail). There is an info marker about the Bald Eagle. Eagles do not develop their white head feathers until they are 4–5 years old. Look for an eagle's nest through the viewing scopes. See how many you can find. Please drive slowly and safely as you exit this refuge. To return to the visitor center, turn left when you reach the highway.

BEST LITTLE BAREFOOTED HIKE IN GRAND MARAIS*

Grand Marais • Off MI 77, 27 miles from Seney • *Gentle Hikes name

- **Grand Marais Lighthouse at trailhead.**
- **Beautiful Lake Superior and Sand Dunes.**

DIRECTIONS & PARKING:

From MI 28 in Seney, turn north on MI 77 and drive 25 miles toward Grand Marais. In Grand Marais, pass H-58 and continue straight on MI 77 passing Grand Marais Ave until sign says "End MI 77." Continue onto Canal Street/Coast Guard Point where the road ends at the Coast Guard Station and Light Keeper's Museum onto a circle drive. Pull into gravel parking lot to the left of museum. Kiosk is at west end of parking lot.

TRAILHEAD FACILITIES & FEES:

No facilities. No fees for trail use.

TOTAL LENGTH/SURFACE:

750'; loose sand.

ALERT:

Walk barefoot at your own risk.

NARRATIVE:

Trailhead begins at Piping Plover kiosk at west end of parking lot. Take some time to read about this endangered species. Views start mounting quickly here, as do photo ops. Enjoy!

MUSKALLONGE LAKE STATE PARK SUPERIOR BEACH VIEW*

Muskallonge Lake State Park, near Deer Park • Off H-37, 27.3 miles from Newberry • *Gentle Hikes name

---

- **Glorious sweeping views of Lake Superior's sandy beach lined with evergreen and birch.**

DIRECTIONS & PARKING:

From MI 28, turn north on MI 123 toward Newberry and drive 7.9 miles to 4 Mile Corner (Deer Park Road, H-37, Muskallonge Lake and CR-407). Turn left and drive 23.3 miles into Deer Park. Follow signs and turn left toward Muskallonge Lake State Park on H-58 and drive to the park entrance on left (south) side of street. Park in paved lot just beyond contact station.

TRAILHEAD FACILITIES & FEES:

Facilities nearby at Muskallonge Lake Picnic Area (pg. 220). Annual or day use state park permit is required and available at park office.

TOTAL LENGTH/SURFACE:

0.2 mile; boardwalk.

ALERT:

No ground fires or camping. Remove all waste. Carry out what you carry in.

NARRATIVE:

Trailhead begins across the highway, up a sandy walkway to boardwalk. One step up (wood, double handrail) leads to boardwalk. Descend 55 steps (wood, double handrail, non-continuous) onto the sandy shores of Lake Superior.

TAHQUAMENON RIVER ALMOST HIKE*

Tahquamenon Falls State Park, Paradise • Off MI 123, 46.6 miles from Newberry • *Gentle Hikes name

---

- **Beautiful river views.**
- **Abundance of seasonal wildflowers.**
- **Somewhat off the beaten path.**

DIRECTIONS & PARKING:

From MI 28, turn north on MI 123 toward Newberry. Drive 41.4 miles to stop sign and continue right on MI 123 toward Tahquamenon Falls State Park Picnic Area and Rivermouth Campground. Drive 5.2 miles to Tahquamenon Falls State Park Rivermouth Campground (0.5 miles past Picnic Area) and turn right (west) into Park. Turn right after Ranger Station toward modern campground. Continue straight for 0.2 miles and see unmarked gravel road on right side. Follow straight and pass service road sign until you come to a dirt parking area by sign indicating "no camping and no ground-fires."

TRAILHEAD FACILITIES & FEES:
No facilities here. Annual or day use state park permit is required and available at park office.

TOTAL LENGTH/SURFACE:
300'; grass (width contingent on mowing).

ALERT:
No camping and no ground fires.

NARRATIVE:
Simply put, a beautiful way to spend 300'. Two benches with lovely river views. Photo-worthy.

WHITEFISH POINT BIRD SIGHTING WALK*

Paradise • Off MI 123, 52.9 miles from Newberry • *Gentle Hikes name

- **Whitefish Point Bird Observatory—among the leading in the USA!**
- **National Wildlife Refuge.**
- **A great place for bird watching.**

DIRECTIONS & PARKING:
From MI 28, turn north on MI 123 toward Newberry. Drive 41.4 miles to the stop sign. From stop sign, turn left (north) onto North Whitefish Point Road and drive about 11.5 miles. Park in paved lot for Whitefish Point Lighthouse. Designated wheelchair accessible and RV parking available.

TRAILHEAD FACILITIES & FEES:
Flush toilets (wheelchair accessible), water, info kiosk, bench, gift shops, museums. No fees for trail use, but fee required for museum entry.

TOTAL LENGTH/SURFACE:
0.1 mile; paved, loose sand.

ALERT:
Overgrowth and uneven path. No off-road vehicles. Pets must be on leash. Stay off dunes, leave no trace. No trespassing on posted private properties.

NARRATIVE:
Trailhead begins near Coast Guard Lookout Tower and behind small red brick building on 2'-wide cement path. Expect overgrowth as the paved path passes through thick shrub area. Tread softly as you look and listen for birds. In 225', this path turns to sand and leads to beach area with beautiful views of Lake Superior. To see bird exhibits and obtain educational materials, we recommend a visit to the Owl's Roost gift shop located on the site of an officially designated Globally Important Bird Area. You will see it from the parking area. There are more trails behind the gift shop, yet

due to the number of entry points we were unable to document a clear route for purposes of this book. We recommend inquiring at this gift shop for more information.

WHITEFISH POINT LIGHT STATION
Paradise • Off MI 123, 52.9 miles from Newberry

- **Great Lakes Shipwreck Museum and the oldest operating lighthouse on Lake Superior!**
- **Whitefish Point Bird Observatory—among the leading in the USA.**
- **National Wildlife Refuge.**

DIRECTIONS & PARKING:
From MI 28, turn north on MI 123 toward Newberry. Drive 41.4 miles to the stop sign. From stop sign, turn left (north) onto North Whitefish Point Road and drive about 11.5 miles and park in paved lot for the lighthouse. Designated wheelchair accessible and RV parking available.

TRAILHEAD FACILITIES & FEES:
Flush toilets (wheelchair accessible), water, info kiosk, bench, gift shops, museums. No fees for trail use, but fee required for museum entry.

TOTAL LENGTH/SURFACE:
0.4 mile; paved, boardwalk.

ALERT:
No off-road vehicles. Pets must be on leash. Stay off dunes, leave no trace. No trespassing on posted private properties.

NARRATIVE:
Trailhead begins from parking area on paved path. Due to the many paths in this area, we thought it best to provide an overview of the grounds and leave the exploring to you. Several benches are placed throughout this area. Boardwalk (wood, double handrail) leads to the "Graveyard on the Great Lakes"—read the info marker to discover why more vessels were lost in the Whitefish Point region than any other part of Lake Superior. The boardwalk is about 100' long and beach access is possible by descending 14 steps (wood, double handrail). Views are spectacular! This area also houses the oldest operating lighthouse on Lake Superior (established 1849), U.S. Coast Guard Station, Lifeboat Station, Shipwreck Museum and several gift shops. Also on public display is the actual rudder and tiller of the *M.M. Drake* (1882–1901). Read about what caused her wreck and how the crew was saved just moments prior to her demise!

Behind the Museum Store and restrooms is a path that leads to boardwalk (no handrail). In 200', the boardwalk takes on a slight incline and now has a double handrail. In another 200', find bench and info on the sand dunes before ascending 48 steps (wood, double handrail). Find more benches as you approach the "Raptor Migration Observatory Platform." Did you know that 15,000 to 25,000 raptors migrate through this area each spring? Furthermore, the views of the dunes, Lake

Superior and Whitefish Point Lighthouse are photo-worthy from this vantage point. Please do not walk out on dunes as this is prohibited.

 **Foot Note:**

Among the leading observatories in the country, the Whitefish Point Bird Observatory is a nonprofit membership organization dedicated to documenting and studying migratory bird populations. Fall highlights include a spectacular migration of up to 100,000 waterbirds! For more information call (906) 492-3596 or visit www.wpbo.org.

 Foot Note:

Did you know that the Great Lakes Shipwreck Museum has been deemed as one of the best small museums in America by *Money Magazine*? For more information call (800) 635-1742 or visit www.ShipwreckMuseum.com.

Whitefish Point Light Station (see pg. 179). Photo by Lisa Vogelsang

KEMP MARINA ALMOST HIKE*

Sault Ste. Marie • Off I-75, 67.4 miles from Newberry • *Gentle Hikes name

- **Great views of the St. Mary's River—see ships preparing to enter the locks!**
- **Home of the Soo Locks and Valley Camp Ship Tours.**

DIRECTIONS & PARKING:

From MI 28, turn north on I-75 and drive 8.8 miles to exit #394. Turn right off exit onto Easterday Ave. Turn left onto Johnston Street and then right on Water Street. Pass the Museum Ship Valley Camp and continue straight into the driveway of a large paved parking area for Valley Camp, The Ship's Store, and farther east in the lot, the Soo Locks Boat Tours. Park in this lot rather than the small parking lot adjacent to the Kemp Marina, which is reserved for marina boaters and their guests. To get to the trailhead, walk back through the parking area entrance past the Valley Camp (to west side of ship) and into the small reserved parking area for marina boaters.

TRAILHEAD FACILITIES & FEES:

Flush toilets, water, bench, gift shop, smoke-free cafe. No fees for trail use.

TOTAL LENGTH/SURFACE:

0.3 mile; paved, boardwalk.

ALERT:

No alcohol, swimming, inline skates, bicycles, skateboards, running, horseplay or fishing lines in marina basin.

NARRATIVE:

Trailhead begins on 5'-wide cement path. Descend 11 steps (cement, double handrail, non-continuous). Turn right to river boardwalk, which runs parallel to Museum Ship Valley Camp. The boardwalk is 10' wide (double handrail). The ship that houses the museum is so close that it's almost touchable. Several benches along the way provide spectacular views of St. Mary's River.

 Foot Note:

Two tour options from this location: Soo Locks Boat Tours (800) 432-6301; www.soolocks.com and Valley Camp Ship Tours (888) 744-7867; www.thevalleycamp.com.

WAYSIDES & SCENIC LOCALES

We have included the most scenic waysides and overlooks that Lake Superior's Shore and Michigan's Upper Peninsula have to offer. Includes stuff you don't even need to leave the car to see!

We tell you which are paved and which have designated wheelchair accessible and RV parking, plus highlights, amenities and a brief narrative of what to expect while you're there.

Keep in mind that many waysides are closed during snow season. Some only operate seasonally (mid-May to mid-October). This being northern Michigan, these are close approximations based on ground freezing and thawing.

Don't forget the camera!

MICHIGAN WELCOME CENTER IN IRONWOOD

Ironwood • On U.S. 2, 12.2 miles from Wakefield

- **See displays of various artifacts such as native copper, Isle Royale greenstone, Keweenaw Thompsonites and a variety of rocks, minerals and mining paraphernalia.**
- **Nicely arranged cases sport the merchandise of area gift shops (although no goods are sold at the Welcome Center).**

DIRECTIONS & PARKING:

On U.S. 2 from the Wisconsin border, drive 0.2 mile east to Welcome Center on the right (south) side. Paved lot (designated wheelchair accessible and RV parking).

AMENITIES:

Flush toilet (wheelchair accessible), water, well-stocked visitor center, picnic area (tables in open area as well as under covered open-sided shelters), grills, benches, information kiosk and map.

NARRATIVE:

Designated dog run provides great leg stretch for Fido as well! Grounds include an abundance of pine and maple. During summer, look for unique planter box under one of the open-sided shelters. Picturesque rock walls adorn much of the outside premises, but please do not climb them. This Visitor Center has a plethora of information—all free to the public.

MEMORY LANE ROADSIDE PARK

Bessemer • Off U.S. 2, 8 miles east of Wisconsin border

- **On Michigan's register of historic sites (Gogebic Iron Range Historical Site)**

DIRECTIONS & PARKING:

From U.S. 2 in Bessemer, drive 1.1 miles east of intersection with CR-513 (to Black Harbor) to first section of park on left (north). Park in paved lot (designated wheelchair accessible parking).

AMENITIES:

Vault toilet (wheelchair accessible), water, picnic tables and information kiosk.

NARRATIVE:

Very convenient as this one is literally right on the highway.

CITY OF WAKEFIELD SOUTH WEST PARK

Wakefield • Off U.S. 2, 11.8 miles from Ironwood

- **Take the Sunday Lake Boardwalk Almost Hike (see pg. 159).**
- **Sweeping views of Sunday Lake.**

DIRECTIONS & PARKING:
From U.S. 2 in Wakefield, turn north on Lakeshore Drive (west side of Sunday Lake). Park in paved lot (no designated spaces).

AMENITIES:
Flush toilet (wheelchair accessible), bench, picnic tables.

NARRATIVE:
Sunday Lake is very nice and can easily be viewed from the car. However, better views wait on the Sunday Lake Boardwalk Almost Hike (see pg. 159) with continuous lake views on one side and mixed wooded forest on the other. The entire path is boardwalk. This wayside also looks like a good fishing spot.

EWEN PINES ROADSIDE PARK

Ewen • Off MI 28, 7.4 miles west of Bruce Crossing

- **Beautiful pine setting**

DIRECTIONS & PARKING:
From junction of U.S. 2 and MI 28 in Wakefield, drive 33 miles northeast on MI 28 (7.4 miles west of Bruce Crossing) until roadside park. Park in paved lot (designated wheelchair accessible and RV parking).

AMENITIES:
Vault toilet (wheelchair accessible), water, picnic tables, grills and dog run.

NARRATIVE:
A great wooded area with towering pines right off the highway combine for a wonderful place for lunch.

WILDERNESS VISITOR CENTER

Porcupine Mountains Wilderness State Park • Off South Boundary Road, 3.6 miles from Silver City

- **Amazing wildlife exhibit and interactive displays!**
- **Displays of logging paraphernalia, native copper and mining.**

DIRECTIONS & PARKING:
From MI 28 in Bergland, turn north on MI 64 and drive 17.7 miles to junction of

MI 64 and MI 107 in Silver City. Turn left (west) on MI 107 and drive 2.7 miles to intersection of MI 107 and South Boundary Road (notice the sign that indicates Visitor Center). Turn left and drive along South Boundary Road for 0.4 mile. Turn right at Entrance Road and find sign indicating "Visitor Center." Drive 0.5 mile to paved parking for Wilderness Visitor Center area. Wheelchair accessible parking available. RV parking in separate nearby lot (follow signs).

AMENITIES:

Flush toilet (wheelchair accessible), water, incredible visitor center, gift shop, small picnic area.

NARRATIVE:

This Wilderness Visitor Center is truly one of those "not-to-be-missed" attractions worth carving out some time for. It's the only place in the Porcupines where you can see on exhibit the Black Bear and cub, wolf, Goshawk, beaver, fisher, owls, Peregrine Falcon, eagle and of course, the porcupine. The exhibits are educational and some are interactive. Feel the coarseness of bear fur and that of the wolf. Learn more about the Black Bear and hear the cry of the wolf. And you can even take a part of the Porcupine Mountains home via the park's gift shop on the premises. Also, the Visitor Center staff is very knowledgeable about the area and can also tell you about the park's numerous seasonal interpretive programs. From the Visitor Center doors, it is 330' back to the parking area.

Sunday Lake (see pg. 159). Photo by Ladona Tornabene

AGATE FALLS ROADSIDE PARK

Agate Falls Park • On MI 28, 8 miles from Bruce Crossing

- **Highly recommended walk to Agate Falls (see pg. 61), which also can be accessed from this wayside.**

DIRECTIONS & PARKING:

From the junction of MI 28 and U.S. 45 in Bruce Crossing, drive 7.6 east on MI 28. Agate Falls Roadside Park is on the right side (south). Park in paved lot (designated wheelchair accessible and RV parking).

AMENITIES:

Vault toilet (wheelchair accessible), water, picnic area, grills and information kiosk.

NARRATIVE:

A lovely wooded forest waits with an invitation to two views (side and from trestle) of Agate Falls (see pg. 61), which can be accessed from this wayside. Enter 6' paved trail at the right of the kiosk and travel 775' to the viewing platform for a side view of the falls. To access trestle view, consult trail write-up (pg. 61). This is a great leg stretch with a gift shop (and ice cream!) across the highway that can be accessed en route to Agate Falls. However, if you access gift shop from this vantage point, it will require ascending a gentle incline. Otherwise, there is parking from the road directly in front of the store.

CANYON FALLS ROADSIDE PARK

On U.S. 41 • 40.5 miles from Bruce Crossing, 9.5 miles from L'Anse

---

- **Highly recommended, the trailhead to the short walk to Canyon Falls (pg. 63) is at this wayside. Very scenic along Sturgeon River.**

DIRECTIONS & PARKING:

From Bruce Crossing, drive east on MI 28 for 38 miles until the intersection at U.S. 41. At intersection, turn north on U.S. 41 toward L'Anse/Houghton and drive about 2.5 miles. Look for Canyon Falls Roadside Park sign and turn left (west) into wayside. Park in paved lot (designated wheelchair accessible and RV parking).

AMENITIES:

Vault toilet (wheelchair accessible), water, picnic area, grills and information kiosk.

NARRATIVE:

The very picturesque Canyon Falls is well worth a few minutes of your time. This easy trail affords a great leg stretch where scenery abounds. Grab the camera.

MILITARY HILL ROADSIDE PARK

Rockland area • On U.S. 45, 11.8 miles north of Bruce Crossing

• **Lovely overlook of Ontonagon River.**

DIRECTIONS & PARKING:
From MI 28 in Bruce Crossing turn north on U.S. 45 and drive 11.8 miles to roadside park on right (east) side of highway. Park in paved lot (designated wheelchair accessible parking).

AMENITIES:
Vault toilet (wheelchair accessible), water, picnic area, grills, information kiosk and dog run.

NARRATIVE:
Nice, peaceful place. Read the monument to see how Abraham Lincoln is connected to this wayside.

KEWEENAW WATERWAY SCENIC TURNOUT

Hancock • On U.S. 41, 1.2 miles north of U.S. 41 and MI 203 junction

• **This is a not-to-be-missed scenic stop!**

• **Keweenaw Waterway was created between 1859 and 1873; it shortened the shipping route by 100 miles.**

DIRECTIONS & PARKING:
From MI 28, turn north on U.S. 45 at Bruce Crossing and drive 14.1 miles. At intersection, turn northeast on MI 26 toward Houghton-Hancock and drive about 57 miles. Look for U.S. 41 north in Houghton and cross lift bridge to Hancock. Follow signs in Hancock and continue to follow U.S. 41 north for 2 miles. Watch sign for Scenic Turnout on right (east). This turnout is located at a curve in the road as you drive out of Hancock. Watch carefully. Turn into small paved pull-through parking area.

AMENITIES:
Information kiosk.

NARRATIVE:
This site overlooks Hancock toward Houghton across the Keweenaw Waterway and east toward a portion of Portage Lake. Enjoy views of Huron Mountains, Mount Ida, Mount Benson and Burnt Mountain. Quincy Mine Shaft is at the top of the hill.

THE RECORD SNOWFALL WAYSIDE

Between Mohawk & Cliff • On U.S. 41, 24.4 miles south of Copper Harbor, 32.7 miles north of Houghton

- **Massive thermometer-shaped measuring "stick" gives an accurate visual of record snowfall—390.4 inches!**

DIRECTIONS & PARKING:
From U.S. 41 in Houghton, drive north across Lift Bridge into Hancock and drive north for 31.7 miles (from junction of MI 203 in Hancock). The wayside is 2.7 miles south of MI 26 in Phoenix and 24.4 miles south of Copper Harbor on U.S. 41. Park in paved lot.

AMENITIES:
Vault toilet (wheelchair accessible), picnic area, grills and bench.

NARRATIVE:
It's worth the stop for a fun photo op! Strategically placed bench makes for family seating and creative Christmas card idea. Take time to read the snowfall record on sign posted nearby.

MEMORIAL AIRPORT ROADSIDE PARK

Between Hancock and Osceola • On U.S. 41, 6.1 miles north of U.S. 41 and MI 203 junction in Hancock

- **Read about the interesting history of copper mining in the Keweenaw Peninsula, which was the leading center of copper production in the country.**

DIRECTIONS & PARKING:
From MI 28, turn north on U.S. 45 at Bruce Crossing and drive 14.1 miles. At intersection, turn northeast on MI 26 toward Houghton-Hancock and drive about 57 miles. Look for U.S. 41 north in Houghton and cross lift bridge to Hancock. Follow signs in Hancock and continue to follow U.S. 41 north for 6.9 miles. Watch sign for Roadside Park. Pull into small paved parking area on right (east). Designated wheelchair and RV parking available at this pull-through wayside.

AMENITIES:
Vault toilets (wheelchair accessible), tables, water, grills and information kiosk.

NARRATIVE:
Convenient stop if you need it. Picnic area is in nice wooded area. A good place to watch for planes!

EAGLE RIVER PARK

Eagle River • On MI 26, 27.7 miles from Houghton, 21.3 miles from Copper Harbor

* **Beautiful Northern Cedar stand.**

DIRECTIONS & PARKING:

From MI 28, turn north on U.S. 45 at Bruce Crossing and drive 14.1 miles. At intersection, turn northeast on MI 26 toward Houghton-Hancock and drive about 57 miles. Look for U.S. 41 north in Houghton and cross lift bridge to Hancock. Follow signs in Hancock and continue to follow U.S. 41 north for about 25 miles to Phoenix. Turn left (northwest) on MI 26 and continue 2.7 miles into Eagle River. Park is on the left. Park in paved pull-through.

AMENITIES:

Vault toilet (wheelchair accessible), water (spigot at west end of pullout near white post), picnic area and gift shop.

NARRATIVE:

A nice place to take a break.

ESREY ROADSIDE PARK

Between Eagle Harbor and Copper Harbor • On MI 26, 5.4 miles from Eagle Harbor and 8.4 miles from Copper Harbor

* **Rugged cliffs of Lake Superior and towering pines.**
* **Glorious sweeping vistas of the lake!**
* **Dine at water's edge.**

DIRECTIONS & PARKING:

From MI 26 in Eagle Harbor drive east 5.4 miles (or drive 8.4 miles west of Copper Harbor). Park on north side near Lake Superior. Park in paved pull-through (designated wheelchair accessible parking).

AMENITIES:

Vault toilet (wheelchair accessible), water, picnic area with small open-sided shelter, grills and information kiosk.

NARRATIVE:

Absolutely breathtaking! Just 24 steps (uneven stone, no handrail) lead to a stone ridge line that offers succulent views of Lake Superior. Two benches under a shelter afford rest and shade with incredible sweeping vistas of the lake. Photo ops abound!

GREAT SAND BAY SCENIC OVERLOOK

Eagle Harbor Area • On MI 26, 3.2 miles from Eagle Harbor

- **Rugged, rocky Lake Superior coastline, sandy beach and rhyolite beach—all visible from one sweeping vista!**

DIRECTIONS & PARKING:

From MI 26 in Eagle Harbor drive 3.2 miles southwest (4.7 miles northeast of Eagle River) to overlook. Park in paved area of highway pull-through.

AMENITIES:

Information kiosk. Just 0.1 mile south is another pullout with picnic tables and grill.

NARRATIVE:

Superior showcases her diversity here and we highly recommend a camera! The info kiosk features Lake Superior, when she was discovered, and her first steamer.

WEST BLUFF SCENIC VIEW ATOP BROCKWAY MOUNTAIN DRIVE

Keweenaw • On Brockway Mountain Drive, between Eagle Harbor and Copper Harbor, 9.5 miles from MI 26 Eagle Harbor and 4.4 miles from Copper Harbor

- **Not to be missed! A 360° panorama of Lake Superior, Lake Upson and Lake Medora all from a drive-to location.**

DIRECTIONS & PARKING:

From the junction of U.S. 41 and MI 26 in Copper Harbor, go west on MI 26 until you come to Brockway Mountain Drive. Turn left and drive up the hill for 4.4 miles until you come to the large circular gravel parking area of the overlook.

AMENITIES:

Vault toilet and seasonal gift shop.

NARRATIVE:

This one is a must-see! Bring the camera as scenery is in abundance here. Take some time to read about Copper County and the copper it produced, then browse through the well-stocked gift shop (seasonal) for a souvenir.

COPPER HARBOR AND LAKE FANNY HOOE SCENIC OVERLOOK

Copper Harbor Area • On Brockway Mountain Drive, 0.8 miles from Copper Harbor

- **A must-stop! Arresting views of Lake Superior, Copper Harbor and Lake Fanny Hooe.**

DIRECTIONS & PARKING:

From the junction of U.S. 41 and MI 26 in Copper Harbor, go west on MI 26 until you come to Brockway Mountain Drive. Turn left and drive up the hill for 0.8 miles until you come to the first pullout. Park in gravel area of highway pull-through. Limited parking.

AMENITIES:
Picnic table.

NARRATIVE:
A very popular stop and with good reason—it's gorgeous!

BARAGA CLIFF ROADSIDE PARK

Baraga County • On U.S. 41, 21.2 miles from Houghton

* **Beautiful sweeping vista of Lake Superior and Keweenaw Bay!**

DIRECTIONS & PARKING:
From U.S. 41 in Houghton, drive 21.2 miles south. Park in paved lot (designated wheelchair accessible parking).

AMENITIES:
Vault toilet (wheelchair accessible), water, picnic area, grills and information kiosk.

NARRATIVE:
Read about Baraga County's 20 Cultural Heritage Preservation Sites as well as Michigan wildflowers.

Esrey Roadside Park (see pg. 189). Photo by Lisa Vogelsang

TIOGA CREEK ROADSIDE PARK

L'Anse • Baraga County, On U.S. 41/MI 28, 45.5 miles east of Bruce Crossing

- **See two small but picturesque waterfalls in Tioga Creek.**

DIRECTIONS & PARKING:

On U.S. 41/MI 28 drive 18.4 miles west of turnoff for Van Riper State Park (or drive 6.5 miles east of MI 28 and U.S. 41 junction). Park in paved lot (designated wheelchair accessible and RV parking).

AMENITIES:

Vault toilet (wheelchair accessible), water, picnic tables, grills, information kiosk and dog run.

NARRATIVE:

The first of the waterfalls is visible from the parking area. A fairly flat but uneven 3'-wide paved path extends 150' to a bridge overlooking the beautiful Tioga Creek and affords a closer view of the first waterfall. The second fall is 775' away and begins on 3'-wide paved path to the left of the information kiosk. The trail soon narrows to a 12"-wide dirt path to the falls, which are also small, but fairly wide. Expect overgrowth on this trail with a moderate section of tree root at 560'. The picnic tables are nicely spread amid a wooded section and can be reached from the parking area. Overall, a very lovely stop.

MICHIGAMME ROADSIDE PARK

Michigamme Area • On U.S. 41, 58.1 miles from Bruce Crossing

- **Beautiful George Lake.**

DIRECTIONS & PARKING:

From MI 28 in Bruce Crossing, drive 58.1 miles east to roadside park (19.1 miles east of MI 28 and U.S. 41 junction and 5.8 miles west of Van Riper State Park). Park in paved lot (designated RV parking).

AMENITIES:

Vault toilet (wheelchair accessible, but there are 27 steps en route to toilet), water, picnic tables, grills and information kiosk.

NARRATIVE:

George Lake is visible from the car and 27 steps (iron grid and concrete, double handrail, non-continuous) lead to toilets, water and picnic area. A nice place for picnicking with views of George Lake.

SCENIC DRIVE THROUGH PRESQUE ISLE PARK

Presque Isle Park, Marquette • Off U.S. 41/MI 28 bypass

- **Gorgeous views of Lake Superior throughout this 2.1-mile loop.**
- **Numerous trails with various entry points offering Superior views!**

DIRECTIONS & PARKING:

From U.S. 41/MI 28 bypass driving east into Marquette, turn left (north) on East Lake Shore Blvd, followed by another left on North Lake Shore Blvd until you reach Presque Isle Park. Continue on the road around to the right (Peter White Drive) beyond the park entrance, past the marina and boat launch and around Presque Isle Park. There are numerous parking areas throughout this drive. Some are paved and have designated wheelchair accessible spaces; others are gravel.

AMENITIES:

Flush toilets (wheelchair accessible), water, benches, picnic tables, grills, reservable pavilion, MooseWood Nature Center, concession stand, swimming pool, playground and band shell.

NARRATIVE:

This is a lovely drive around the island but use extreme caution as cyclists and hikers share the no-shoulder road. There are numerous trails, in addition to the two featured in this book (see pg. 89 & 91), that vary in length depending upon entry point and erosion. Some of these trails are right along a ridge overlooking Lake Superior and others can be challenging through wooded terrain. Alert: Please pay close attention to signs as erosion is a serious problem. For your safety, do not cross barricades and do use common sense in problem areas. Please note that this road is closed to motor vehicles Saturday and Sunday 7am–10am; Monday and Wednesday 6pm–8pm and Tuesday and Thursday 7am–1pm.

MARQUETTE WELCOME CENTER

Marquette • On U.S. 41/MI 28, 1.4 miles west of junction MI 28 and U.S. 41 (south)

- **Beautiful sweeping vista of Lake Superior!**
- **A variety of paths lead to semi-secluded picnic areas.**
- **Access to paved bike path with continuous views of the lake.**

DIRECTIONS & PARKING:

From U.S. 41/MI 28 drive 1.4 miles west of junction MI 28 and U.S. 41 (south). Park in paved lot (designated wheelchair accessible and RV parking).

AMENITIES:

Flush toilet (wheelchair accessible), water, well-stocked visitor center, picnic area, grills and information kiosk. No dogs permitted in picnic area.

NARRATIVE:

This is a delightful wayside with a secluded flavor even though it is directly on MI 28 West. The layout of tables amid a wooded setting within close proximity to Lake Superior makes this a great place to picnic. Should you need a longer leg stretch, the paved bike path runs through here with continuous views of the lake!

DEER LAKE PARK ROADSIDE PARK

Deerton area • On MI 28, 23.7 miles from Munising

* **Beautiful views of Deer Lake.**

DIRECTIONS & PARKING:

From the Visitor Center in Munising (junction of MI 28 & H-58), turn west on MI 28 and drive for 23.7 miles to roadside park. Park in paved lot (designated wheelchair accessible and RV parking).

AMENITIES:

Vault toilet (wheelchair accessible), water, grills, picnic area, information kiosk, dog run.

NARRATIVE:

Dine within a stone's throw of water's edge with sweeping views of Deer Lake amid towering conifers. Worth the stop.

One of the many waysides in the Marquette Area. Photo by Lisa Vogelsang

LAKE SUPERIOR ROADSIDE PARK

Marquette Area • On MI 28, 7.1 miles from Michigan Welcome Center in Marquette

• **Incredible Lake Superior views with stair access to beach.**

DIRECTIONS & PARKING:

From Michigan Welcome Center in Marquette, drive east on U.S. 41/MI 28 for 1.3 miles. Continue east on MI 28 at junction of U.S. 41 (turning south) and drive for 5.8 miles until you come to roadside park. Park in paved lot. Designated wheelchair accessible parking.

NOTE: There are many other unnamed waysides (paved and unpaved) along this stretch of MI 28 between Marquette and Munising. New scenic turnouts were being built and paved with stair access to beach and designated wheelchair accessible parking during August 2005.

AMENITIES:

Vault toilet (wheelchair accessible), water, picnic tables, grills, benches and information kiosk.

NARRATIVE:

If it's close proximity to Lake Superior that you are seeking, this would be it. Just 32 stairs (wood, double handrail, non-continuous) lead to the beautiful sandy beaches of Superior.

LAKE SUPERIOR SCENIC VIEW

Munising area, On MI 28, 12.2 miles from Munising

• **Definitely lives up to its title, delivering breathtaking vistas of Lake Superior!**

DIRECTIONS & PARKING:

From the Visitor Center in Munising (junction of MI 28 & H-58), turn west on MI 28 and drive for 12.2 miles Lake Superior Scenic View pullout. Paved lot. Designated wheelchair accessible and RV parking.

NOTE: There are many other unnamed waysides (paved and unpaved) along this stretch of MI 28 between Marquette and Munising. New scenic turnouts were being built and paved with stair access to beach and designated wheelchair accessible parking during August 2005.

AMENITIES:

Vault toilets (wheelchair accessible), volleyball, changing area for beach.

NARRATIVE:

Scenery at its finest! Definitely worth a stop. The beaches are beautiful.

GRAND ISLAND HARBOR SCENIC TURNOUT–ROADSIDE PARK

Hiawatha National Forest, Munising • Off MI 28, 1.8 miles from junction of MI 28 and East Munising Ave (H-58) near Visitor Center

- **We highly recommend the short walk to Grand Island Overlook (see Almost Hike, pg. 173).**

DIRECTIONS & PARKING:
From junction of MI 28 and East Munising Ave (H-58) near Visitor Center, turn west on MI 28 and drive 1.8 miles. Turn left into driveway for Grand Island Harbor Scenic Turnout–Roadside Park. Park in paved lot (wheelchair accessible parking available).

AMENITIES:
Vault toilet (wheelchair accessible), water, info kiosk, grills, picnic tables.

NARRATIVE:
Sweeping vista of Grand Island and Lake Superior at overlook. Grab the camera.

SCOTT FALLS ROADSIDE PARK

Munising area • On MI 28, 11.5 miles from Munising

- **Gorgeous picnic area overlooking Lake Superior.**
- **Wheelchair accessible boardwalk to stunning views of Lake Superior.**
- **Scott Falls is located nearby.**

DIRECTIONS & PARKING:
From the Visitor Center in Munising (junction of MI 28 & H-58), turn west on MI 28 and drive for 11.5 miles to roadside park (north side) across the street from Scott Falls. Paved lot. Designated wheelchair accessible and RV parking.

AMENITIES:
Vault toilets (wheelchair accessible), grills, info kiosk, dog run.

NARRATIVE:
Simply a great place to stop for a picnic and leg stretch. Several tables scattered about offer some privacy with glorious lake views. Or you can choose a semi-wooded area closer to the road. A 75' (150' round-trip) wheelchair accessible boardwalk leads to stunning views of Lake Superior and small cliffs. Five steps down (wood, double handrail) lead to beach. Scott Falls (small, but picturesque) is across the highway. Please use caution if you go, as it is a two-lane, fairly busy road.

SENEY STRETCH REST AREA

Seney • On MI 28, 3.9 miles west of Seney (junction MI 77 South)

- **Unique log cabin-like structure houses very clean modern restrooms.**
- **Great place for a picnic and leg stretch among towering pines.**

DIRECTIONS & PARKING:

From MI 28 at junction of MI 77 South in Seney, drive west for 3.9 miles to the entrance of rest area (approximately 30 miles east of Munising). Paved lot. Designated wheelchair accessible and RV parking.

AMENITIES:

Flush toilets (wheelchair accessible), water, grills, info kiosk, bench, dog run.

NARRATIVE:

See highlights.

 SAYS WHO?

In a bad mood? Stride toward a better attitude!

Walking 30 minutes 4-6 days per week at a moderate pace can improve mood, self esteem and feelings of well-being.

Exercising Your Way to Better Mental Health [40, 41, 42]

OLD FLOWING WELL ROADSIDE PARK

Newberry • On MI 28, 19.2 miles east of Seney, 4 miles west of Newberry

* **Nicely wooded, well groomed, clean wayside.**

DIRECTIONS & PARKING:

From MI 28 in Seney, continue east for 19.2 miles past junction of MI 77 south (4 miles west of junction of MI 28 and M123 in Newberry). Paved lot. Designated wheelchair accessible and RV parking.

AMENITIES:

Vault toilets (wheelchair accessible), water, grills, picnic tables, info kiosk.

NARRATIVE:

Very nice place to take a break—clean and accommodating. Note: No camping or overnight parking.

Lake Superior Scenic View (see pg. 195). Photo by Lisa Vogelsang

SAULT REST AREA

Sault Ste. Marie • Off I-75, 3.6 miles north of MI 28 and I-75 junction, 5.2 miles south of Sault Ste. Marie (exit #394)

- **Several lovely shaded picnic tables scattered about this wayside make it a great stop for lunch.**
- **Kiosk of Historic Lighthouse poster depicting all of the state's 55 beacons for safety since 1825.**

DIRECTIONS & PARKING:

From MI 28, turn north on I-75 and drive 3.6 miles to turnoff on right after mile marker #389 (right turn off interstate). Park in paved lot (designated wheelchair accessible and RV parking).

AMENITIES:

Flush toilet (wheelchair accessible), water, grills, picnic area, benches, info kiosk.

NARRATIVE:

Take the miniature, outdoor, self-guided kiosk info tour!

MISSION HILL SCENIC OVERLOOK

Point Iroquois area • Off Lakeshore Drive, 25 miles from Sault Ste. Marie

- **Glorious scenic overlook of Spectacle Lake and Lake Superior in the distance.**

DIRECTIONS & PARKING:

Leaving Sault Ste. Marie on I-75 South, take the #392 exit and turn right on 3 Mile Road. Drive 1.2 miles and turn left on Baker Road toward Brimley. Drive 3.2 miles and turn right on 6 Mile Road. After passing Brimley State Park, 6 Mile Road becomes West Lakeshore Drive at junction of MI 221. Follow road and signs for Iroquois Point for about 6 miles and turn left at the sign for Mission Hill Cemetery and Scenic Overlook. Take the winding dirt road to the top of the overlook near the horse hitching post. Dirt lot.

AMENITIES:

None

NARRATIVE:

Worth the drive and you can even see this view from the car.

MICHIGAN WELCOME CENTER IN SAULT STE. MARIE

Sault Ste. Marie • Off I-75, 65.7 miles from Newberry, 9.2 miles north of MI 28/I-75 junction

- **Lots of beautiful blooms in the summer on premises.**
- **Very knowledgeable staff and a plethora of travel information make this a must-stop for tourists!**

DIRECTIONS & PARKING:

From MI 28, turn north on I-75 and drive 8.8 miles to exit #394. From exit #394, turn left on overpass. At bottom of overpass turn right onto Portage Ave and follow signs to the Michigan Welcome Center. Park in paved lot (designated wheelchair accessible and RV parking).

AMENITIES:

Flush toilet (wheelchair accessible), water, well-stocked visitor center, picnic area, benches, information kiosk, dog run, mailbox.

NARRATIVE:

Nice grounds for a leg stretch.

PICNIC AREAS

Whether you grill it or pack it, we have selected some of the most scenic picnic areas along Lake Superior's South Shore and in Michigan's Upper Peninsula. From woods to rivers and the big lake, you'll find all kinds of picnic spots listed here. Bon appetit!

We had a little fun writing the picnic areas in a "Menu" format featuring Appetizers, Main Course and Dessert.

APPETIZER:
Typically we list what is nearby and en route to the picnic area (what precedes it— as an appetizer precedes a meal), be it an Almost Hike, trail or wayside.

MAIN COURSE:
Here's where we describe what the actual picnic area is like.

DESSERT:
Usually we list what is nearby the picnic area—be it an Almost Hike, trail or area to explore. It's what we recommend as a great finish to a good meal, but actually burns calories instead!

In addition, we include amenities (located at the picnic area sites), applicable fees, parking surface and designated wheelchair accessible spaces.

Please note: All tables are park and carry.

BLACK RIVER HARBOR PICNIC AREA

Black River Harbor Area • Off U.S. 2, 15.1 miles from Bessemer

- **Appetizer: En route is a smorgasbord of falls from which to choose: Rainbow, Sandstone, Gorge, Potawatomi and Great Conglomerate (p. 24–30)**
- **Main Course: Dine in a beautiful wooded setting. Some tables host views of Black River and harbor—simply gorgeous.**
- **Dessert: Take Black River Harbor Almost Hike (pg. 158)**

PICNIC AREA DIRECTIONS & PARKING:

From U.S. 2 in Bessemer, turn north on CR-513 (Black River Road). Drive 15.1 miles to paved parking area for Black River Harbor. Designated wheelchair parking.

AMENITIES & FEES:

Flush and vault toilets (both wheelchair accessible), water, enclosed shelter, grills, playground, small gift shop and concessions. No fees for picnic area use.

Black River. Photo by Lisa Vogelsang

EDDY PARK PICNIC AREA

Wakefield • On MI 28, 14 miles from Ironwood

- **Appetizer: Get acquainted with beautiful Lake Sunday by taking the Sunday Lake Boardwalk Almost Hike (pg. 159).**
- **Main Course: Dining options range from water's edge, to under shelters, to swimming beach.**
- **Dessert: For a good leg stretcher with fantastic lake views, take the Sunday Stroll on Sunday Lake Almost Hike (pg. 159). We bet you'll want seconds!**

PICNIC AREA DIRECTIONS & PARKING:

From U.S. 2 in Wakefield, turn left (northeast) on MI 28 (Chicago Mine Road) and drive 0.9 mile. Turn left (west) at park sign indicating Eddy Park. Park in gravel parking area along paved road.

AMENITIES & FEES:

Flush toilets (wheelchair accessible, except in area near swimming beach), water, grills, two enclosed shelters, playground, benches, beach, volleyball. Please note that dogs and bicycles are not allowed in picnic area or on Eddy Park's paved path.

PICNIC BUFFET—SUPERIOR STYLE!*

Porcupine Mountains Wilderness State Park, Ontonagon • On MI 107, 3.2–3.5 miles from Silver City • *Gentle Hikes name

- **Appetizer: Stop off at the Union River Almost Hike (pg. 160) to work up an appetite strolling along Lake Superior's shoreline.**
- **Main Course: Your pick—five different pullouts await with each offering a bit of privacy for your Superior dining experience.**
- **Dessert: Lake of the Clouds (pg. 34). The perfect dessert "topper!"**

PICNIC AREA DIRECTIONS & PARKING:

From MI 28 in Bergland, turn north on MI 64 and drive 17.7 miles to the junction of MI 64 and MI 107 in Silver City. Turn left (west) on MI 107 drive for 3.2 miles and look right for the first of five picnic areas. The first offers roadside parking, the second has a small parking area, the third has a small lot, the fourth is a pull-through (can accommodate RVs) and the last has a circular parking area.

AMENITIES & FEES:

Tables & grills. Annual or day use state park permit is not required.

EN ROUTE TO LAKE OF THE CLOUDS PICNIC PULLOVER*

Porcupine Mountains Wilderness State Park, Ontonagon • On MI 107, 7.9 miles from Silver City • *Gentle Hikes name

- **Appetizer: Take the En Route to Lake of the Clouds Almost Hike (pg. 161) for a sweeping vista of Lake Superior.**
- **Main Course: Enjoy a picnic meal in a wooded setting just off the main road to Lake of the Clouds.**
- **Dessert: Since you are en route to it—go see Lake of the Clouds (pg. 34)!**

PICNIC AREA DIRECTIONS & PARKING:
From MI 28 in Bergland, turn north on MI 64 and drive 17.7 miles to the junction of MI 64 and MI 107 in Silver City. Turn left (west) on MI 107 drive for 7.9 miles; look right for picnic area. Park along side of road. Picnic area is 1.6 miles past sign for Government Peak Trail en route to Lake of the Clouds.

AMENITIES & FEES:
Tables, grills, vault toilet, historical site. Annual or day use state park permit is not required.

PRESQUE ISLE PICNIC AREA OF THE PORCUPINE MOUNTAINS*

Porcupine Mountains Wilderness State Park • Off CR-519, 28.1 miles from Silver City, 47.8 miles from Bergland • *Gentle Hikes name

- **Appetizer: Go see Manido Falls (pg. 56).**
- **Main Course: Have lunch in an incredibly beautiful wooded area with appropriately spaced tables for privacy.**
- **Dessert: Relax with a stroll over to Manabezho Falls (pg. 53).**

PICNIC AREA DIRECTIONS & PARKING:
From MI 28 in Bergland, turn north on MI 64 and drive 17.7 miles to the junction of MI 64 and MI 107 in Silver City. Turn left (west) on MI 107, drive for 2.7 miles to the intersection of MI 107 and South Boundary Road (notice sign that indicates Visitor Center). Turn left and drive along South Boundary Road for 24.4 miles and turn right (north) at CR-519. Proceeding north, you will pass the ranger station and the first parking area and come to a Y intersection in 0.9 mile. Go right and follow signs to paved picnic parking lot.

AMENITIES & FEES:
Tables, grills, vault toilet, open-sided shelter. Annual or day use state park permit is required and available at Wilderness Visitor Center, Park Headquarters and Presque Isle Ranger Station.

GREEN PARK PICNIC AREA

Ontonagon • Off MI 64, 6.6 miles from Silver City

- **Appetizer: Take a leisurely stroll along the sandy beaches of Lake Superior.**
- **Main Course: Dine within a beautiful birch setting or looking out at the vastness of the lake.**
- **Dessert: If you've had a late lunch, catch a spectacular sunset over the water.**

PICNIC AREA DIRECTIONS & PARKING:

From MI 28 in Bergland, turn north on MI 64 and drive 17.7 miles to the junction of MI 64 and MI 107 in Silver City. Turn right going east on MI 64 for 6.6 miles. Park in gravel lot on the left (north).

AMENITIES & FEES:

Tables, vault toilet, covered shelter, changing area for beach access. No fees for picnic area use.

ONTONAGON TOWNSHIP PARK PICNIC AREA

Ontonagon • Off Lakeshore Drive, 13.9 miles from Silver City

- **Appetizer: Take the Ontonagon Marina and Boardwalk Stroll Almost Hike (pg. 162) for a lovely preview of the town's water and wildlife.**
- **Main Course: Dine among the pines within a "cone's throw" of Lake Superior. Great place to catch a sunset at water's edge.**
- **Dessert: Take a stroll around this wonderful park. Many benches beckon and several playgrounds make this a great family outing!**

PICNIC AREA DIRECTIONS & PARKING:

From MI 28 in Bergland, turn north on MI 64 and drive 17.7 miles to the junction of MI 64 and MI 107 in Silver City. Turn right, going east on MI 64 for 12.8 miles to River Street and turn right again. In 0.1 mile, turn left on Houghton Street (Note: Road changes name to Lakeshore Drive as it parallels Lake Superior) and follow for one mile to first parking area on left. Park in hardpacked dirt parking areas.

AMENITIES & FEES:

Several beach pullouts en route give access to Lake Superior, tables, grills, water spigot, vault toilet, benches and campground (tent and RV). No fees for picnic area use.

BOND FALLS PICNIC AND DAY USE AREA

Bond Falls Scenic Site • Off U.S. 45, 13.3 miles from Bruce Crossing, 3.7 miles from Paulding

- **Appetizer: See beautiful Bond Falls (pg. 59).**

- **Main Course: Dine at water's edge overlooking beautiful Bond Lake with beach access and much shade.**

- **Dessert: If you enjoy photography, the Bond Falls area and river are wonderfully scenic.**

PICNIC AREA DIRECTIONS & PARKING:

From MI 28 in Bruce Crossing, turn south on U.S. 45 and drive 9.5 miles into Paulding. Turn left onto Bond Falls Road and drive 3.2 miles to sign on left indicating "Bond Falls Scenic Site." Keep straight and continue just past concessions area on the right into picnic area driveway.

AMENITIES & FEES:

Vault toilet, grills, beach, volleyball. No fees for picnic area use.

TWIN LAKES STATE PARK PICNIC AREA

Twins Lakes State Park • On MI 26, 47.2 miles from Bruce Crossing, 23.4 miles from Houghton

- **Appetizer: If you have a boat, this is the place to bring it.**

- **Main Course: Dine with splendid views of Twin Lakes under a canopy of oak and maple.**

- **Dessert: Stroll along the lake's edges as the views deliver.**

PICNIC AREA DIRECTIONS & PARKING:

From MI 28, turn north on U.S. 45 at Bruce Crossing and drive 14.1 miles. At intersection, turn northeast on MI 26 toward Houghton-Hancock and drive about 33.1 miles. Park is on the right (east) side of MI 26. Park in paved lot (designated wheelchair accessible parking).

AMENITIES & FEES:

Vault toilets (wheelchair accessible), water, grills, information kiosk, open and enclosed shelter (rentable), bench and playground. Annual or day use state park permit is required and available at park office.

HOUGHTON WATERFRONT PARK PICNIC AREA

Houghton • Off MI 26, 70.6 miles from Bruce Crossing

- **Appetizer: Stroll around this huge park on a paved path to secure the ideal picnic spot.**
- **Main Course: Dine with lovely views of the Portage Waterway and Portage Lift Bridge.**
- **Dessert: Walk the Houghton Waterfront Trail (pg. 70).**

PICNIC AREA DIRECTIONS & PARKING:
From MI 28, turn north on U.S. 45 at Bruce Crossing and drive 14.1 miles. At intersection, turn northeast on MI 26 toward Houghton-Hancock and drive about 56.5 miles. Before coming down the hill into Houghton, look to your left for City RV Park–Lakeshore Drive sign and turn left into the paved area. Wheelchair accessible and RV parking available.

AMENITIES & FEES:
Flush toilet (wheelchair accessible), water, grills, bench, open-sided shelter. No fees for picnic area use.

HANCOCK RECREATIONAL PICNIC AREA

Hancock • On MI 203, 3.1 miles from Houghton

- **Appetizer: For an unobstructed view of the Waterway, stroll onto the dock.**
- **Main Course: Dine amid pine with lovely views of the Keweenaw Waterway.**
- **Dessert: Be adventurous and take the drive out to F.J. McLain State Park for the very scenic Bear Lake Trail (pg. 77).**

PICNIC AREA DIRECTIONS & PARKING:
From MI 28, turn north on U.S. 45 at Bruce Crossing and drive 14.1 miles. At intersection, turn northeast on MI 26 toward Houghton-Hancock and drive about 57 miles. Follow signs for U.S. 41 north in Houghton and cross Lift Bridge to Hancock. Stay on U.S. 41 until the intersection of MI 203. Turn left (north) on MI 203 and drive 1.2 miles to entrance. Gravel parking area. Designated wheelchair parking.

AMENITIES & FEES:
Flush toilets (wheelchair accessible), water, grills, pits, open-sided shelter, playground, benches, volleyball. No fees for picnic area use. No dogs. No lifeguard on duty.

F.J. MCLAIN STATE PARK ENTRANCE PICNIC AREA

F.J. McLain State Park • Off MI 203, 11.1 miles from Lift Bridge in Hancock

- **Appetizer: You could work up an appetite just by exploring this picnic area, as it is the largest we've ever seen!**
- **Main Course: Immediate seating available. Tables as far as the eye can see with terrific Lake Superior views.**
- **Dessert: Take the Breakwater & Fitness Trail (pg. 80).**

PICNIC AREA DIRECTIONS & PARKING:

From MI 28, turn north on U.S. 45 at Bruce Crossing and drive 14.1 miles. At intersection, turn northeast on MI 26 toward Houghton-Hancock and drive about 57 miles. Follow signs for U.S. 41 north in Houghton and cross Lift Bridge to Hancock. Stay on U.S. 41 until the intersection of MI 203. Turn left (north) on MI 203 and drive 9.8 miles to entrance of F.J. McLain State Park. Once in the park, follow road toward left to large paved lot just past entrance (wheelchair accessible parking available).

AMENITIES & FEES:

Flush toilets (not wheelchair accessible), vault toilet (wheelchair accessible), water, open-sided shelter, semi-enclosed shelter (rentable), grills, volleyball and playground. Annual or day use state park permit is required and available at park office.

BREAKWATER BEACH HOUSE PICNIC AREA

F.J. McLain State Park • Off MI 203, 12.2 miles from Lift Bridge in Hancock

- **Appetizer: Explore the wonderful Bear Lake Trail (pg. 77).**
- **Main Course: Take your pick of covered shelters (reservable) or dine in wooded settings.**
- **Dessert: For a picturesque stroll, take the F.J. McLain Scenic Boardwalk and Gazebo Almost Hike (pg. 164).**

PICNIC AREA DIRECTIONS & PARKING:

From MI 28, turn north on U.S. 45 at Bruce Crossing and drive 14.1 miles. At intersection, turn northeast on MI 26 toward Houghton-Hancock and drive about 57 miles. Follow signs for U.S. 41 north in Houghton and cross Lift Bridge to Hancock. Stay on U.S. 41 until the intersection of MI 203. Turn left (north) on MI 203 and drive 9.8 miles to entrance of F.J. McLain State Park. Once in park, follow road toward left past the Park Entrance Picnic Area for 1.1 miles to large paved parking area (wheelchair accessible parking available).

AMENITIES & FEES:

Flush toilets (wheelchair accessible), water, grills, open-sided shelter, playground, benches, volleyball, basketball, horseshoe pit. No pets on beach. Pack in/pack out. Annual or day use state park permit is required and available at park office.

CALUMET WATERWORKS PARK PICNIC AREA

Calumet • Off MI 203, 18.3 miles from Lift Bridge in Hancock

- **Appetizer: Stroll along the many paths to pick the perfect site.**

- **Main Course: From covered shelters to wooded tables with fantastic Lake Superior views, this area has it all.**

- **Dessert: There is a trail (Gardener's Creek) across from this park that was closed at time of writing due to logging. If it is open, we encourage you to inquire about it at the Keweenaw Tourist Information center in Calumet.**

PICNIC AREA DIRECTIONS & PARKING:

From MI 28, turn north on U.S. 45 at Bruce Crossing and drive 14.1 miles. At intersection, turn northeast on MI 26 toward Houghton-Hancock and drive about 57 miles. Look for signs for U.S. 41 north in Houghton and cross Lift Bridge to Hancock. Follow signs in Hancock and continue to follow U.S. 41 north for about 13.1 miles until the northern loop of MI 203 intersects MI 41. Turn left onto MI 203 and go 2.5 miles to Calumet Waterworks Road. Turn right, drive 2.7 miles until you see Calumet Waterworks Park on the right side. Park in paved lot (designated wheelchair accessible parking).

AMENITIES & FEES:

Vault toilets (wheelchair accessible), water, grills, open-sided shelter, information kiosk, bench, playground and volleyball. No fees required for picnic area use.

HEBARD PARK PICNIC AREA

Keweenaw • On MI 26 between Eagle Harbor and Copper Harbor, 10.9 miles from Eagle Harbor and 2.7 miles from Copper Harbor

- **Appetizer: Hunter's Point Trail (pg. 86) is not too far away.**

- **Main Course: This park has two picnic areas, both with stunning views of Lake Superior! The first is more obvious and in a semi-wooded section; the second is 0.1 mile farther, offering spectacular view of Superior's vastness and rock formations.**

- **Dessert: See Esrey Roadside Park (pg. 189)—it is not to be missed.**

PICNIC AREA DIRECTIONS & PARKING:

From MI 28, turn north on U.S. 45 at Bruce Crossing and drive 14.1 miles. At intersection, turn northeast on MI 26 toward Houghton-Hancock and drive about 57 miles. Look for U.S. 41 north in Houghton and cross Lift Bridge to Hancock. Follow signs in Hancock and continue to follow U.S. 41 north for about 25 miles to

Phoenix. Turn left (northwest) on MI 26 and continue past Eagle River and Eagle Harbor for 21.3 miles toward Copper Harbor. The first picnic area is on the right (south) side away from the Lake. The second is 0.1 mile farther on the left or Lake Superior side of MI 26 with covered benches, more picnic tables and grills. Paved lot.

AMENITIES & FEES:
Vault toilets (wheelchair accessible), grills, open-sided shelter and bench. No fees for picnic area use.

FORT WILKINS STATE PARK PICNIC AREA

Fort Wilkins State Park, Copper Harbor • Off MI 26, 49.5 miles from Houghton

- **Appetizer: Take the Fort Cemetery Almost Hike (pg. 170), which begins from this parking area**
- **Main Course: Dine amid towering pines.**
- **Dessert: Savor this one! Spend some time exploring Fort Wilkins Historic Site via the Almost Hike (pg. 168).**

PICNIC AREA DIRECTIONS & PARKING:
From MI 28, turn north on U.S. 45 at Bruce Crossing and drive 14.1 miles. At intersection, turn northeast on MI 26 toward Houghton-Hancock and drive about 57 miles. Look for U.S. 41 north in Houghton and cross lift bridge to Hancock. Follow signs in Hancock and continue on U.S. 41 north to Copper Harbor for about 48 miles. At intersection of U.S. 41 and MI 26 in Copper Harbor, turn right (east) and drive 1.5 miles to Fort Wilkins State Park. Turn right into large paved parking area. Designated wheelchair and RV parking.

AMENITIES & FEES:
Flush toilets (wheelchair accessible) near park store, vault toilet (wheelchair accessible), water, open-sided shelter, grills, info kiosk, bench, volleyball, playground and gift shop. Annual or day use state park permit is required and available at park office.

BARAGA STATE PARK PICNIC AREA

Baraga State Park • On U.S. 41, 30.5 miles from Houghton

- **Appetizer: Feel like getting away from it all? Drive over to DeVriendt Nature Trail (pg. 67) and enjoy its wildlife.**
- **Main Course: Dine overlooking Keweenaw Bay and Lake Superior.**
- **Dessert: Drive a few miles to L'Anse for a short but scenic trek to a very lovely set of cascades (See Falls River Falls, pg. 65).**

PICNIC AREA DIRECTIONS & PARKING:
From U.S. 41 in Houghton, drive south 30.5 miles. You will see Baraga State Park Day Use Picnic Area on the left (east) bordering Lake Superior. Park in paved lot (designated wheelchair accessible parking).

AMENITIES & FEES:
Vault toilets (wheelchair accessible), grills, info kiosk, bench and playground. Annual or day use state park permit is required and available at park office.

L'ANSE WATERFRONT PARK PICNIC AREA
L'Anse • Off U.S. 41, 33.9 miles Houghton

- **Appetizer: This is a fairly large area—have fun choosing the best dining spot.**
- **Main Course: Enjoy your picnic in the shade of a covered shelter. There may be waterfowl to observe paddling near the mouth of Falls River.**
- **Dessert: See Falls River Falls (pg. 65)!**

PICNIC AREA DIRECTIONS & PARKING:
From Houghton, turn south on U.S. 41 toward L'Anse. Drive 33.1 miles (from MI 28 turn north on U.S. 41). Turn left (north) on Broad Street into downtown L'Anse under the Welcome sign and travel 0.6 mile. At Main Street, turn left and continue to stop sign just before bridge. There are two sections of picnic area: One with amphitheater and play area divided by fishing piers and boat landing. West area has designated wheelchair accessible parking.

AMENITIES & FEES:
Water, grills, open-sided shelter, playground, benches, volleyball, horseshoe pits. No fees for picnic area use.

 SAYS WHO?

Hiking + soda pop = discomfort!

Soft drinks are not recommended as a fluid replacement because of their concentrated sugars, carbonation and/or caffeine contents. Carbonation takes up space in the stomach that could be used by additional fluids. And caffeine causes you to lose more fluid than is contained in the drink itself!

Nutrition: Concepts and Controversies [43]

VAN RIPER PICNIC AREA

Van Riper State Park, Champion • Off U.S. 41/MI 28, 35 miles from Marquette

- **Appetizer: Explore the state park in the heart of moose country.**
- **Main Course: Dine next to beautiful Lake Michigamme!**
- **Dessert: Relax on the beaches of Lake Michigamme.**

PICNIC AREA DIRECTIONS & PARKING:

Drive 35 miles west on U.S. 41/ MI 28 from Marquette. Turn right (north) into state park and follow signs to picnic area. Park in paved lot. Designated wheelchair accessible parking available.

AMENITIES & FEES:

Flush toilets (wheelchair accessible), water, grills, reservable enclosed shelter, playground, beach, volleyball, concession stand. Annual or day use state park permit is required and available at park office.

PRESQUE ISLE PICNIC AREA IN MARQUETTE

Presque Isle Park, Marquette • Off U.S. 41/MI 28 bypass and Lakeshore Blvd.

- **Appetizer: Take the Presque Isle Nature Trail (pg. 91) for some quiet wooded time and a wonderful overlook of Lake Superior's rugged cliff side.**
- **Main Course: Dine with unobstructed views of an active ore dock or amid towering maples while overlooking Lake Superior.**
- **Dessert: Weather permitting, stroll onto the Presque Isle Breakwall (pg. 170) for nearly 360° views of Lake Superior and more of her rocky shore.**

PICNIC AREA DIRECTIONS & PARKING:

From U.S. 41 bypass in Marquette, follow Lakeshore Blvd north along Marquette Bay to Presque Isle Park. Picnic area is to your immediate right prior to entering the one-way road that loops around the island. Park in paved circular parking area. Designated wheelchair accessible parking available.

AMENITIES & FEES:

Water, grills, gazebo, benches. Nearby are flush toilets (wheelchair accessible), playground, concession stand and MooseWood Nature Center.

MARQUETTE SESQUICENTENNIAL PAVILION

Presque Isle Park, Marquette • Off U.S. 41/MI 28 bypass and Lakeshore Blvd.

- **Appetizer: Feed your appetite for knowledge by taking the interpretive**

Presque Isle Bog Walk just prior to entering Presque Isle Park (pg. 89).

- **Main Course: Picnic with spectacular Lake Superior views. This pavilion (wheelchair accessible) can also be reserved and has a full kitchen and huge outdoor grill.** Additional tables scattered about near the lake.

- **Dessert: Stroll along nearby footpaths (use caution as erosion is nibbling away at trails) for incredible lake views. A great place to take in a sunset over Lake Superior is at Sunset Point, across the road from this pavilion.**

PICNIC AREA DIRECTIONS & PARKING:

From U.S. 41 bypass in Marquette, follow Lakeshore Blvd north along Marquette Bay to Presque Isle Park. Turn left on Peter White Drive near marina and soon pavilion and dirt parking will be on your right. Designated wheelchair accessible parking.

AMENITIES & FEES:

Flush toilets (wheelchair accessible and open even if pavilion is reserved), water, open-sided and enclosed shelter, grills, benches. No fees for picnic area use.

PICNIC ROCKS AT SHIRAS PARK

Marquette • Off U.S. 41/MI 28 Bypass and Lakeshore Blvd

- **Appetizer: The paved bike path is accessible from here with views of Lake Superior, so take a stroll for as long or short as you wish.**

- **Main Course: Beautiful views of Lake Superior and Marquette's Lighthouse.**

- **Dessert: Popular beach area that affords picturesque views of Marquette's Lighthouse. Great photo ops.**

PICNIC AREA DIRECTIONS & PARKING:

From U.S. 41 Bypass in Marquette, follow Lakeshore Blvd north along Marquette Bay toward Presque Isle. Shiras Park is near the intersection of Fair Ave on the shore of Lake Superior. Park in paved parking area.

AMENITIES & FEES:

Flush toilets (wheelchair accessible), benches, playground. No fees for picnic area use. No dogs allowed.

TOURIST PARK PICNIC AREAS 1, 2 & 3

Marquette • Off U.S. 41/ MI 28 Bypass and Sugarloaf Ave (CR-550)

- **Appetizer: Veer over to view the Dead River and see the bottom of a lake that drained due to dam breakage. At time of writing (summer 2005) the intriguing rock formations offered unsurpassed beauty of color and texture.**

- **Main Course: Dine in a semi-wooded setting.**

- **Dessert: See the waterfall created by the dam breakage near the Frank J. Russell Hydroplant.**

PICNIC AREA DIRECTIONS & PARKING:

From U.S. 41/MI 28 just west of Marquette, turn left (north) on Wright Street and follow until Sugarloaf Ave (CR-550). Turn left (north) on CR-550 (Sugarloaf Ave) and drive about 0.5 miles to Marquette Tourist Park entrance. Gravel with designated wheelchair accessible parking.

AMENITIES & FEES:

Flush toilets (wheelchair accessible), water, grills and playground. No fees for picnic area use.

CINDER POND PICNIC AREA

Marquette • Off U.S. 41/MI 28 Bypass, 41 miles from Munising

- **Appetizer: Kids Cove truly has something for the entire family. Portions of playground are wheelchair accessible and each piece of equipment has a different sponsor. Interesting wood carvings serve as entrance greeters.**

- **Main Course: Smorgasbord of views ranging from Lake Superior, Lower Harbor Breakwall Light and the city of Marquette.**

- **Dessert: Take a stroll on the paved path (wheelchair accessible) to see the city's original fire bell on the Cinder Pond Almost Hike (pg. 171).**

PICNIC AREA DIRECTIONS & PARKING:

From U.S. 41/MI 28 Bypass driving east into Marquette, turn left (north) on East Lake Shore Blvd, followed by another left on North Lake Shore Blvd. Turn right into the Cinder Pond Marina paved parking lot (designated wheelchair accessible and RV parking).

AMENITIES & FEES:

Flush toilets (wheelchair accessible), water, open-sided shelter, benches, playground and concession. No fees for picnic area use.

 SAYS WHO?

Want to improve your relationship? Take a hike—together.

Walking together can help improve relationships because of the time spent talking without distractions.

Health [27]

AU TRAIN PICNIC AREA

Au Train, Hiawatha National Forest • Off MI 28 on H-03, 19 miles from Munising

- **Appetizer: Relax along swimming area beach.**
- **Main Course: Dine with sweeping views of Au Train Lake.**
- **Dessert: Enjoy a beautiful wooded hike at Au Train Songbird Trail (pg. 104).**

PICNIC AREA DIRECTIONS & PARKING:
From MI 28 turn south on H-03 (also called Forest Lake Road). Drive 4.3 miles to FR-2276 (also called BuckBay Road). Turn left (east) onto FR-2276 (Alert: Road is paved but can be rough with potholes) and drive 0.6 mile. Turn left on Campground Road (FR-2596) and stay on pavement until you reach picnic area in about 1.5 miles (you will pass campground). Paved lot with designated RV parking.

AMENITIES & FEES:
Vault toilet (wheelchair accessible), water, grills, info kiosk. No fees for picnic area use.

BAY FURNACE PICNIC AREA

Christmas, Hiawatha National Forest • On MI 28, 3 miles from Munising.

- **Appetizer: Take the interpretive Bay Furnace Historic Site (pg. 107) and quench your appetite for history.**
- **Main Course: Dine with gorgeous views of Lake Superior and beautiful sandstone cliffs that are common in this area.**
- **Dessert: The North Pole has never been so close. Drive 0.3 mile east for a photo with the world's largest Santa—in Christmas!**

PICNIC AREA DIRECTIONS & PARKING:
From MI 28 in Munising, drive 3 miles west to Christmas. Turn right (north) at sign indicating "Bay Furnace Historic Site." Park in gravel lot. Designated wheelchair accessible and RV parking.

AMENITIES & FEES:
Vault toilet, water, grills, bench, info kiosk. No fees for picnic area use.

MUNISING FALLS PICNIC AREA

Pictured Rocks National Lakeshore • Off H-58, 2 miles from MI 28 in Munising

- **Appetizer: See Munising Falls (pg. 111), a short walk that's big on beauty!**
- **Main Course: Dine in a semi-wooded setting.**
- **Dessert: Looking for wildlife? Take the fully accessible Sand Point Marsh Trail (pg. 113).**

PICNIC AREA DIRECTIONS & PARKING:

From MI 28, go east on H-58 (East Munising Ave) for 1.3 miles to Washington Street. Turn left and drive 0.5 miles to Sand Point Road. Turn right and follow for 0.2 mile to Visitor Center paved parking area. Designated wheelchair and RV parking. Alert: Use caution when traveling through residential area.

AMENITIES & FEES:

Flush toilets (wheelchair accessible), water, info kiosk, visitor center, gift shop. No fees for picnic area use.

SAND POINT PICNIC AREA

Pictured Rocks National Lakeshore • Off H-58, 4 miles from MI 28 in Munising

- **Appetizer: Munising Falls (pg. 111) is en route to this picnic area and well worth the stop.**
- **Main Course: Forget lunch! Come here for dinner. Dine close to water's edge and watch the sunset over Munising Bay.**
- **Dessert: Take the accessible and interpretive Sand Point Marsh Trail (pg. 113).**

PICNIC AREA DIRECTIONS & PARKING:

From MI 28, go east on H-58 (East Munising Ave) for 1.3 miles to Washington Street. Turn left and drive 0.5 mile to Sand Point Road. Turn right and follow for 2.2 miles to the Sand Point Marsh Trail and Sand Point Beach/Picnic Area paved parking area. Designated wheelchair and RV parking. Alert: Use caution when traveling through residential area.

AMENITIES & FEES:

Vault toilet (wheelchair accessible), grills, bench, info kiosk, volleyball. No fees for picnic area use.

MINERS BEACH PICNIC AREA

Pictured Rocks National Lakeshore • Off H-58, 11.7 miles from MI 28 in Munising

- **Appetizer: Take the Miners Beach Almost Hike (pg. 173) to scope out the best picnic area.**
- **Main Course: Dine in a beautiful forest with sites that offer privacy.**
- **Dessert: Head to Miners Castle (pg. 118) for spectacular views!**

PICNIC AREA DIRECTIONS & PARKING:

From MI 28 in Munising, turn east on H-58 and drive 5.3 miles. Turn left on Miners Castle Road. Drive for 5.1 miles and turn right at Y intersection. Soon road changes from paved to gravel to dirt. In about 1 mile, turn left at intersection to Miners Beach and in 0.3 mile park in gravel lot.

AMENITIES & FEES:
Vault toilet (wheelchair accessible), grills, info kiosk, bench. No fees for picnic area use.

MINERS CASTLE PICNIC AREA

Pictured Rocks National Lakeshore • Off H-58, 10.7 miles from MI 28 in Munising

- **Appetizer: Head to Miners Castle (pg. 118) for spectacular views!**
- **Main Course: Dine in a lovely wooded setting with Lake Superior views.**
- **Dessert: If you are able to stay for a sunset, the view from atop Miners Castle is a photo op.**

PICNIC AREA DIRECTIONS & PARKING:
From MI 28 in Munising, turn east on H-58 and drive 5.3 miles to Miners Castle Road. Turn left and drive 5.1 miles to Y intersection. Turn left and continue 0.3 mile into paved parking area. Wheelchair accessible and RV parking available.

AMENITIES & FEES:
Flush toilets (wheelchair accessible), water, grills, bench, visitor center, gift shop. No fees for picnic area use.

GRAND SABLE LAKE OVERLOOK PICNIC AREA

Pictured Rocks National Lakeshore • On H-58, 25 miles from Seney

- **Appetizer: See beautiful Sable Falls (pg. 125).**
- **Main Course: Glorious view of Grand Sable Lake.**
- **Dessert: Make the trip to Au Sable Light Station (pg. 131). It's worth it!**

PICNIC AREA DIRECTIONS & PARKING:
From MI 28 in Seney, turn north on MI 77 and drive 25 miles toward Grand Marais. In Grand Marais, turn left on H-58 and drive 3.8 miles to turnoff for Grand Sable Lake Overlook Picnic Area with a gravel, pull-through parking area and wheelchair accessible parking.

AMENITIES & FEES:
Grills. No fees for picnic area use.

SABLE FALLS PICNIC AREA

Pictured Rocks National Lakeshore • On H-58, 26.6 miles from Seney

- **Appetizer: See beautiful Sable Falls (pg. 125).**
- **Main Course: Dine under a maple canopy with the sounds of Sable Creek.**
- **Dessert: Hike the Grand Sable Dunes Trail (pg. 127). It puts you atop the dunes with stunning Lake Superior views!**

PICNIC AREA DIRECTIONS & PARKING:

From MI 28 in Seney, turn north on MI 77 and drive 25 miles toward Grand Marais. In Grand Marais, turn left on H-58 and drive 1.4 miles to turnoff for Sable Falls and Dunes area. Park in paved lot (designated wheelchair accessible and RV parking available).

AMENITIES & FEES:

Flush toilets (wheelchair accessible), water, grills, info kiosk, bench. No fees for picnic area use.

HURRICANE RIVER PICNIC AREA

Pictured Rocks National Lakeshore • Off H-58, 37.1 miles from Seney

- **Appetizer: Take the 16 steps (wood, double handrail) down to the beach for a stroll. Mouth of Hurricane River is very picturesque.**
- **Main Course: Dining options include views of Lake Superior or the rumbling Hurricane River. Very scenic!**
- **Dessert: Au Sable Light Station (pg. 131) is near and worth the easy walk.**

PICNIC AREA DIRECTIONS & PARKING:

From MI 28 in Seney, turn north on MI 77 and drive 25 miles toward Grand Marais. In Grand Marais, turn left on H-58 and drive 12.1 miles to turnoff for Lower Hurricane River Campground (comes after Upper Hurricane River Campground). Park in gravel area (designated wheelchair accessible parking).

AMENITIES & FEES:

Nearby vault toilet (wheelchair accessible), water, grills, info kiosk, bench. No fees for picnic area use.

LOG SLIDE TRAIL PICNIC AREA

Pictured Rocks National Lakeshore • Off H-58, 33.2 miles from Seney

- **Appetizer: Take Log Slide Overlook (pg. 129) to breathtaking views of Grand Sable Dunes and Au Sable Point.**
- **Main Course: Dine in a beautiful mature hardwood forest and take in some local history at interpretive markers for Jones Cabin and more.**
- **Dessert: Make the trip to Au Sable Light Station (pg. 131). It's worth it!**

PICNIC AREA DIRECTIONS & PARKING:

From MI 28 in Seney, turn north on MI 77 and drive 25 miles toward Grand Marais. In Grand Marais, turn left on H-58 and drive 7.4 miles to the stop sign and turnoff for Log Slide Overlook Area. It is 0.8 mile to gravel lot. Wheelchair accessible and RV parking available.

AMENITIES & FEES:

Vault toilet (wheelchair accessible), water, grills, info kiosk. No fees for picnic area use.

BAYSHORE PARK PICNIC AREA

Grand Marais • Off MI 77, 26 miles from Seney

- **Appetizer: Take the Best Little Barefooted Hike in Grand Marais (pg. 176).**

- **Main Course: Relaxation abounds with numerous tables overlooking the harbor. You can also dine near Lake Superior's shore.**

- **Dessert: Drive on over to two fabulous hikes (Sable Falls, pg. 125 and Grand Sable Dunes, pg. 127).**

PICNIC AREA DIRECTIONS & PARKING:

From MI 28 in Seney, turn north on MI 77 and drive 25 miles toward Grand Marais. In Grand Marais, pass H-58 and continue straight on MI 77. Just past Grand Marais Ave you'll see the driveway into Bayshore Park on the right (east) side prior to Canal Street. Park in paved lot.

AMENITIES & FEES:

Flush toilets, grills, open-sided shelter, bench, playground, volleyball. No fees for picnic area use.

Grand Sable Dunes (see pg. 127). Photo by Lisa Vogelsang

MUSKALLONGE LAKE PICNIC AREA

Muskallonge Lake State Park, near Deer Park • Off H-37, 27.3 miles from Newberry

- **Appetizer: Work up a "superior" appetite on the very scenic Muskallonge Lake State Park Section of the North Country Trail (pg. 140).**
- **Main Course: Dine within feet of Muskallonge Lake and don't be surprised if a flock of geese decides to join you!**
- **Dessert: Take the Muskallonge Lake State Park Superior Beach View Almost Hike (pg. 177).**

PICNIC AREA DIRECTIONS & PARKING:

From MI 28, turn north on MI 123 toward Newberry and drive 7.9 miles to 4 Mile Corner (Deer Park Road, H-37, Muskallonge Lake and CR-407). Turn left and drive 23.3 miles into Deer Park. Follow signs and turn left toward Muskallonge Lake State Park on H-58. Park entrance is on left side of street. Pull into gravel lot near picnic area.

AMENITIES & FEES:

Vault toilet (wheelchair accessible), grills, playground. Annual or day use state park permit is required and available at park office.

UPPER TAHQUAMENON FALLS PICNIC AREA

Tahquamenon Falls State Park, Paradise • Off MI 123, 24.2 miles from Newberry

- **Appetizer: See one of the largest waterfalls west of Niagara—Upper Tahquamenon Falls (pg. 142)!**
- **Main Course: Dine in the heart of Tahquamenon Falls State Park. This is a very popular area and full of life!**
- **Dessert: See beautiful Lower Tahquamenon Falls (pg. 147).**

PICNIC AREA DIRECTIONS & PARKING:

From MI 28, turn north on MI 123 toward Newberry. Drive 27.1 miles to Upper Falls entrance for Tahquamenon Falls State Park. Park in large paved lot (wheelchair accessible and RV parking available).

AMENITIES & FEES:

Flush toilets (wheelchair accessible), water, grills, info kiosk, bench. Restaurant and gift shop are privately owned and operated. They are not on state park property. Annual or day use state park permit is required and available at park office.

LOWER TAHQUAMENON FALLS PICNIC AREA

Tahquamenon Falls State Park, Paradise • Off MI 123, 29.3 miles from Newberry

- **Appetizer: See beautiful Lower Tahquamenon Falls (pg. 147).**
- **Main Course: Dine in a wonderful wooded setting overlooking Tahquamenon River or feast with a view of Lower Falls in the distance.**
- **Dessert: See one of the largest waterfalls west of Niagara—Upper Tahquamenon Falls (pg. 142)! It's a short drive to the trailhead.**

PICNIC AREA DIRECTIONS & PARKING:
From MI 28, turn north on MI 123 toward Newberry. Drive 30.9 miles to Lower Falls entrance for Tahquamenon Falls State Park. Once inside park, continue 0.8 mile past first campground entrance to large paved parking area. Wheelchair accessible and RV parking available.

AMENITIES & FEES:
Flush toilets (wheelchair accessible), grills, open-sided shelter, info kiosk, bench, gift shop, concession stand. Annual or day use state park permit is required and available at park office.

STABLES PICNIC AREA

Tahquamenon Falls State Park, Paradise • On MI 123, 25 miles from Newberry

- **Appetizer: See one of the largest waterfalls west of Niagara—Upper Tahquamenon Falls (pg. 142)!**
- **Main Course: Dine in close proximity to other hiking trails in Tahquamenon Falls State Park. These trails exceeded Gentle Hikes length criteria, but feel free to inquire of park staff regarding their difficulty level.**
- **Dessert: See beautiful Lower Tahquamenon Falls (pg. 147).**

PICNIC AREA DIRECTIONS & PARKING:
From MI 28, turn north on MI 123 toward Newberry. Drive 27.4 miles to Stables Picnic Area. Gravel parking.

AMENITIES & FEES:
Nearby at Upper Tahquamenon Falls (pg. 142) or Lower Tahquamenon Falls (pg. 147). Annual or day use state park permit is required and available at park office.

TAHQUAMENON RIVERMOUTH PICNIC AREA

Tahquamenon Falls State Park, Paradise • On MI 123, 43.7 miles from Newberry

- **Appetizer: Take the Tahquamenon Rivermouth Walk (pg. 149), which is very close by.**

- **Main Course: Fine dining overlooking Lake Superior. Especially interesting is the caramel color of the lake in this area.**

- **Dessert: Take a stroll on the small beach area located just north of the parking lot. At time of writing (summer 2004) there were some large, beautiful pieces of driftwood in the region for creative photos.**

PICNIC AREA DIRECTIONS & PARKING:
From MI 28, turn north on MI 123 toward Newberry. Drive 41.4 miles to the stop sign and continue right on MI 123 toward Tahquamenon Falls State Park Picnic Area and Rivermouth Campground. Drive 4.7 miles and turn left into picnic area. Paved parking.

AMENITIES & FEES:
Vault toilet (wheelchair accessible), grills, info kiosk. Annual or day use state park permit is required and available at park office.

SAWMILL CREEK PARK PICNIC AREA
Paradise • Off MI 123, 41.7 miles from Newberry

- **Appetizer: Take the short trail within Sawmill Creek Park**
- **Main Course: Enjoy lunch in this literal "Park in Paradise!"**
- **Dessert: It's well worth the 11.2-mile drive to Whitefish Point Light Station, which has several attractions, a great beach and an Almost Hike (pg. 179).**

PICNIC AREA DIRECTIONS & PARKING:
From MI 28, turn north on MI 123 toward Newberry. Drive 41.4 miles to the stop sign. From stop sign, turn left (north) onto North Whitefish Point Road, drive about 0.3 mile and turn left into gravel parking area.

AMENITIES & FEES:
Vault toilet (wheelchair accessible), water, grills, info kiosk. No fees for picnic area use.

 SAYS WHO?

Have trouble drinking enough? (Water, that is!)

Studies show that some people have an easier time drinking sports drinks than water during physical activity because sports drinks taste good.

Appetite [39]

BIG PINES PICNIC AREA

Hiawatha National Forest • Off West Lakeshore Drive, 34.4 miles from Sault Ste. Marie

- **Appetizer: Explore the numerous paths that lead to various tables and find the perfect picnic place.**
- **Main Course: Incredible sites amid towering pine all with Lake Superior views. This location has a very remote feeling.**
- **Dessert: Explore sandy beach or simply relax among the glorious pines.**

PICNIC AREA DIRECTIONS & PARKING:

Leaving Sault Ste. Marie on I-75 South, take the #392 exit and turn right on 3 Mile Road. Drive 1.2 miles and turn left on Baker Road toward Brimley. Drive 3.2 miles and turn right on 6 Mile Road. After passing Brimley State Park, 6 Mile Road becomes West Lakeshore Drive at junction of MI 221. Follow road and signs for Iroquois Point (Big Pines is 6.4 miles past Point Iroquois Lighthouse) for about 15.4 miles, entrance on the right. Paved lot with designated RV parking.

AMENITIES & FEES:

Vault toilet (wheelchair accessible), water, grills, bench. No fees for picnic area use.

BRIMLEY STATE PARK PICNIC AREA

Brimley State Park, Brimley • Off West Lakeshore Drive, 19 miles from Sault Ste. Marie

- **Appetizer: At time of writing (summer 2004), plans for a trail at this park were underway. Inquire of park staff for details.**
- **Main Course: Dine with a view of Lake Superior or in a fully enclosed shelter.**
- **Dessert: Kick back at the beach area where several benches await. Be aware that these benches are very low to the ground.**

PICNIC AREA DIRECTIONS & PARKING:

Leaving Sault Ste. Marie on I-75 South, take the #392 exit and turn right on 3 Mile Road. Drive 1.2 miles and turn left on Baker Road toward Brimley. Drive 3.2 miles and turn right on 6 Mile Road. Continue for about 7.5 miles to Brimley State Park. Turn right into park on South Park Street and follow road to picnic area. Park in paved lot. Designated wheelchair accessible and RV parking.

AMENITIES & FEES:

Flush toilets (wheelchair accessible in campground only), water, grills, reservable enclosed shelter, bench, playground, volleyball. Annual or day use state park permit is required and available at park office.

BRADY PARK PICNIC AREA

Sault Ste. Marie • Off I-75, 67.8 miles from Newberry

- **Appetizer: Watch for ships entering the Soo Locks.**
- **Main Course: Dine within very close proximity to the Locks.**
- **Dessert: A must-see! Visit Soo Locks Walk-About (pg. 152), located just around the corner!**

PICNIC AREA DIRECTIONS & PARKING:

From MI 28, turn north on I-75 and drive 8.8 miles to exit #394. Turn left off exit and follow signs to the Michigan Welcome Center. Turn right on West Portage Ave and after passing the Welcome Center, follow signs to Soo Locks. At the curve, continue right onto East Portage Ave and drive for about 1.7 miles (just past Soo Locks Park) and turn left on Gov. Osborn Blvd, which leads into a right turn on Waters Street. Brady Park is 0.2 mile ahead on the left (north toward water) with paved parking.

AMENITIES & FEES:

Nearby at Soo Locks Park and Visitor Center. No pets permitted at this picnic area. No fees for picnic area use.

SOLDIER LAKE RECREATION AND PICNIC AREA

On MI 28, 34.7 miles from Newberry

- **Appetizer: Park and explore on foot as there are many sites to choose from at these two picnic areas.**
- **Main Course: Dine among pines at an open-sided shelter or right on the sandy beaches of Soldier Lake.**
- **Dessert: Take the stroll out to the beach. Two benches and with campground in close proximity, expect plenty of lake action in the summer. If here in August, watch for butterflies on Spotted Knapweed—beautiful!**

PICNIC AREA DIRECTIONS & PARKING:

From Newberry turn south on MI 123 go 2.4 miles until the junction with MI 28. Turn left (east) on MI 28 drive for 32.3 miles (passing east side of MI 123) to Soldier Lake National Lakeshore Picnic and Recreation Area. Park in paved lot.

AMENITIES & FEES:

Vault toilet (wheelchair accessible), water, grills, open-sided shelter, info kiosk. No fees but please note the D&D Enterprises rules posted on kiosk. No lifeguard on duty. No animals on beach, except Seeing Eye dogs.

HIKING FOR HEALTH
INCREDIBLE STUFF WE COULDN'T EVEN MAKE UP!

Imagine being able to take a pill that could:

- help you lose weight and keep it off
- reduce your risk of heart disease
- reduce your risk of cancer and stroke
- lower your risk of developing high blood pressure
- lower high blood pressure if you already have it
- improve your cholesterol levels
- lower your risk for type 2 diabetes
- help you sleep better
- manage lower back and knee pain
- function better if you have arthritis
- lower your risk of falls and injury
- sustain the ability to live independently
- improve the quality of your life!

No such pill exists; however, all of the above benefits and more can be derived from doing one thing. That one "thing" you can do to get all of these benefits: physical activity.[1,2,31] If the benefits of physical activity could be packaged in pill form, it could easily be a trillion-dollar seller!

But currently our nation as a whole is not capitalizing on these benefits because approximately a quarter of a million deaths occur annually in the United States because of sedentary living.[3] Other major causes of death include heart disease, cancer and stroke.

Heart Disease

The bad news: Cardiovascular disease has killed almost a million men and women each year for the past decade. More women die from cardiovascular disease than men each year.[4] As a matter of fact, nearly 500,000 women die of cardiovascular disease annually.[4] Approximately 41,000 die from breast cancer.[5]

The good news: Regular moderate intensity physical activity (such as brisk walking) offers considerable protection against heart disease.[8,9] Even walking for short durations several times throughout the day are associated with decreased cardiovascular disease risk.[4,10]

Cancer

The bad news: Cancer will kill over a half million men and women in 2006.[5] Lung cancer is the number-one cancer killer, claiming almost twice as many women as does breast cancer.[5] Smoking can be credited for nearly 82% of lung cancer deaths.[11] Colorectal cancer cases increase markedly after age 50.[6]

The good news: Quitting smoking pays enormous health benefits. Kick butt with physical activity as it helps to ease withdrawal symptoms, stress and weight gain.[12] Several studies have observed a 30–40% reduction in breast cancer risk among women who were the most physically active.[13] Risk of colon cancer as well as other cancers can be reduced through exercise.[14]

Stroke

The bad news: Stroke will cause or contribute to over a quarter million deaths in 2006.[7] About 46,000 more women than men have a stroke each year.[7]

The good news: Physical activity, including moderate-intensity exercise such as walking, is associated with substantial reduction in risk of strokes.[15]

Let's use our FEET to DE-FEAT these many disease risks due to inactivity!

How Much Do The Feet Have To Move?

The Centers for Disease Control and the American College of Sports Medicine recommend 30 minutes of moderate-intensity activities on most days of the week.[16] Examples of moderate-intensity activities include a 30-minute brisk walk for 2 miles, a 15-minute run for 1.5 miles, wheeling self in a wheelchair for 30 minutes, shoveling snow for 15 minutes, or bicycling 5 miles in 30 minutes.[3] Certain trails in this book can accommodate all of the above activities depending on the season! For weight management or improved cardiovascular benefits, 60 minutes of moderate-to-vigorous-intensity activity on most days of the week is recommended while not exceeding caloric intake requirements.[17] Note: If you are new to a vigorous physical activity program and are over age 40 (men) or over age 50 (women), it is recommended that you first consult your doctor to ensure that you do not have heart disease or other health problems.[3]

How Fast Do The Feet Have To Move?

Hiking can be done at light-, moderate- or vigorous-intensity levels depending on the speed at which you walk and diversity of terrain. If you hike at a light intensity, do so for longer than 30 minutes—60 minutes if possible. Trails with a ⬤ rating are relatively flat, providing an excellent location for light-intensity hiking. For vigorous intensity seek out our ⬤ rating trails with steps and inclines or jog along the ⬤ rated trails.

What If The Feet Can't Move Much?

If you are unable to engage in 30 minutes of continuous activity, start slowly, increasing no more than 10% of total minutes or mileage per week. If you are inactive, even increments of 5 minutes, 6 times per day, on most days of the week can improve heart health.[18] Our Almost Hikes (p. 157–181) range from 80' to 0.6 miles, making them ideal for smaller increments of physical activity. Note: If you have chronic health problems, such as heart disease, obesity, diabetes, or are at high risk for these problems, you are advised to consult your physician prior to beginning a new program of physical activity.[3]

Health Is More Than Just The Physical...

PHYSICAL ACTIVITY IS GOOD FOR MENTAL HEALTH

Depression can have devastating effects on people's lives, relationships, employment or academic achievement.[19] Depression is also the leading cause of disability worldwide and is associated with increased death and disease.[19] Over 100 studies have been done since the early 1900s on the relationship between exercise and decreased depression.[20] Results consistently showed that a significant reduction in depression was achieved through exercise regardless if the activity was a single bout or done on a regular basis.[20] These results were consistent across age and gender.[20] So, whether you go out for one hike or adhere to a regular exercise program, physical activity can reduce depression.

Other mental and emotional benefits of physical activity include reducing stress, anxiety and feelings of loneliness while promoting overall psychological well-being.[21]

Cognitive functioning, such as memory and thinking ability, has also been shown to improve in older men and women who engage in regular walking.[22,23]

FOR BETTER HEALTH ON THE INSIDE—GET OUTSIDE!

Hiking outdoors produces many benefits for mental health that go beyond the effects of the exercise itself. Simply being in the outdoors adds a sense of calm and peace.[24] Actually, just looking at the color green has been shown to have a calming effect.[25,26]

SOCIAL BENEFITS OF WALKING/HIKING

Many therapists utilize outdoor pursuits to effect changes in interpersonal relationships. Hiking may be more of a social activity than walking. Most people take along another person or more when venturing out for a hike for safety as well as other reasons. Additionally, people often want to share the special beauty, sights and sounds of the outdoors with someone. There are no TVs blaring, no phones ringing (leave the cell phone off!), no chores calling while outside. New terrain to explore and discuss gives additional advantage to hiking. Couples and friends can improve their relationships by talking while walking. In one study, couples found themselves growing closer because of the additional time spent together without competing distractions.[27]

So, grab a friend and/or loved one to share a trail with you. But please remember that others on the trail may be seeking solitude or a spiritual experience. Therefore, remember to keep conversation volume down as voices travel a long way in the woods, especially near water.

SPIRITUAL BENEFITS OF WALKING/HIKING

There is no question that being out in nature can awaken a deep part of us like nothing else can. For many people, walking in the woods or other natural settings can help them to realize or even access feelings of spirituality in ways not possible through other methods. One article found that people often use such recreational activities as camping, canoeing, walking or riding in wooded areas, and even gardening to connect to their inner spirituality.[28] It seems that natural environments serve as a type of connection to spiritual experience.[24] Appreciating the world's natural beauty has been a part of most spiritual traditions from the very beginning of time. Since time is at such a premium in most people's lives, it has been suggested to use exercise time (walking, running, hiking, etc.) to commune with God or to pray.[29]

Until our paths meet again...

It is the authors' hope that all of this information will encourage you to get out and explore the trails in this guide. But don't wait until you are near Michigan's Upper Peninsula area to hike. Explore local trails and neighborhood parks. Start or join a walking/hiking club in your own community. Treat yourself to a mental workout by reading other reputable health and fitness books (see Appendix A, pg. 246 for suggestions).

Remember: the steps you take toward a healthy lifestyle today will eventually create a path to that same destination. Wishing you a lifetime of healthy trails—however you travel them.

Note: The information presented herein is in no way intended to substitute for medical advice. It is best to seek medical advice from a reputable medical professional. For your maximum well-being, we strongly recommend getting your doctor's approval before beginning any physical activity program.

FOR TRAVELERS WITH SPECIFIC NEEDS
FOR OUR READERS WITH PHYSICAL CHALLENGES

This chapter contains information about features on trails, Almost Hikes, picnic areas and waysides that are designed for persons with disabilities. For more general information about trails, Almost Hikes, picnic areas and waysides, please see their respective sections.

A Candid Message

After hearing the true story of a man who took his wife (in a wheelchair) on a trail that contained over 300 steps (spread throughout) and inclines at 36% grade—we had to pause and reflect on what we say regarding accessibility. While we are hesitant to label hikes as accessible or not, we do aspire to present the trails in our book with honesty, integrity and straightforwardness. As we reviewed the Regulatory Negotiation Committee on Accessibility Guidelines for Outdoor Developed Areas (Final Report, September 30, 1999), we knew we were not qualified to assess our trails according to these standards, nor have we attempted to do so. Although a few of our trails may be barrier-free, we only indicate those the state parks or other entities claim as officially meeting such standards. See Wheelchair Accessible Trails section below.

For the remainder of trails in this book, we have developed our own rating criteria (see pg. 20). We note those things that may present challenges (e.g. inclines, rocks, roots, steps, etc.) as well as those features that may be helpful (i.e. benches, handrails, paved trails, etc.). On each trail we state total trail length, trail surface, average tread width, total number of inclines and the steepest and longest (exceeding 30') incline. We report all inclines exceeding 10 degrees (18% grade). We used a clinometer to measure the inclines (running slope, not cross-slope) and chose to report in degrees rather than % grade (see Appendix C for conversion chart).

We put significant detail on each trail so our readers would know the locations (rounded to tenths of a mile) of various features. This way each person could make an informed decision based on his/her abilities as to how far to go on a certain trail or whether to choose another altogether.

Inclines on the Trails

On all of our trails, we report inclines. If a trail states that there are no inclines exceeding 10 degrees (18% grade), it does not necessarily mean that it is flat. The trail could (and often does) have inclines of lesser degrees. To alert our readers to the flattest trails (flattest defined by what our naked eye could perceive), we formed a list displayed in Authors' Corner (pg. 12).

Wheelchair Accessible Trails

The following trails are designated barrier-free or wheelchair accessible. For general descriptions, see trail write-ups at page numbers provided.

Additional Accessibility Information

Rainbow Falls (pg. 24) The first 300' of trail up until the bridge is about 6' wide, hardpacked dirt/gravel and is flat. We speculate that a wheelchair could be used in this section as it is through a beautiful wooded area.

Manido Falls (pg. 56) We strongly suspect that the first 900' of Manido Falls trail could accommodate a wheelchair if weather conditions are dry. Although neither of the falls are visible, the strikingly beautiful old-growth hemlocks are spectacular!

At time of publication, Porcupine Mountains Wilderness State Park was developing a wheelchair accessible gravel path that leads to a view of the beautiful Scenic Presque Isle River. The trail is approximately 800 feet long and is located near the Presque Isle Ranger Station. Inquire for more details at the Ranger Station or Wilderness Visitor Center.

Bond Falls (pg. 59)* For the first time, one of the most spectacular waterfalls in the Upper Peninsula is now wheelchair accessible (summer 2005) and we highly recommend a visit! Amenities from parking area that are also accessible include vault toilet, picnic table & grill. Paved to all amenities.

Agate Falls (pg. 61) Agate Falls is wheelchair accessible from the Agate Falls Roadside Park parking area (see pg. 186). Enter 6' paved trail at the right of the kiosk and travel 775' to the viewing platform for a side view of the falls. En route see glimpses of the Ontonagon River between towering pines.

Houghton Waterfront Trail (pg. 70) Paralleling the lovely Portage Waterway with continuous views of the Portage Lift Bridge, this paved and wheelchair accessible path has much to offer.

Presque Isle Bog Walk (pg. 89)* Denoted as wheelchair accessible; however, we found a section of mulch 0.2 mile into the trail that may be challenging for a self-pushed chair. Also, grass trail width is contingent on mowing.

Bay Furnace Historic Site (pg. 107) We speculate that a wheelchair could be taken on this hardpacked gravel/boardwalk trail that is of historical significance. However, spur trail has stairs.

Wagner Falls (pg. 109) There is one 10° incline for about 20'; otherwise, trail is on a gentle grade of hardpacked gravel. Beautiful Wagner Falls can be seen prior to steps from the bridge. Alert: Bridge is slippery when wet. This trail does not meet ADA standards but we think it may be able to be self-pushed by someone in good health.

Munising Falls (pg. 111)* Paved to main overlook of these wonderful falls towering down over sandstone cliff! Although there are no inclines over 10°, the trail is not completely flat. We think it may be able to be self-pushed by someone in good health.

Miners Castle (pg. 118) Not to be missed is this spectacular feature of the Pictured Rocks Boat Tour that can be viewed from land on an easy accessible paved path! Viewing window is wheelchair accessible as well. However, trail atop Miners Castle has stairs en route.

Oswald's Bear Ranch Walk-About (pg. 137) This is the only trail is this book where a bear sighting is guaranteed! Although trail surface is loose sand, the staff is happy to assist those needing accommodations via golf cart. Inquire in gift shop.

Tahquamenon Falls (Upper, pg. 142) One of the biggest waterfalls west of Niagara is accessible up to the second viewing platform of falls!

Tahquamenon Falls (Lower, pg. 147) This trail is paved, boardwalk and no steps, yet is not officially accessible because small incline en route to trailhead does not meet ADA standards. However, park personnel have observed that many people who use wheelchairs have successfully accessed the lower falls. If this incline is problematic, park advises contacting their office for other arrangements.

Soo Locks Walk-About (pg. 152) See the award-winning Soo Locks via a park that is wheelchair accessible. Although viewing platforms have steps, access to lock area can be attained by contacting security stationed therein.

Point Iroquois Lighthouse & Boardwalk (pg. 155) Although the lighthouse is not accessible, we suspect grounds are via boardwalk. Spectacular views of Lake Superior and lighthouse.

ALMOST HIKES

Black River Harbor (pg. 158) The main path is paved (watch for uneven surfaces on blacktop) up to the Suspension Bridge and affords lovely views of the Black River. Beyond the bridge, there is one gentle descent that might pose a challenge for a self-pushed wheelchair on the return. Amenity considerations: Flush and vault toilets are accessible; however, vault toilet has a 2" lip prior to cement platform entry.

Sunday Stroll at Sunday Lake (pg. 159) We speculate that a wheelchair could access this paved trail along beautiful Sunday Lake.

Ontonagon Marina & Boardwalk Stroll (pg. 162) Under construction at time of writing (summer 2004) but we speculate that it could accommodate a wheelchair. Nice views of Ontonagon River.

F.J. McLain Scenic Boardwalk and Gazebo (pg. 164) Fully accessible.

Eagle River Falls and Historic Bridge (pg. 165) Accessible and no motorized vehicles with which to contend.

Copper Harbor Boat Launch (pg. 166) Accessible with distant views of Copper Harbor Lighthouse.

Copper Harbor Lighthouse Overlook (pg. 167) Accessible trail via 6' wide gravel path and accessible viewing platform (decking). Amenity considerations: No extension on picnic table.

Fort Wilkins Historic Site (pg. 168) This is an incredible preservation of mid-19th century life and we highly recommend a visit. Parade Ground buildings are accessible via ramps and the grassy area is level. First part of trail is paved. Park service recommends allowing between 1–2 hours.

Fort Cemetery (pg. 170) Path is paved with uneven blacktop. Spur to cemetery is grass and a bit uneven but we speculate that a wheelchair could be used.

Cinder Pond (pg. 171) Accessible. Portions of playground, fishing area with bench and picnic tables affording beautiful views of Lake Superior shoreline are accessible.

Grand Island Overlook (pg. 173) We speculate that a wheelchair could be used en route to this lovely vista. A flat boardwalk trail leads to a stunning overlook of Grand Island and Lake Superior.

Seney Visitor Center Stroll (pg. 174) Viewing scope is wheelchair accessible! Incredible visitor center worth setting aside time to visit.

Marshland Wildlife Drive—The Almost Hike That's a Drive Through! (pg. 175) A must-see. Observation decks having wheelchair accessible viewing scopes. Wildlife can be seen from your vehicle. Drawback is seriously limited parking at observation decks. Speed limit 15 mph. Daylight visits only.

Tahquamenon River Almost Hike (pg. 177) This area is flat, grassy and fairly level. We speculate a wheelchair could be used contingent on mowing level.

Whitefish Point Light Station (pg. 179) The paved path (although uneven in spots) that meanders through the area would most likely accommodate a wheelchair as would most boardwalk areas prior to steps. Especially noteworthy are the views of Lake Superior along "Shipwreck Coast," which is accessible via boardwalk. The Shipwreck Museum is also wheelchair accessible.

Waterfalls visible from the car

We were unable to include all falls visible from your car in this guide; therefore, we highly recommend *A Guide to 199 Michigan Waterfalls* (see Appendix A, pg. 246) as it lists falls that are visible from your vehicle.

Waysides

These waysides have one or more accessible features. U.D. = Universal Design. U.D. is barrier-free access to both sides of table whereas extensions are only on one side. Narrative of views from car are described below under name of wayside/scenic locale. Additional information on accessibility is provided in narrative below this chart.

WAYSIDE/SCENIC LOCALE	PAGE NUMBER	RESTROOM TYPE	RESTROOM ACCESSIBLE	SURFACE TO RESTROOM	SURFACE TO TABLES	SURFACE UNDER TABLE	TABLE EXTENSION	DESIGNATED PARKING	VIEWS FROM CAR	VISITOR CENTER
Michigan Welcome Center (Ironwood)	183	Flush	X	Paved	Grass	Paved, grass	X	X	X	X
Memory Lane	183	Vault	X	Paved	Paved	Paved	U.D.	X		
City of Wakefield SW Park	184	Flush	X	Paved	Gravel	Paved, grass	X		X	
Ewen Pines Roadside Park	184	Vault	X		Paved, grass	Paved	U.D.	X		
Wilderness Visitor Center	184	Flush	X	Paved	Grass	Grass		X	X	X
Agate Falls Roadside Park	186	Vault	X	Paved	Paved, grass	Paved	U.D.	X	X	
Canyon Falls Roadside Park	186	Vault	X	Paved	Paved, grass	Paved, grass	U.D.	X	X	
Military Hill Roadside Park	186	Vault	X	Paved	Paved, grass	Paved	U.D.	X	X	
Keweenaw Waterway Scenic Turnout	187								X	
The Record Snowfall Wayside	188	Vault	X	Paved	Gravel, grass	Paved, gravel	U.D.			

WAYSIDE/SCENIC LOCALE	PAGE NUMBER	RESTROOM TYPE	RESTROOM ACCESSIBLE	SURFACE TO RESTROOM	SURFACE TO TABLES	SURFACE UNDER TABLE	TABLE EXTENSION	DESIGNATED PARKING	VIEWS FROM CAR	VISITOR CENTER
Memorial Airport Roadside Park	188	Vault	X	Paved	Paved, grass	Paved, grass	U.D.	X		
Eagle River Park	189	Vault	X	Paved	Grass	Paved, grass	U.D.			
Esrey Roadside Park	189	Vault	X	Paved	Grass	Paved, grass	U.D.	X	X	???
Great Sand Bay Scenic Overlook	190								X	
West Bluff Scenic View atop Brockway Mountain Drive	190	Vault		Paved					X	
Copper Harbor and Lake Fanny Hooe Scenic Overlook	190								X	
Baraga Cliff Roadside Park	191	Vault	X	Paved	Paved, grass	Paved	U.D.	X	X	
Tioga Creek	192	Vault	X	Paved	Paved, grass	Paved	U.D.	X	X	
Scenic Drive Through Presque Isle Park	193								X	
Marquette Welcome Center	193	Flush	X	Paved	Paved, dirt	Paved, dirt	U.D.	X		X
Deer Lake Park Roadside Park	194	Vault	X	Paved	Paved, dirt	Paved, dirt	U.D.	X	X	
Lake Superior Roadside Park	195	Vault	X	Paved	Paved	Paved	U.D.		X	

WAYSIDE/SCENIC LOCALE	PAGE NUMBER	RESTROOM TYPE	RESTROOM ACCESSIBLE	SURFACE TO RESTROOM	SURFACE TO TABLES	SURFACE UNDER TABLE	TABLE EXTENSION	DESIGNATED PARKING	VIEWS FROM CAR	VISITOR CENTER
Lake Superior Scenic View	195	Vault	X	Paved	Loose sand	Paved	U.D.	X	X	
Grand Island Harbor	196	Vault	X	Paved	Paved, grass	Paved	U.D.	X		
Scott Falls Roadside Park	196	Vault	X	Paved	Paved, dirt	Paved, dirt	U.D.	X	X	
Seney Stretch Rest Area	197	Flush	X	Paved	Paved	Paved	U.D.	X	X	
Old Flowing Well Roadside Park	198	Vault	X	Paved	Paved, grass	Paved, grass	U.D.	X		
Sault Rest Area	199	Flush	X	Paved	Paved, grass	Paved, grass	U.D.	X		
Mission Hill Scenic Overlook	199								X	
Michigan Welcome Cntr (Sault Ste. Marie)	200	Flush	X	Paved	Paved	Paved, grass	U.D.	X		X

Michigan Welcome Center in Ironwood has two entirely separate restrooms for men and women that are wheelchair accessible. Ladies, you are in for a treat as the women's restroom has a full wall sporting a variety of brochures—yours for the taking. The picnic area at this visitor center has one site that is completely paved to table and under table with grill access. Michigan welcomes you in style!

Memory Lane: Between table and paved surface is slightly sloped grassy area.

City of Wakefield SW Park: Views of Sunday Lake can be seen from parking area but are especially nice when driving on MI 28.

Parking area at Wilderness VC is surrounded by, er—wilderness! Very nice area can be seen from the car.

Ewen Pines: This rest area was under construction at time of writing (summer 2005).

Agate Falls: View of lovely wooded forest from vehicle.

Canyon Falls: Falls are not visible from car, but nice wooded area near parking lot.

Military Hill: View of Ontonagon River from vehicle.

Keweenaw Waterway Scenic Turnout: All very visible from vehicle!

The Record Snowfall: For picnic table, a 3" lip may prevent complete wheelchair access under table.

Eagle River Park: For picnic table, a 3" lip may prevent complete wheelchair access under table.

Esrey: View of the majestic rugged Lake Superior Shoreline.

Great Sand Bay: This vista showcases views of the rhyolite beach and Lake Superior from vehicle.

West Bluff Scenic View atop Brockway Mountain Drive: See highlights (pg. 190) as it's all viewable by vehicle.

Copper Harbor and Lake Fanny Hooe: See highlights (pg. 190). From vehicle, partially obstructed by trees.

Baraga Cliff: Lake Superior view from vehicle, but partially obstructed by trees.

Tioga Creek: Picturesque Tioga Creek with small bridge.

Scenic Drive Presque Isle: This is simply one very nice scenic drive with views virtually everywhere of Lake Superior, rugged cliffs and woods.

Lake Superior Roadside Park: Under construction at time of writing (summer 2005). Sweeping vista of Lake Superior!

Lake Superior Scenic View: Glorious views of Lake Superior and small sand dunes from vehicle.

Deer Lake Park: View of Deer Lake Park from vehicle.

Scott Falls: Falls is across road from wayside and can be seen but traffic flow was too fast a pace to slow down. View at wayside is of Lake Superior through the trees.

Seney Stretch: Beautiful pine grove.

Mission Hill Scenic Overlook: See highlights (pg. 199) as view is visible from vehicle.

Picnic Areas

These picnic areas have one or more accessible features. U.D. = Universal Design. U.D. is barrier-free access to both sides of table whereas extensions are only on one side. Additional information on accessibility is provided in narrative below this chart.

PICNIC AREA	PAGE NUMBER	RESTROOM TYPE	RESTROOM ACCESSIBLE	SURFACE TO RESTROOM	SURFACE TO TABLES	SURFACE UNDER TABLE	TABLE EXTENSION	DESIGNATED PARKING
Black River Harbor	202	Flush, vault	X	Paved	Grass	Grass	X	X
Eddy Park	203	Flush	X	Paved	Paved, grass	Paved, grass	X	
En Route to Lake of the Clouds	204	Vault	X	Grass	Grass	Grass		
Presque Isle River	204	Vault	X	Gravel	Paved, grass	Paved, grass		
Ontonagon Township Park	205	Vault		Grass	Sand, dirt	Sand, dirt		
Bond Falls Picnic and Day Use Area	206	Vault	X	Dirt	Dirt	Dirt		
Twin Lakes State Park	206	Vault	X	Paved	Grass, decking	Grass, decking		X
Houghton Waterfront Park	207	Flush	X	Paved	Paved, grass	Paved	U.D.	X
Hancock Recreational Area	207	Flush	X	Paved	Paved	Paved	X	X
F.J. McLain State Park Entrance	208	Vault	X	Paved	Paved, grass	Paved	U.D.	X
Breakwater Beach House	208	Flush	X	Paved	Paved, dirt, grass	Paved, grass	U.D.	X

PICNIC AREA	PAGE NUMBER	RESTROOM TYPE	RESTROOM ACCESSIBLE	SURFACE TO RESTROOM	SURFACE TO TABLES	SURFACE UNDER TABLE	TABLE EXTENSION	DESIGNATED PARKING
Calumet Waterworks Park	209	Vault	X	Paved	Paved, grass	Paved, grass	U.D.	X
Hebard Park	209	Vault	X	Grass	Grass	Grass		
Fort Wilkins State Park	210	Flush, vault	X (near store)	Paved, gravel	Paved, grass	Paved, grass	X	X
Baraga State Park	210	Vault	X	Paved, gravel	Grass	Grass	X	X
Van Riper	212	Flush	X	Paved	Paved, grass	Paved, grass	U.D.	X
Presque Isle (Marquette)	212	Flush	X (nearby)	Paved	Grass	Grass	X	X
Marquette Sesqui-centennial Pavilion	212	Flush	X	Paved	Paved, grass	Paved, grass	X	X
Picnic Rocks at Shiras Park	212	Flush	X	Paved	Grass	Grass	X	
Tourist Park	213	Flush	X	Paved, grass	Grass	Grass	X	X
Cinder Pond	214	Flush	X	Paved	Paved, dirt, grass	Paved, dirt, grass	X	X
Au Train	215	Vault	X	Gravel	Grass	Grass	X	
Bay Furnace	215	Vault		Gravel	Grass	Grass	X	
Munising Falls	215	Flush	X	Paved	Grass	Dirt	X	X
Sand Point	216	Vault	X	Paved	Paved, sand	Paved, sand	X	X
Miners Beach	216	Vault	X	Paved, boardwalk	Dirt, boardwalk	Dirt	X	
Miners Castle	217	Flush	X	Paved	Paved, grass	Paved, grass	X	X

PICNIC AREA	PAGE NUMBER	RESTROOM TYPE	RESTROOM ACCESSIBLE	SURFACE TO RESTROOM	SURFACE TO TABLES	SURFACE UNDER TABLE	TABLE EXTENSION	DESIGNATED PARKING
Grand Sable Lake Overlook	217				Gravel, grass	Gravel, grass	X	
Sable Falls	217	Flush	X	Paved	Paved, grass	Paved, grass	X	X
Hurricane River	218	Vault (nearby)	X	Paved, dirt	Dirt	Dirt		X
Log Slide Trail	218	Vault	X	gravel	Gravel	Gravel	U.D.	X
Muskallonge Lake	220	Vault	X	Paved	Grass	Grass		
Upper Tahquamenon Falls	220	Flush	X	Paved	Grass	Grass	X	X
Lower Tahquamenon Falls	221	Flush	X	Paved	Grass	Paved, grass	U.D.	X
Tahquamenon Rivermouth	221	Vault	X	Paved	Paved	Paved	U.D.	X
Sawmill Creek Park	222	Vault	X	Gravel	Gravel	Dirt, gravel, grass		
Big Pines	223	Vault	X	Paved, gravel	Dirt	Dirt		
Brimley State Park	223	Flush	X (campground)	Paved	Paved, grass	Grass	X	X
Soldier Lake Recreation	224	Vault	X	Paved	Grass	Grass		

Eddy Park Picnic Area: There are two sets of restrooms at Eddy Park. The set by the swimming beach is not wheelchair accessible.

En Route to Lake of the Clouds Picnic Area: There is a steep slope of 18° en route to this picnic area.

Ontonagon Township Park Picnic Area: Has tables on a gentle grade and path to bench is on a very gentle slope from selected parking areas.

Bond Falls Picnic and Day Use Area: Note: This is in a totally different area from Bonds Falls Trail.

Calumet Waterworks Park Picnic Area: There is a ramp to beach; but no accommodations follow. Therefore, we suspect it is used by kayakers carrying their boats down or as an alternative to the stairs by others.

Baraga State Park Picnic Area: Vault toilets are located a distance from the designed accessible parking. However, there is small gravel pullout near the vault toilets.

Van Riper State Park Picnic Area: This park has a reservable picnic shelter but it may be challenging getting a wheelchair to it as it involves traversing over grass with uneven surface and/or gentle incline. We recommend contacting park staff to inquire about alternative parking if such requirements are needed.

Presque Isle (Marquette) Picnic Area: Benches at picnic area are accessible with great views of ore docks, Presque Isle Light and Lake Superior.

Marquette Sesquicentennial Pavilion: Pavilion is a fully enclosed accessible shelter with open-sided shelter in front sporting lovely Lake Superior views! Restrooms are open to public even if shelter is reserved.

Cinder Pond: Portions of the playground are accessible.

Restroom Accessibility

Please refer to individual Trail, Almost Hike, Wayside and Picnic Area descriptions throughout this book.

When Snowflakes Fly

At time of writing no trails are plowed in winter.

RESOURCES

Superior Alliance for Independent Living (SAIL) promotes the inclusion of people with disabilities into our communities on a full and equal basis through empowerment, education, participation and choice.

(906) 228-5744 or 1-800-379-7245
Fax: 906-228-5573
www.upsail.com/
email: pamela@upsail.com

FOR OUR READERS TRAVELING IN RVS

This chapter summarizes some of the information included throughout this book regarding state parks, trails, Almost Hikes, waysides and picnic areas that may be of assistance to our readers traveling in RVs. For a full description of each of the trails, Almost Hikes, waysides and picnic areas, please see their respective chapters.

Trails

Parking areas for the following trails have designated RV spaces:

Wilderness Visitor Center Nature Trail 36
Canyon Falls 63
Houghton Waterfront Trail 70
Fort Wilkins State Park Lake Superior Trail 82
Lake Fanny Hooe View Trail 84
Hunter's Point Trail 86
Munising Falls 111
Sand Point Marsh Trail 113
Miners Falls 116
Miners Castle 118
Sable Falls 125
Grand Sable Dunes 127
Log Slide Overlook 129
Tahquamenon Falls (Upper) 142
Tahquamenon Falls (Lower) 147
Point Iroquois Lighthouse & Boardwalk 155

Note: Oswald's Bear Ranch Walk-About has RV parking available but spots are not designated.

Almost Hikes

Parking areas for the following Almost Hikes have designated RV spaces:

Copper Harbor Boat Launch 166
Fort Wilkins Historic Site 168
Fort Cemetery 170
Cinder Pond 171
Whitefish Point Bird Sighting Walk 178
Whitefish Point Light Station 179

Waysides & Scenic Locales

While we encourage you to read through our detailed descriptions of the waysides and scenic locales starting on pg. 182, for your convenience we have included here those that have designated RV parking and highway pull-throughs (plus we tell you other information at a glance that may be helpful). We have listed them in chart format (pg. 243) for your convenience and state the following information:

Designated parking: Indicates that there are spaces specifically designed to accommodate RVs.

Highway pull-through: A designated area with an easy exit off the highway and an easy entrance back onto the highway.

Type of restroom: Indicates toilet type—flush (modern), vault (pit), portable (port-a-pottys, portalets).

Picnic tables: Ideal for a quick lunch when traveling, but do check out our entire "spread" on picnic areas (pg. 201).

Visitor center: Indicates if there is a center at the site or nearby.

Also, many of the waysides are closed during snow season as they are not plowed.

Picnic Areas

While we encourage you to read through our detailed descriptions of the picnic areas in this book starting on pg. 201, for your convenience we have included here those that have designated RV parking.

These as well as all picnic areas featured in this book have a knack for working up an appetite for scenic beauty. Bon appetit!

RVs not recommended or prohibited

Greenstone Falls and Overlooked Falls (Almost Hike): Not enough room to turn around. Do not attempt to take an RV to Clark Lake trailhead as road en route to trailhead is VERY narrow with bumps, loose sand and problematic brush (read: scratches!).

Questionable: Bond Falls Scenic Site entails a steep slope, which may pose a challenge for some RVs.

These waysides and scenic locales have features useful for those traveling in RVs.

WAYSIDE/ SCENIC LOCALE	PAGE NUMBER	RV PARKING	HWY PULL-THROUGH	RESTROOM TYPE	PICNIC TABLES	VISITOR CENTER
Michigan Welcome Center (Ironwood)	183	X		Flush	X	X
Memory Lane Roadside Park	183		X	Vault	X	
Ewen Pines Roadside Park	184	X		Vault	X	
Wilderness Visitor Center	184	Separate lot		Flush	X	X
Agate Falls Roadside Park	186	X		Vault	X	
Canyon Falls Roadside Park	186	X		Vault	X	
Keweenaw Waterway Scenic Turnout	187		X			
The Record Snowfall Wayside	188		X	Vault	X	
Memorial Airport Roadside Park	188		X	Vault	X	
Eagle River Park	189		X	Vault	X	
Esrey Roadside Park	189		X	Vault	X	
Great Sand Bay	190		X			

WAYSIDE/SCENIC LOCALE	PAGE NUMBER	RV PARKING	HWY PULL-THROUGH	RESTROOM TYPE	PICNIC TABLES	VISITOR CENTER
Baraga Cliff	191		X	Vault	X	
Tioga Creek Roadside Park	192	X		Vault	X	
Michigamme Roadside Park	192	X		Vault	X	
Marquette Welcome Center	193	X		Flush	X	X
Deer Lake Park Roadside Park	194	X		Vault	X	
Lake Superior Roadside Park	195	X	X	Vault	X	
Lake Superior Scenic View	195	X		Vault	X	
Scott Falls196	X		Vault	X		
Seney Stretch Rest Area197	X		Flush	X		
Old Flowing Well Roadside Park	198	X		Vault	X	
Sault Rest Area	199	X		Flush	X	
Michigan Welcome Cntr (Sault Ste. Marie)	200	X		Flush	X	X

APPENDICES

APPENDIX A: RECOMMENDED READINGS, RESOURCES AND REFERENCES

The following are recommended resources for your health and enjoyment.

Hiking Michigan

Dufresne, J. *Best Hikes with Children*. Seattle: The Mountaineers Books, 2001.

Dufresne, J. *Porcupine Mountains Wilderness State Park: A Backcountry Guide for Hikers, Campers, Backpackers and Skiers, 2nd Edition*. Holt, MI: Thunder Bay Press, 1999.

Dufresne, J. *50 Hikes in Michigan: The Best Walks, Hikes, and Backpacks in the Lower Peninsula, 2nd Edition*. Woodstock, VT: Countryman Press, 1999.

Hansen, E. *Hiking Michigan's Upper Peninsula*. A Falcon Guide. Guilford, CT: Globe Pequot Press, 2005.

Penrose, L. *A Guide to 199 Michigan Waterfalls, Revised Edition*. Davision, MI: Friede Publications, 1996.

Storm, R. and S. Wedzel. *Hiking Michigan*. Champaign, IL: Human Kinetics, 1997

Hiking Wisconsin

Tornabene, L., M. Morgan and L. Vogelsang. *Gentle Hikes: Wisconsin's Most Scenic Lake Superior Hikes Under 3 Miles*. Cambridge, MN: Adventure Publications, Inc., 2004.

Hiking Minnesota's North Shore

Tornabene, L., M. Morgan and L. Vogelsang. *Gentle Hikes: Minnesota's Most Scenic North Shore Hikes Under 3 Miles*. Cambridge, MN: Adventure Publications, Inc., 2002.

State Parks

Rafferty, M. and R. Spraque. *Porcupine Mountains Companion: Inside Michigan's Largest State Park, 4th Edition*. White Pine, MI: Nequaket National History Association, 2001.

Field Guides

Tekiela, S. *Birds of Michigan Field Guide, Second Edition*. Cambridge, MN: Adventure Publications, Inc., 2004.

Tekiela, S. *Mammals of Michigan Field Guide*. Cambridge, MN: Adventure Publications, Inc., 2005.

Tekiela, S. *Reptiles & Amphibians of Michigan Field Guide*. Cambridge, MN: Adventure Publications, Inc., 2004.

Tekiela, S. *Trees of Michigan Field Guide*. Cambridge, MN: Adventure Publications, Inc., 2002.

Tekiela, S. *Wildflowers of Michigan Field Guide*. Cambridge, MN: Adventure Publications, Inc., 2000.

Family Fun

Shanberg, K. and S. Tekiela. *Plantworks: A Wild Plant Cookbook, Field Guide and Activity Book.* Cambridge, MN: Adventure Publications, Inc., 1991.

Tekiela, S. and K. Shanberg. *Nature Smart: A Family Guide to Nature.* Cambridge, MN: Adventure Publications, Inc., 1995.

Tekiela, S. and K. Shanberg. *Start Mushrooming: The Easiest Way to Start Collecting 6 Edible Mushrooms.* Cambridge, MN: Adventure Publications, Inc., 1993.

For Educators

Gilbertson, K., T. Bates, T. McLaughlin and A. Ewert. *Outdoor Education: Methods and Strategies.* Champaign, IL: Human Kinetics, 2006.

Mahan, J. and A. Mahan. *Lake Superior: Story and Spirit.* Gaylord, MI: Sweetwater Visions 1998.

Health and Wellness

Alsbro, D. *The Best Little Book of Wellness.* Benton Harbor, MI: Rainbow Wellness, 2000.

Cooper, K. *Faith-Based Fitness.* Nashville, TN: Thomas Nelson Publishers, 1997.

Leith, L.M. *Exercising Your Way to Better Mental Health.* Morgantown, WV: Fitness Information Technology, 1998.

Walking

Sweetgall, R. *Walk the Four Seasons: Walking and Cross-training Logbook.* Clayton, MO: Creative Walking, Inc., 1992.

Stretching

Anderson, B. and J. Anderson. *Stretching (Revised).* Berkeley, CA: Publishers Group West, 2000.

Photography

Blacklock, C. *The Lake Superior Images.* Moose Lake, MN: Blacklock Nature Photography, 1993.

Brimm, S. *Spirit of Place.* Copper Harbor, MI: Tidal Creek Press, 2004.

Mahan, J. and A. Mahan. *Lake Superior: Story and Spirit.* Gaylord, MI: Sweetwater Visions, 1998.

Additional Resources, Including Websites

North Country Trail Association
229 East Main Street
Lowell, MI 49331
(616) 897-5987 or 1-866-hikeNCT (1-866-445-3628)
Fax: (616) 897-6605

Friends of Presque Isle
City of Marquette
400 West Baraga Avenue
Marquette, MI 49855

Want to help support a pathway to separate motor vehicles and bikes from pedestrians? Consider donating to "Friends of Presque Isle." The Pedestrian Pathway will provide access for people with physical challenges. All donations are tax deductible.

Vacation Planning (by region)
BLACK RIVER HARBOR AREA
Ottawa National Forest
East 6248 U.S. Hwy 2
Ironwood, MI 49938
(906) 932-1330 ext. 350

PORCUPINE MOUNTAIN WILDERNESS AREA
Porcupine Mountains Wilderness State Park
412 South Boundary Road
Ontonagon, MI 49953
(906) 885-5275

KEWEENAW PENINSULA AREA
Baraga County Tourist and Recreation Association
755 East Broad Street
L'Anse, MI 49946
(906) 524-7444

Isle Royale National Park
800 East Lakeshore Drive
Houghton, MI 49931-1869
(906) 482-0984 or www.nps.gov/isro
Email: ISRO_ParkInfo@nps.gov

Keweenaw Convention and Visitors Bureau
56638 Calumet Avenue
Calumet, MI 49913
(906) 337-4579 or 1-800-338-7982

Keweenaw Peninsula Chamber of Commerce
902 College Avenue
Houghton, MI 49931
1-866-304-5722

MARQUETTE AREA
Marquette Country Convention & Visitors Bureau
337 West Washington
Marquette, MI 49855
1-800-544-4321 or www.marquettecountry.org

MUNISING/PICTURED ROCKS NATIONAL LAKESHORE AREA
Hiawatha National Forest Visitor Center
400 East Munising Avenue
Munising, MI 49862
(906) 387-2512

Pictured Rocks National Lakeshore

P.O. Box 40
Munising, MI 49862-0040
(906) 387-3700 or www.nps.gov.piro

TAHQUAMENON FALLS AREA

Tahquamenon Falls State Park
41382 West M-123
Paradise, MI 49768
(906) 492-3415

Great Lakes Shipwreck Museum
18335 North Whitefish Point Road
Paradise, MI 49768
800-635-1742 or www.ShipwreckMuseum.com

Whitefish Point Bird Observatory
16914 North Whitefish Road
Paradise, MI 49768
(906) 492-3596 or www.wpbo.org

SAULT STE. MARIE AREA

Sault Ste. Marie Convention & Visitors Bureau
536 Ashmun Street
Sault Ste. Marie, MI 49783
(906) 632-3366 or 1-800-MI-SAULT (1-800-647-2858)
email: info@saultstemarie.com

The Soo Locks Visitors Center Association
P.O. Box 666
Sault Ste Marie, MI 49783
1-800-MI-SAULT (1-800-647-2858) or www.soolocksvisitorscenter.com

General

Hunts' Guide to Michigan's Upper Peninsula
http://hunts-upguide.com

Schmidt, B. and G. Schmidt. *Foghorn Outdoors Great Lakes Camping: The Complete Guide to More than 750 Campgrounds in Minnesota, Wisconsin, and Michigan.* Emeryville, CA: Avalon Travel, 2002.

APPENDIX B:TRAIL HEADQUARTERS INFORMATION

The following is a topic-specific list of phone numbers, addresses and applicable websites of all trail headquarters pertaining to the trails featured in this book.

National Park

Pictured Rocks National Lakeshore
P.O. Box 40
Munising, MI 49862-0040
(906) 387-3700 or www.nps.gov.piro

National Wildlife Refuge

Seney National Wildlife Refuge
HCR #2, Box 1
Seney, MI 49883
(906) 586-9851 (ext. 15 for Visitor Center) or www.midwest.fws.gov/seney

State Parks

common web address for all state parks: www.michigan.gov/dnr

Baraga State Park
1300 U.S. 41 South
Baraga, MI 49908
(906) 353-6558

F.J. McLain State Park
18350 Michigan State Highway 203
Hancock, MI 49930
(906) 482-0278

Fort Wilkins State Park
P.O. Box 71, U.S. 41 East
Copper Harbor, MI 49918
(906) 289-4215

Muskallonge Lake State Park
30042 County Road 407
Newberry, MI 49868
(906) 658-3338

Porcupine Mountains Wilderness State Park
412 South Boundary Road
Ontonagon, MI 49953
(906) 885-5275

Tahquamenon Falls State Park
41382 West M-123
Paradise, MI 49768
(906) 492-3415

Van Riper State Park
P.O. Box 88
Champion, MI 49814-0088

(906) 339-4461

Chambers of Commerce and Visitor Centers
Baraga County Tourist and Recreation Association
755 East Broad Street
L'Anse, MI 49946
(906) 524-7444

Keweenaw Peninsula Chamber of Commerce
902 College Avenue
Houghton, MI 49931
1-866-304-5722

Marquette Country Convention & Visitors Bureau
337 West Washington
Marquette, MI 49855
1-800-544-4321 or www.marquettecountry.org

State and National Forests
Hiawatha National Forest Visitor Center
400 East Munising Avenue
Munising, MI 49862
(906) 387-2512

Ottawa National Forest
East 6248 U.S. Hwy 2
Ironwood, MI 49938
(906) 932-1330 ext. 350

Department of Natural Resources Service Center Location
DNR
1990 U.S. 41 South
Marquette, MI 49855
(906) 228-6561

North Country Trail
North Country Trail Association
229 East Main Street
Lowell, MI 49331
(616) 897-5987 or 1-866-hikeNCT (1-866-445-3628)
Fax: 616-897-6605

Other
Agate Falls Gift Shop
On M-28 (8 miles east of Bruce Crossing)
Open May 31–October 15
(906) 852-3666

Great Lakes Shipwreck Museum
18335 North Whitefish Point Road
Paradise, MI 49768

(800) 635-1742 or www.ShipwreckMuseum.com

Hunter's Point Project
P.O. Box 76
Copper Harbor, MI 49918
www.hunters-point.org

MooseWood Nature Center
Located in the Shiras Pool building at Presque Isle Park
Marquette, MI
(906) 228-6250 or www.moosewood.org

Oswald's Bear Ranch
13814 County Road 407
Deer Park Road
Newberry, MI 49868
(906) 293-3147

Point Iroquois Lighthouse
12942 West Lakeshore Drive
Brimley, MI 49715
(906) 437-5272

The Soo Locks Visitors Center Association
P.O. Box 666
Sault Ste Marie, MI 49783
1-800-MI-SAULT (1-800-647-2858) or www.soolocksvisitorscenter.com

Whitefish Point Bird Observatory
16914 North Whitefish Road
Paradise, MI 49768
(906) 492-3596 or www.wpbo.org

Woman's National Farm and Garden Association, Inc.
P.O. Box 1175
Midland, MI 48641-1175
www.wnfga.org

APPENDIX C: TECHNICAL SPECIFICATIONS

Forgive us, but remember that two of us are professors and the other—a former accountant!

Measuring distances

All trails were rolled with a Rolotape (400 series—professional). Distances were recorded in feet, then rounded to the nearest tenth of a mile.

Measuring inclines

Inclines were measured with a clinometer (Suunto MC-2G Global Navigator).

Inclines were reported on an average of various places on the slope when applicable.

Inclines were reported in this book in degrees. The following is a conversion chart for those desiring the same information reported in % grade.

Conversion of degrees to % grade
10 degrees is 18% grade
12 degrees is 21% grade
14 degrees is 25% grade
16 degrees is 29% grade
18 degrees is 32% grade
20 degrees is 36% grade
22 degrees is 40% grade

Formula: To convert degrees to % grade, use a calculator with a tangent function. Enter the number of degrees, then press the "tan" button. For an approximation, double the degrees and the answer will be close to the % grade.

Trail hiking time frame

All trails in this book were hiked by at least one of the authors in the summer and fall of 2004 and the summer/fall of 2005. Conditions were reported as accurately as possible; however, conditions can change due to environmental factors. Improvements continue to be made on trails.

We advise you to call ahead to the respective trail headquarters for current conditions (phone numbers are provided after Inclines and Alerts on all hiking trails. When available, the North Country Trail Association posts conditions on their website at www.northcountrytrail.org).

Photography Credits

All photos were taken digitally by the authors. Tornabene (Fuji FinePix S3 and Konica Minolta DiMAGE A2); Vogelsang (Canon EOS 20D and Canon PowerShot Pro 1); Morgan (Olympus Camedia C-730).

Wilderness Blessing

May you feel the warmth of a fire
on the coldest days.

May you see light from the brightest star
on the darkest nights.

May you hear music in the wind
on the loneliest trails.

May you taste the sweetness of honey
in the bitterness of life.

May you smell the freshness of spring
in the stifling pressures of the day.

May you know the way of the wilderness.

peeje

Written as a tribute to Gentle Hikes, and to those who seek to find the way of the wilderness.

copyright 2004

"Thoughts by peeje" is a collection of poems and thoughts featuring the North Shore and Lake Superior. For more information, contact pjellis11@juno.com

APPENDIX D: BIBLIOGRAPHY
References used in writing this book

Dufresne, J. *Best Hikes With Children*. Seattle: The Mountaineers Books, 2001.

Dufresne, J. *Porcupine Mountains Wilderness State Park: A Backcountry Guide for Hikers, Campers, Backpackers and Skiers, 2nd Edition*. Holt, MI: Thunder Bay Press, 1999.

Penrose, L. *A Guide to 199 Michigan Waterfalls, Revised Edition*. Davison, MI: Friede Publications, 1996.

References for Hiking for Health and Says Who

1. Brozic A., editor, "Physical Inactivity," Healthy Heart Society of British Columbia, Vancouver General Hospital, Vancouver, BC; 2005, Nov. Retrieved March 17, 2006 from www.heartbc.ca/public/exercise.htm **2.** "Physical Activity and Health: A Report of the Surgeon General," U.S. Department of Health and Human Services, Center for Disease Control and Prevention; 1996. Retrieved March 17, 2006 from www.cdc.gov/nccdphp/sgr/pdf/execsumm.pdf **3.** Booth F.W., et al, "Waging War on Modern Chronic Diseases: Primary Prevention Through Exercise Biology," *Journal of Applied Physiology*. 2000;88:774–787. **4.** "American Heart Association Special Report: Women & Heart Disease," Vitality Communications, The Staywell Company; 2004. Retrieved March 17, 2006 from www.americanheart.org/downloadable/heart/10878331778411Go%20Red_Toolkit_S R.pdf **5.** "Estimated New Cancer Cases and Deaths by Sex for All Sites, US, 2006." American Cancer Society, Inc. Surveillance Research. Retrieved March 30, 2006 from www.cancer.org/downloads/stt/CAFF06EsCsMc.pdf **6.** "Colorectal Cancer: Early Detection," American Cancer Society, Inc. Retrieved March 29, 2006 from www.cancer.org/docroot/CRI/content/CRI_2_6X_Colorectal_Cancer_Early_Detection_10.asp?sit earea=&level= **7.** Thom T., et al, "Heart Disease & Stroke Statistics—2006 Update," A Report From the American Heart Association Statistics Committee and Stroke Statistics Subcommittee, *Circulation*. 2006;113:e85–e151. **8.** Manson J.E., et al, "A Prospective Study of Walking as Compared with Vigorous Exercise in Prevention of Coronary Heart Disease in Women," (Abstract). *New England Journal of Medicine*. 1999;341:650–658. **9.** Press V., "Physical Activity: The Evidence of Benefit in the Prevention of Coronary Heart Disease," *QJ Medicine*. 2003;96:245–251. **10.** Lee I.M., et al, "Physical Activity and Coronary Heart Disease Risk in Men," *Circulation*. 2000;102:981–986. **11.** American Cancer Society, "Anti-Smoking Efforts Cut Lung Cancer Deaths," ACS News Center; 2003/08/21. Retrieved March 30, 2006 from www.cancer.org/docroot/NWS/content/NWS_2_1x_Anti-Smoking_Efforts_Cut_Lung_Cancer_Deaths.asp **12.** Leontos C. & Christy D., "Smoke-free & Fit: Weight Management After Quitting Smoking," Fact sheet 97–38 Cooperative Extension University of Nevada Reno. Retrieved March 29,2006 from www.unce.unr.edu/publications/FS97/FS9738.pdf **13.** Friedenreich C.M. & Orenstein M.R., "Physical Activity and Cancer Prevention: Etiological Evidence and Biological Mechanisms," *Journal of Nutrition*. 2002;132:3456S–3464S. **14.** Roberts C.K. & Barnard J.R., "Effects of Exercise and Diet on Chronic Disease," *Journal of Applied Physiology*. 2005;98:3–30. **15.** Hu F.B., et al, "Physical Activity and Risk of Stroke in Women" (Abstract). *Journal of the American Medical Association*. 2000;283(22). **16.** Weyer C, Linkeschowa R, Heise T, Giesen HT, & Spraul M., "Implications of the Traditional and the New ACSM Physical Activity Recommendations on Weight Reduction in Dietary Treated Obese Subjects," *International Journal of Obesity and Related Metabolic Disorders*. 1998;Nov;22(11):1071–8. **17.** Chapter 4: Physical Activity in "Dietary Guidelines for Americans 2005," U.S. Department of Health and Human Services, Retrieved on March 18, 2006 from www.health.gov/dietaryguidelines/dga2005/document/html/chapter4.htm **18.** Coleman K.J., Raynor H.R., Mueller D.M. and others, "Providing Sedentary Adults with Choices for Meeting Their Walking Goals," *Preventive Medicine.* 1999;28:510–519. **19.** DPSA. "The State of Depression in American," Depression and Bipolar Support Alliance: Executive Summary; February, 2006. Retrieved on March 30, 2006 from www.wfmh.org/documents/DEPINAMERICAExSum.pdf **20.** Landers D.M., "The Influence of Exercise on Mental Health," originally published as series 2, number 12 of the *PCPFS Research Digest.* nd. **21.** World Health Organization, "Benefits of Physical Activity," Retrieved on March 30, 2006 from www.who.int/moveforhealth/advocacy/information_sheets/benefits/en/print.html **22.** Abbott R.D., et al, "Walking and Dementia in Physically Capable Elderly Men," *Journal of the American Medical Association.* 2004;292:1447–1453. **23.** Weuve J., et al, "Physical Activity, Including Walking, and Cognitive Function in Older Women," *Journal of the American Medical Association.* 2004;292:1454–1461. **24.** Cohen M.J., *Reconnecting with Nature.* Corvallis, OR: Ecopress; 1997. **25.** Sharpe D., *The Psychology of Color.* Chicago: Nelson-Hall; 1974. **26.** Grill T., Scanlon M. *Photographic Composition.* New York: Amphoto; 1990. **27.** Foltz-Gray D., "Exercise in Romance: What's the Best Way to Renew Your Commitment to Fitness—and to Your Relationship? (walking)," *Health.* 2001, May;15(4):48(3). **28.** McChesney J., Knight S., Boswell B., & Hamer M., "Interrelatedness Between Recreational Activity and Spirituality: The Perspectives of Persons with Disabilities," *Research Quarterly for Exercise and Sport.* 2000, Mar;71(1) Supplement:A-50. **29.** Bauman A., "Running on Faith," *Runners World.* 1999, Jun;34(6):86 (1). **30.** Bartholomew J.B., et al, "Effects of Acute Exercise on Mood and Well-Being in Patients with Major Depressive Disorder," *Medicine & Science in Sports & Exercise.* 2005;37(12):2032–2037. **31.** "Physical Activity and Older Americans: Benefits & Strategies," Agency for Healthcare Research and Quality and the Centers for Disease Control. 2002, June. Retrieved on March 18, 2006 from www.ahrq.gov/ppip/activity.htm **32.** Colcombe S., Erickson K.I., Raz N., Webb A.G., Cohen N.J., McAuley E., & Kramer A.F., "Aerobic Fitness Reduces Brain Tissue Loss in Aging Humans," *Journals of Gerontology Series A: Biological Sciences & Medical Sciences.* 2003, Feb;58A(2):176–181. **33.** Eichner E.R., "Infection, Immunity and Exercise: What to Tell Patients," *The Physician and Sportsmedicine.* 1993;Jan 21:125–135. **34.** Colcombe S., Kramer A.F., "Fitness Effects on the Cognitive Function of Older Adults: A Meta-analytic Study," *Psychological Science.* 2003;Mar14(2):125–131. **35.** Ross R., Freeman J.A., & Janssen I., "Exercise Alone Is an Effective Strategy for Reducing Obesity and Related Comorbidities," *Exercise and Sports Sciences Reviews.* 2000;28(4):165–170. **36.** Fontain K.R., "Physical Activity Improves Mental Health," *The Physician and Sportsmedicine.* 2000;28(10):83–83. **37.** "American Hiking Society Fact Sheet: A Step in the Right Direction," American Hiking Society. Silver Springs, MD, nd. Retrieved on April 5, 2006 from www.americanhiking.org/news/pdfs/health_ben.pdf **38.** "Hitting the Trail in Good Form," *Harvard Women's Health Letter.* 2000;June:7(10):na. **39.** Passe D.H., Horn M., & Murray R., "Impact of Beverage Acceptability on Fluid Intake During Exercise," *Appetite.* 2000;35:219–229. **40.** Seraganian P., editor. *Exercise Psychology: The Influence of Physical Exercise on Psychological Processes.* New York: John Wiley & Sons; 1993. **41.** Leith L.M., *Foundations of Exercise and Mental Health.* Morgantown, WV: Fitness Information Technology; 1994. **42.** Leith L.M., *Exercising your Way to Better Mental Health.* Morgantown, WV: Fitness Information Technology; 1998. **43.** Sizer F. & Whitney E., *Nutrition: Concepts and Controversies (8th edition).* Belmont, CA: Wadsworth; 2000.

GLOSSARY OF TERMS

This is not a conclusive list; however, we have included terms that may not be familiar to our readers that were used in our trails, Almost Hikes, waysides and picnic areas.

Amenities/Facilities: Indicates availability of such things as restrooms, water fountains, visitor centers, picnic tables, playgrounds, grills, shelters, concessions, gift shops, etc. Note: For clarity, we indicate restrooms by toilet type: flush (modern), vault (pit), portable (port-a-pottys, portalets).

Boardwalk: Long boards laid side by side or end to end, to make walking easier over a particular section. These may be slippery when wet or frosted; may be loose in some areas; may be difficult to use with hiking poles or challenging to navigate if narrow. Always use caution when crossing them.

Laid log paths: Sometimes referred to as cut-log paths, these are normally laid side by side across the trail to facilitate crossing a muddy section, are often unsecured or loose. These may be challenging to navigate regardless of conditions. Always use caution when crossing them.

Seasonal: Some of our trailhead facilities and amenities will have a seasonal notation. Seasonal is typically defined as the period of time from mid-May to mid-October. This being Michigan's Upper Peninsula, these are close approximations based on ground freezing/thawing. Many of the waysides are closed during snow season as they are not plowed.

Spur Trail: A trail that connects to the main trail, typically leading to a point of interest or scenic overlook.

Universal Design Standards: Universal Design means that the trail meets accessibility standards for persons of all physical abilities.

Wheelchair accessible: We have used this term throughout the book regarding parking and other amenities/facilities. It is defined as a location that can be accessed by someone using a wheelchair.

CHECKLIST (USE THE BOXES TO CHECK THE TRAILS YOU'VE HIKED!)

TRAILS

Region One: Black River Harbor Area

- ☐ Rainbow Falls
- ☐ Sandstone Falls
- ☐ Gorge Falls
- ☐ Potawatomi Falls
- ☐ Great Conglomerate Falls

Region Two: Porcupine Mountain Area

- ☐ Government Peak Trail
- ☐ Lake of the Clouds
- ☐ Wilderness Visitor Center Nature Trail
- ☐ Union Mine Interpretive Trail
- ☐ Nonesuch Mine
- ☐ Summit Peak Tower
- ☐ Greenstone Falls
- ☐ Suspension Bridge – Quick Route
- ☐ Manabezho Falls, Presque Isle River & Suspension Bridge Loop
- ☐ Manido Falls

Region Three: Keweenaw Peninsula Area

- ☐ Bond Falls
- ☐ Agate Falls
- ☐ Canyon Falls
- ☐ Falls River Falls
- ☐ DeVriendt Nature Trail
- ☐ Houghton Waterfront Trail
- ☐ Peepsock Trail
- ☐ Nara Nature Trail
- ☐ Nara River Boardwalk
- ☐ Bear Lake Trail
- ☐ Breakwater & Fitness Trail
- ☐ Fort Wilkins State Park Lake Superior Trail
- ☐ Lake Fanny Hooe View Trail
- ☐ Hunter's Point Trail

Region Four: Marquette Area

- ☐ Presque Isle Bog Walk
- ☐ Presque Isle Nature Trail
- ☐ The Pedestrian Pathway (Wheelchair Accessible Route)
- ☐ Sugarloaf Mountain
- ☐ Little Presque Isle Song Bird Trail
- ☐ Little Presque Isle Point
- ☐ Laughing Whitefish Falls

Region Five: Munising/Pictured Rocks National Lakeshore Area

- ☐ Au Train Songbird Trail
- ☐ Bay Furnace Historic Site
- ☐ Wagner Falls
- ☐ Munising Falls
- ☐ Sand Point Marsh Trail
- ☐ Miners Falls
- ☐ Miners Castle
- ☐ Chapel Falls
- ☐ White Pine Self Guiding Nature Trail
- ☐ Sable Falls
- ☐ Grand Sable Dunes
- ☐ Log Slide Overlook
- ☐ Au Sable Light Station
- ☐ Pine Ridge Nature Trail

Region Six: Tahquamenon Falls Area

- ☐ Oswald's Bear Ranch Walk-About
- ☐ Muskallonge Lake State Park Section of North Country Trail
- ☐ Tahquamenon Falls (Upper)
- ☐ Clark Lake
- ☐ Tahquamenon Falls (Lower)
- ☐ Tahquamenon Rivermouth Walk

Region Seven: Sault Ste. Marie Area

- ☐ Soo Locks Walk-About
- ☐ Point Iroquois Lighthouse & Boardwalk

ALMOST HIKES
Region One: Black River Harbor Area

- ☐ Black River Harbor

Region Two: Porcupine Mountain Area

- ☐ Sunday Lake Boardwalk
- ☐ Sunday Stroll at Sunday Lake
- ☐ Bonanza Falls
- ☐ Union River
- ☐ En Route to Lake of the Clouds
- ☐ Overlooked Falls
- ☐ Ontonagon Marina & Boardwalk Stroll

Region Three: Keweenaw Peninsula Area

- ☐ Bishop Baraga Shrine & Historical Site
- ☐ F.J. McLain Scenic Boardwalk and Gazebo
- ☐ Eagle River Falls and Historic Bridge
- ☐ Eagle Harbor Lighthouse

- [ ] Copper Harbor Boat Launch
- [ ] Copper Harbor Lighthouse Overlook
- [ ] Fort Wilkins Historic Site

Region Four: Marquette Area

- [ ] Fort Cemetery
- [ ] Presque Isle Breakwall
- [ ] Cinder Pond

Region Five: Munising/Pictured Rocks National Lakeshore Area

- [ ] Grand Island Overlook
- [ ] Miners Beach
- [ ] Seney Visitor Center Stroll
- [ ] Marshland Wildlife Drive—The Almost Hike That's a Drive Through!
- [ ] Best Little Barefooted Hike in Grand Marais

Region Six: Tahquamenon Falls Area

- [ ] Muskallonge Lake State Park Superior Beach View
- [ ] Tahquamenon River Almost Hike
- [ ] Whitefish Point Bird Sighting Walk
- [ ] Whitefish Point Light Station

Region Seven: Sault Ste. Marie Area

- [ ] Kemp Marina Almost Hike

WAYSIDES AND SCENIC LOCALES
Region One: Black River Harbor Area

- [ ] Michigan Welcome Center in Ironwood
- [ ] Memory Lane Roadside Park

Region Two: Porcupine Mountain Area

- [ ] City of Wakefield South West Park
- [ ] Ewen Pines Roadside Park
- [ ] Wilderness Visitor Center

Region Three: Keweenaw Peninsula Area

- [ ] Agate Falls Roadside Park
- [ ] Canyon Falls Roadside Park
- [ ] Military Hill Roadside Park
- [ ] Keweenaw Waterway Scenic Turnout
- [ ] The Record Snowfall Wayside
- [ ] Memorial Airport Roadside Park
- [ ] Eagle River Park
- [ ] Esrey Roadside Park
- [ ] Great Sand Bay Scenic Overlook

- [ ] West Bluff Scenic View Atop Brockway Mountain Drive
- [ ] Copper Harbor and Lake Fanny Hooe Scenic Overlook
- [ ] Baraga Cliff Roadside Park

Region Four: Marquette Area

- [ ] Tioga Creek Roadside Park
- [ ] Michigamme Roadside Park
- [ ] Scenic Drive Through Presque Isle Park
- [ ] Marquette Welcome Center
- [ ] Deer Lake Park Roadside Park

Region Five: Munising/Pictured Rocks National Lakeshore Area

- [ ] Lake Superior Roadside Park
- [ ] Lake Superior Scenic View
- [ ] Grand Island Harbor Scenic Turnout–Roadside Park
- [ ] Scott Falls Roadside Park
- [ ] Seney Stretch Rest Area

Region Six: Tahquamenon Falls Area

- [ ] Old Flowing Well Roadside Park

Region Seven: Sault Ste. Marie Area

- [ ] Sault Rest Area
- [ ] Mission Hill Scenic Overlook
- [ ] Michigan Welcome Center in Sault Ste. Marie

PICNIC AREAS

Region One: Black River Harbor Area

- [ ] Black River Harbor Picnic Area

Region Two: Porcupine Mountain Area

- [ ] Eddy Park Picnic Area
- [ ] Picnic Buffet—Superior Style!
- [ ] En Route to Lake of the Clouds Picnic Pullover
- [ ] Presque Isle Picnic Area of the Porcupine Mountains
- [ ] Green Park Picnic Area
- [ ] Ontonagon Township Park Picnic Area

Region Three: Keweenaw Peninsula Area

- [ ] Bond Falls Picnic and Day Use Area
- [ ] Twin Lakes State Park Picnic Area
- [ ] Houghton Waterfront Park Picnic Area
- [ ] Hancock Recreational Picnic Area
- [ ] F.J. McLain State Park Entrance Picnic Area
- [ ] Breakwater Beach House Picnic Area

- [ ] Calumet Waterworks Park Picnic Area
- [ ] Hebard Park Picnic Area
- [ ] Fort Wilkins State Park Picnic Area
- [ ] Baraga State Park Picnic Area
- [ ] L'Anse Waterfront Park Picnic Area

Region Four: Marquette Area

- [ ] Van Riper Picnic Area
- [ ] Presque Isle Picnic Area in Marquette
- [ ] Marquette Sesquicentennial Pavilion
- [ ] Picnic Rocks at Shiras Park
- [ ] Tourist Park Picnic Areas 1, 2 & 3
- [ ] Cinder Pond Picnic Area

Region Five: Munising/Pictured Rocks National Lakeshore Area

- [ ] Au Train Picnic Area
- [ ] Bay Furnace Picnic Area
- [ ] Munising Falls Picnic Area
- [ ] Sand Point Picnic Area
- [ ] Miners Beach Picnic Area
- [ ] Miners Castle Picnic Area
- [ ] Grand Sable Lake Overlook Picnic Area
- [ ] Sable Falls Picnic Area
- [ ] Hurricane River Picnic Area
- [ ] Log Slide Trail Picnic Area
- [ ] Bayshore Park Picnic Area

Region Six: Tahquamenon Falls Area

- [ ] Muskallonge Lake Picnic Area
- [ ] Upper Tahquamenon Falls Picnic Area
- [ ] Lower Tahquamenon Falls Picnic Area
- [ ] Stables Picnic Area
- [ ] Tahquamenon Rivermouth Picnic Area
- [ ] Sawmill Creek Park Picnic Area

Region Seven: Sault Ste. Marie Area

- [ ] Big Pines Picnic Area
- [ ] Brimley State Park Picnic Area
- [ ] Brady Park Picnic Area
- [ ] Soldier Lake Recreation and Picnic Area

INDEX

ABOUT THE AUTHORS

Trails of a "Champ"-ion

To support health education majors in pursuing their passion, Ladona Tornabene has started the Trails of a "Champ"-ion Scholarship Fund through the University of Minnesota Duluth. A portion of the proceeds from the sale of this book go to that scholarship fund.

From left to right, Ladona Tornabene, Champ (UMD's mascot), Melanie Morgan, Lisa Vogelsang

About the Authors

Ladona Tornabene, Ph.D., CHES is an Associate Professor of Health Education and Certified Health Education Specialist at the University of Minnesota Duluth. Her focus lies in confronting the number one public health problem in America today—lack of physical activity. This fact, combined with what she knows about nature's ability to reduce stress, fueled a passion. That passion is to promote better health through opening the outdoors to people of all abilities. She believes the marvelous scenery that Michigan's Upper Peninsula and its Lake Superior Region boasts is prime incentive for accomplishing such a mission. Though an advocate for active lifestyles, she desires for people to know that health is more than just being in good physical shape. Health has a psychological, social, environmental and spiritual dimension as well. Her advice? For better health on the inside—Get outside!

Lisa Vogelsang, Ph.D. is an assistant professor (part-time) at the College of St. Scholastica in Duluth, Minnesota, teaching Psychology and American Sign Language (ASL). Additionally, she is a part-time professional photographer specializing in nature photography from the Lake Superior region. (For more information about Lisa Vogelsang Photography, please call (218) 340-9431, write P.O. Box 3152, Duluth, MN 55803-3152, or visit www.lisavphoto.com.) A former two-time Olympian, she loves the outdoors, especially Lake Superior and the shores around it. Lisa enjoys photography, hiking, biking, sea kayaking, cross country skiing and snowshoeing. After five ankle surgeries and developing severe ankle arthritis from a previous athletic injury, she must keep her hikes short and less rugged. Her disability was, in part, a catalyst in the conception of this and the previous two books, *Gentle Hikes: Minnesota's Most Scenic North Shore Hikes Under 3 Miles* and *Gentle Hikes: Northern Wisconsin's Most Scenic Lake Superior Hikes Under 3 Miles*.

Melanie Morgan is a Minnesota native who loved walking in the woods near her family cabin as a child. Being involved in the hiking and writing of *Gentle Hikes* seemed like an extension of those good feelings and brought back a sense of nostalgia and fond memories. She has always enjoyed a sense of adventure and the love of exploration leads her to many beautiful locations. Though traveling the Lake Superior Circle Tour was a highlight of several family vacations during her childhood, this book gave her more opportunity to explore Michigan's Upper Peninsula and enjoy its particular beauty. Melanie and her husband enjoy hiking and snowshoeing in the woods out the back door of their rural Duluth home.

For more information and additional pictures from *Gentle Hikes* (Minnesota, Wisconsin, Michigan) books, or to let the authors know what you think of the books, please visit the Gentle Hikes website at www.d.umn.edu/~ltornabe/gh